£40-00

Rational expectations and efficiency in futures markets

Do traders in futures markets make use of all relevant information? Is this information fully reflected in prices? This collection of original essays by a team of international economists considers these and other questions which are central to futures markets.

The formation of expectations and the issue of efficiency are of prime importance to economic researchers and market participants alike. The Rational Expectations Hypothesis (REH) is a powerful analytical tool for examining the formation and consequences of expectations in economic activity. Another is the Efficient Markets Hypothesis (EMH): a market is said to be informationally efficient if prices in that market reflect all relevant information as fully as possible. In his introduction the editor surveys recent research on these two hypotheses, while the contributors present new theoretical and empirical analyses of these issues and of the common ground between them. They analyse a wide range of financial and commodity market topics, including the welfare effects of futures markets, the modelling and efficiency of livestock, grain and wool markets, the profitability and risk in currencies, the performance of interest rates markets, and the significance of evidence from experimental markets.

These state-of-the-art papers extend the frontiers of research on futures markets, and will be of interest to researchers in academic and financial institutions as well as to market participants.

Barry A. Goss is Reader in Economics at Monash University, Victoria, Australia. He has written widely on futures markets, and his previous books include *Futures Markets: Their Establishment and Performance, The Economics of Futures Trading* and *The Theory of Futures Trading*.

Rational expectations and efficiency in futures markets

Edited by
Barry A. Goss

ROUTLEDGE

London and New York

First published 1992
by Routledge
11 New Fetter Lane, London EC4P 4EE

Simultaneously published in the USA and Canada
by Routledge
a division of Routledge, Chapman and Hall, Inc.
29 West 35th Street, New York, NY 10001

Typeset by Leaper & Gard Ltd, Bristol
Printed and bound in Great Britain by
Biddles Ltd, Guildford and King's Lynn

British Library Cataloguing in Publication Data
Rational expectations and efficiency in futures markets.
1. Futures markets
I. Goss, B. A. (Barry Andrew) *1939–*
332.645

ISBN 0–415–02343–2

Library of Congress Cataloging in Publication Data
Goss, B. A.
Rational expectations and efficiency in futures markets / Barry A. Goss.
Includes bibliographical references and index.
ISBN 0–415–02343–2
1. Futures market – Mathematical models. 2. Financial futures – Mathematical models. 3. Commodity futures – Mathematical models. 4. Rational expectations (Economic theory) I. Title.
HG6024.A3G66 1991
332.64′5–dc20 90–26524
CIP

Contents

Figures

Tables

Contributors

S. Gulay Avsar is Lecturer in Mathematical Economics at the Victoria University of Technology, Australia. She was previously a Senior Research Assistant at Monash University, Australia, and is co-author (with B.A. Goss) of several papers on futures markets.

Siang-Choo Chan is an official with the Singapore government. She was previously a student at Monash University, Australia, where she gained her B.Ec degree with first class honours in economics and econometrics.

Philip Garcia is Professor in the Department of Agricultural Economics at the University of Illinois, Urbana. He has published numerous scholarly articles and book chapters on topics related to US agricultural markets and was, until recently, a Senior Associate Editor for the *American Journal of Agricultural Economics.*

Barry A. Goss is Reader in Economics at Monash University, Australia and the editor of this volume. He has a major interest in the theoretical and applied economics of futures markets. Dr Goss has published many articles and books on futures markets, including *The Theory of Futures Trading* and *Futures Markets: Their Establishment and Performance.* He has been a consultant to the World Bank, the International Commodities Clearing House and wrote the feasibility study for the Hong Kong futures exchange.

Glenn W. Harrison is the Dewey H. Johnson Professor of Economics at the College of Business Administration, University of South Carolina. Professor Harrison has been a consultant to the World Bank, the Office of the US Trade Representative and the US Department of Energy. He has published numerous articles and chapters in several books on the economics of futures markets.

Raymond M. Leuthold is Professor of Agricultural Economics at the University of Illinois at Urbana-Champaign. He has published (with co-authors Joan Junkus and Jean Cordier) a major textbook entitled *The Theory and Practice of Futures Markets.*

Thomas H. McCurdy is Associate Professor of Economics at Queen's University, Canada. His paper with Ieuan Morgan, 'Evidence of risk premia in foreign currency futures markets', won a prize for best paper at the Northern Finance Meetings in 1989. He has published widely in leading international journals.

Ieuan G. Morgan is Professor of Economics at Queen's University, Canada. He is a member of the American, Western and Northern Finance Associations, as well as the American Statistical Association. He has contributed to many leading international journals.

Thomas Schneeweis is Professor of Finance at the University of Massachusetts at Amherst. He is co-author (with Joanne Hill) of *Financial Futures: Fundamental Strategies and Applications* and has published widely in leading academic finance and management journals. He is on the Board of Trustees of national and international investment funds and is a consultant to various American and European investment firms.

Jerome L. Stein is Professor of Economics at Brown University, Providence, RI. Amongst Professor Stein's many book are *Monetarist, Keynesian and Neo-Classical Economics* and *The Economics of Futures Markets.* He has been an associate editor of the *Journal of Finance*, a member of the editorial board of the *American Economic Review* and a consultant to the Federal Reserve Board of Governors.

Ting-Yean Tan is Lecturer at the National University of Singapore. Mr Tan recently obtained his Ph.D with a thesis on the semi-strong form efficiency of the Australian Interest Rate Futures Market, from Monash University.

Stephen J. Taylor is Reader in Finance at Lancaster University, UK. His studies include futures markets for interest rates, exchange rates, crops and the Sydney wool market. He is the author of *Modelling Financial Time Series*, and recently directed a NATO research workshop on a 'Reappraisal of the Efficiency of Financial Markets'. Dr Taylor has published in leading academic, statistical, finance, and economics journals, including his prize-winning paper on models of price trends in the *Journal of the Royal Statistical Society*, 1980.

Uttama Savanayana lectures at the School of Business Administration, National Institute of Development Administration in Bangkok. Dr Savanayana has published articles in the area of futures markets.

Jot Yau is Assistant Professor of Finance at George Mason University, USA. Previously Dr Yau worked for Shearson/American Express and Dow Chemical in the Pacific area. He has published several articles in the areas of international investments and futures markets.

Introduction

Barry A. Goss

If market prices do not reflect information as fully as possible, then agents are not responding to the best possible signals. Under such circumstances agents will make decisions which will prove to be unjustified, and corrections and adjustments, which are costly, will have to be made. There will have been a misallocation of resources. Hence the issue of informational efficiency in markets of all types remains of prime importance to economists.

The concept of rational expectations evidently originated with Muth's (1961) observation that mean expectations in an industry are as accurate as 'elaborate equation systems', and with his suggestion that informed or 'rational' expectations are the same as the predictions of the 'relevant' economic theory (Muth 1961: 316). Since then the rational expectations hypothesis (REH) has become one of the major hypotheses about the formation and consequences of expectations in economic research.

To some economists the concepts of rational expectations and market efficiency coincide, with the efficient markets hypothesis (EMH) being simply an application of the REH to markets for assets and financial instruments. To others, as we shall see, market efficiency requires more than rational expectations. This introduction surveys recent research on these two hypotheses in the futures markets area, and introduces the various chapters in this book.

RATIONAL EXPECTATIONS HYPOTHESIS

The REH assumes first that agents use all relevant publicly available information at time t in forming their expectations about an economic variable at time $t + 1$. The REH also assumes that agents use such information efficiently (Minford and Peel 1986: 4–5). Second, the REH assumes that agents correctly anticipate future prices, in the sense that the subjective probability distributions of agents equal the objective probability distribution of the system. This does not require identical expectations (Muth 1961: 317; Sheffrin 1985: 10). Operationally, this implies that the mean of agents' subjective probability distributions of prices coincides with the one-step-ahead prediction of the model.

Third, the REH implies that agents have the economic model, under review, in mind in forming their expectations, so that any test of the REH is necessarily a joint test of the REH and the economic model in question (Maddock and Carter 1982). That is, the REH implies that the model which agents believe determines returns is the same as the model driving returns in reality (Minford and Peel 1986: 122). Otherwise abnormal returns would occur.

Fourth, since the REH assumes that agents use all information efficiently, expectational errors will have an expected value of zero, and will not be serially correlated with elements of the information set, and will be uncorrelated with past expectational errors.

The question is then: how do agents learn to form rational expectations? Some answers suggested to this question are that agents acquire this ability by having a long history in the industry in question (Hirsch and Lovell 1969) and by using the same forecasting rule consistently for a long period (Blume *et al.* 1982). On the likelihood of agents learning to form rational expectations, a pessimistic note was struck by Frydman (1982) who investigated whether agents can learn the parameters of the model which forecasts rational expectations equilibrium (REE) when the model is not in equilibrium. In his model of decentralized separated markets, Frydman argued that agents who do not know the model parameters cannot form optimal price forecasts. He observed that autoregressive behaviour of prices and outputs in practice may be a result of agents' learning processes with mis-specified models. The conclusions of Bray and Savin (1986) are more optimistic. They investigated whether agents could learn to form rational expectations by estimating the parameters of a linear model which is correctly specified in REE but mis-specified when there is learning. They concluded that agents' parameter estimates converge to the REE values.

The next question considers what support there is for the idea that markets achieve REE in the relevant (short) time period as required by futures market models. Experimental evidence to support this view was presented by Friedman *et al.* (1983), who found that in a given market situation spot prices converged to the full information equilibrium more rapidly (within four 'trading weeks') with futures markets operating than without them. Plott and Sunder (1982) also found experimental support for the notion that prices converge to REE in security markets. In this volume Harrison (Chapter 4) surveys the experimental literature for evidence against the concept of rational expectations at three different levels of rigour; these are, in ascending order, the 'rationalizable' level, the 'realizable' level and the Muthian level.

The estimation of simultaneous rational expectations models has been discussed in the literature by McCallum (1975, 1979), Flood and Garber (1980), Wallis (1980), Wickens (1982), Cumby *et al.*(1983), Pesaran (1987) and others. Both full information and limited information methods have been discussed, and while the former estimators are potentially more efficient, they require a full specification of all economic processes affecting the model. In practice, as pointed out by Pesaran (1987: 162), limited information estimators have the advantages, first, that they are more robust to specification errors, and second, that they are computationally less complex.

In Chapter 8 of this volume, Goss and Avsar present a simultaneous rational expectations model of the Australian wool spot and futures markets, and estimate it using the instrumental variable (IV) method of McCallum (1979), in which the instrument for the future expectation of an endogenous variable is obtained as a fitted value on the information set of current exogenous and all predetermined variables (including lagged endogenous variables) in the model. The structural equations of the model are then estimated using the IV method. If serial correlation is present, a simple correction for autocorrelation is not appropriate, as noted by Flood and Garber (1980). In such a case, fitted values of all variables in the transformed equation are required, in the interests of consistency, prior to the IV estimation of that equation.

In the area of futures markets Dewbre (1981) developed a two-equation theoretical model of the determination of spot and futures prices, incorporating the REH, Kawai (1983) proposed a theoretical model of price determination for non-storable commodities with rational expectations and Bray (1985) developed a theoretical rational expectations model of futures markets which required futures transactions to be paid for in full at the time of transaction. Giles *et al.* (1985) developed a simultaneous rational expectations model of the corn and soybeans spot and futures markets. Stein (1986) exploited the property of asymptotically rational expectations, which converge to Muth rational expectations over time with repeated sampling. He analysed the welfare implications of price determination by separating the futures price forecast error into three components: first, 'unavoidable error' due to random shifts in demand or production; second, 'Bayesian error' due to misuse of information; and third, the presence of a risk premium.

In this volume Stein (Chapter 1) applies these ideas to the interest rate futures market. His social loss measure of informational efficiency permits markets to be ranked in order of performance, which cannot be done using conventional tests of the EMH. Against these social losses must be set the welfare gains from the existence of futures markets (see, for example, Telser and Higinbotham 1977).

EFFICIENT MARKETS HYPOTHESIS

A market is said to be informationally efficient if prices in that market reflect all relevant information as fully as possible. In particular, a market is defined as efficient with respect to a given information set if the expected profit from a trading programme based on elements of that information set is nil. Since Fama (1970), it has been customary to distinguish three senses of market efficiency based on information sets at three different levels. Weak form efficiency is defined with respect to information in own past prices, while semi-strong form efficiency refers to all relevant publicly available information; strong form efficiency requires that prices also reflect private information as fully as possible.

Grossman and Stiglitz (1976) showed that it is impossible for markets to be fully efficient in the presence of costly information. Pesaran (1987) has argued that the idea that, under these conditions, agents will utilize information up to the point where the marginal cost of acquiring information equals the expected marginal benefit from its utilization is unhelpful, because if the benefits from information processing are uncertain, agents may make systematic errors. On the other hand, these agents, like all others facing uncertain outcomes, must make decisions on the basis of expected values, and are likely to improve their expertise by repeated sampling.

To some authors (for example, Sheffrin 1985: 112), the REH and the EMH are identical. To others (for example, Minford and Peel 1986: 123), the EMH is a joint hypothesis requiring rational expectations, risk neutrality and negligible transaction costs. The latter would seem to be the more persuasive viewpoint, given that market efficiency requires the elimination of all abnormal returns.

In the area of futures markets, Larson (1960), Stevenson and Bear

(1970), Leuthold (1972), Cargill and Rausser (1975), Praetz (1975), Taylor (1985) and others have investigated whether futures prices follow a random walk, using data from a wide range of agricultural commodities, precious and non-ferrous metals and financial futures contracts.[1] Using methodologies borrowed from previous research on share prices, they have found some dependence in past prices, although there is no clear evidence that significant profits could have been made on the basis of this information once transactions costs are taken into account.[2]

Semi-strong form efficiency in futures markets has been studied using three different methodologies: the forecast error approach, the model forecasting approach and the event study procedure.

The forecast error approach exploits the notion that futures prices are market anticipations of delivery date spot prices. A forecast error is defined as the difference between a delivery date cash price and a prior futures price with delivery or maturity on the date of the cash price observation. Such a forecast error contains information, and if the EMH holds, there should be no systematic relationship between the current forecast error for the commodity or financial instrument under review and the immediately prior forecast errors for own and related commodities, which are assumed to form the elements of the set of publicly available information. If the coefficients of these prior forecast errors are estimated by regression methods, the EMH can be addressed by testing the joint hypothesis that all these coefficients are zero.[3]

This methodology has been used for currencies by Hansen and Hodrick (1980), for non-ferrous metals at the London Metal Exchange by Goss (1986: 168–71), MacDonald and Taylor (1988) and Sephton and Cochrane (1990), and for the Australian wool market by Goss (1987). Hansen and Hodrick (1980) found evidence against the EMH for the Canadian dollar, the Deutschmark and the Swiss franc. All authors who studied non-ferrous metals at the London Metal Exchange rejected the EMH for some of the metals traded there, especially zinc, while Goss (1987) found only slight evidence of inefficiency in the Australian wool market.

The second method which has been used to address the semi-strong form EMH in futures markets is the model forecasting approach. This procedure, which also exploits the predictive quality of futures prices, requires the development of a quantitative economic model of the market under review, with this model being used to predict the spot price during a post-sample period. If the economic model outperforms the futures price as a predictor of the cash price, the EMH must be rejected, since the model evidently contains information not reflected in the futures price.[4] Non-rejection of the EMH, of course, is no proof of market efficiency but, as with the previous methodology, may simply reflect inappropriate model specification. This method has been employed by Leuthold and Hartmann (1979) for US hogs, Rausser and Carter (1983) for the US soybeans complex, Brasse (1986) for tin at the London Metal Exchange and Goss (1990) for the Australian wool market, all of whom found some evidence of inefficiency in the markets studied.

In this volume Leuthold and Garcia (Chapter 3) extend the work of Leuthold and Hartmann (1979) by employing the model forecasting approach, together with an assessment of the returns from various trading strategies, to investigate the efficiency of the US live cattle and live hogs markets. These authors also estimate the social loss ratios for cattle and hogs, based on Stein (1986), which permit a ranking of the relative efficiency of these two markets. In Chapter 6, Goss, Chan and Avsar develop a simultaneous model of the much neglected US oats market, and compare the performance of post-sample forecasts of the cash price, derived from this model, with the performance of forecasts provided by futures prices. Also in this volume, Goss and Avsar (Chapter 8) employ the simultaneous rational expectations model of the Australian wool market, referred to above, to test the semi-strong form EMH using the model forecasting methodology.

A third methodology which has been used to test the semi-strong form EMH with futures market data is the event studies approach. In this procedure the behaviour of futures price changes is studied during the days immediately prior and subsequent to an announcement which is assumed to contain information relevant to the futures contract under review. The efficiency hypothesis assumes that any expected information in the announcement should already be reflected in futures prices, and that any unanticipated information (i.e. the news component) should be reflected in prices within a day, possibly within hours, of the announcement. Hence, on the announcement day, under the EMH prices should not respond to the expected component of the announcement but should respond immediately to the unanticipated component. Unless independent expectations data are used (such as survey data), it would seem that such a test is a joint test of the expectations hypothesis employed and of the EMH. Chance (1985a) used this methodology to study the behaviour of Government National Mortgage Association futures prices on days surrounding inflation rate announcements, where the expected inflation rate was assumed to be equal to the difference between the 30 day treasury bill rate and the real rate of inflation, and the unexpected inflation rate was assumed to be zero. His results were consistent with the EMH.

Chance (1985b) reached a similar conclusion for the treasury bond futures market. Colling and Irwin (1990) studied the response of US live hog futures prices to US Department of Agriculture *Hogs and Pigs Reports*, using survey data on market analysts' expectations of breeding and inventory changes, to estimate the anticipated component of the announcements. Again, their results are consistent with the EMH. In Chapter 9 of this volume Tan studies the response of the price of the 90 day bank accepted bills of exchange futures contract on the Sydney Futures Exchange to announcements of inflation rates, money supply and balance of payments. In Chapter 7, Yau, Savanayana and Schneeweis survey recent theoretical and empirical research on interest rate futures, with emphasis on hedging effectiveness from a portfolio viewpoint.

While tests of the EMH according to different methodologies may lead to inferences about market efficiency, a sufficient condition for inefficiency, as Leuthold and Garcia point out in Chapter 3, is the possibility of employing a trading rule to produce significant profits, net of transaction costs. In Chapter 5, Taylor uses forecasts of return and volatility, the latter based on the autoregressive conditional heteroscedasticity (ARCH) models of Engle and Bollerslev (1986) and Bollerslev (1987), to generate a trading rule based on the price trend models of Taylor (1980, 1982) and to show that significant profits could have been made in yen futures on the International Monetary Market in Chicago.

Dusak (1973) found the systematic risk, in the sense of the Sharpe (1964) – Lintner (1965) capital asset pricing model (CAPM), to be near zero for traders in wheat, corn and soybean futures. Lee and Leuthold (1986) reached a similar conclusion for the systematic risk between a wide range of futures contracts, including grains, livestock and precious metals, and the Standard & Poor's Index. On the other hand, Robichek and Eaker (1978) found some evidence of systematic risk premiums for four currencies, including the French franc and the Japanese yen, using forward market data, and in Chapter 2 McCurdy and Morgan investigate this issue with futures price spread data for a group of five currencies.

ACKNOWLEDGEMENTS

Special thanks are due to Mrs Margaret Coates who typed the manuscript to her own meticulous standards, to the draughtsmen of the Geography Department at Monash University who produced the Figures, and to the Australian Wool Corporation and the Monash University Publications Committee, each of which provided a grant to support the publication of this volume.

NOTES

1 Rejection of the random walk hypothesis is not necessarily rejection of weak form efficiency, since the random walk, which requires that changes in futures prices are independently and identically distributed, is a special case of weak form efficiency (Fama 1970). A less restrictive characterization of weak form efficiency is the martingale which hypothesizes that futures prices follow a martingale if the change in futures prices is a fair game (see LeRoy 1989: 1589).

2 Larson (1960: 318) observed that the distributions of futures price changes have 'an excessive number of extreme values', a phenomenon which Mandelbrot (1963) hypothesized is best described by the family of stable Paretian distributions, although Rainbow and Praetz (1986) argued that the Student distribution is more appropriate. More recently, Hall *et al.* (1989) found support for the hypothesis that the distribution of futures price changes is a combination of normal distributions with different variances. See also Hsieh (1988).

3 It would seem that the regression constant should not be included in such a test, because a significant constant (due, for example, to the spot commodity's commanding a premium over the maturing future because of uncertainities about delivery location) is not evidence of inefficiency in pricing.

4 If a linear combination of the model-derived predictor and the futures price outperforms the futures price as a predictor of the maturity date spot price, this also has been used as evidence to reject the EMH, because again it implies the presence of information in the model which is not reflected in the futures price (see Chapters 3, 6 and 8).

REFERENCES

Blume, L.E., Bray, M.M. and Easley, D. (1982) 'Introduction to the stability of rational expectations equilibrium', *Journal of Economic Theory* 26: 313–17.

Bollerslev, T. (1987) 'A conditionally heteroskedastic time series model for security prices and rates of return data', *Review of Economics and Statistics* 59: 542–7.

Brasse, V. (1986) 'Testing the efficiency of the tin futures market on the LME', in K. Tucker and C. Baden Fuller (eds) *Firms and Markets: Essays in Honour of Basil Yamey*, London: Croom Helm.

Bray, M.M. (1985) 'Rational expectations, information and asset markets: an introduction', *Oxford Economic Papers* 37: 151–95.
Bray, M.M. and Savin, N.E. (1986) 'Rational expectations equilibria, learning and model specification', *Econometrica* 54 (5): 1129–60.
Cargill, T.F. and Rausser, G.C. (1975) 'Temporal price behaviour in commodity futures markets', *Journal of Finance* 30 (4): 1043–53.
Chance, D.M. (1985a) 'A semi-strong form test of the efficiency of the treasury bond futures market', *Journal of Futures Markets* 5 (3): 385–405.
—— (1985b) 'The reaction of the Chicago Board of Trade GNMA future contract to the announcement of inflation rates: a study of market efficiency', *Review of Research in Futures Markets* 4 (1): 132–53.
Colling, P.L. and Irwin, S.H. (1990) 'The reaction of live hog futures prices to USDA Hog and Pigs Reports', *American Journal of Agricultural Economics* 72 (1): 84–94.
Cumby, R.E., Huizinga, J. and Obstfeld, M. (1983) 'Two-step two-stage least squares estimation in models with rational expectations', *Journal of Econometrics* 21: 333–55.
Dewbre, J.H. (1981) 'Interrelationships between spot and futures markets: some implications of rational expectations', *American Journal of Agricultural Economics* 63: 926–33.
Dusak, K. (1973) 'Futures trading and investor returns: an investigation of commodity market risk premium', *Journal of Political Economy* 81 (6): 1387–406.
Engle, R.F. and Bollerslev, T. (1986) 'Modelling the persistence of conditional variances', *Econometric Reviews* 5: 1–50.
Fama, E.F. (1970) 'Efficient capital markets: a review of theory and empirical work', *Journal of Finance* 25: 383–417.
Flood, R.P. and Garber, P.M. (1980) 'A pitfall in estimation of models with rational expectations', *Journal of Monetary Economics* 6: 433–5.
Friedman, D., Harrison, G.W. and Salmon, J.W. (1983) 'The informational role of futures markets: some experimental evidence', in M.E. Streit (ed.) *Futures Markets: Modelling, Managing and Monitoring Futures Trading*, Chapter 6, Oxford: Basil Blackwell.
Frydman, R. (1982) 'Individual rationality, decentralization and the rational expectations hypothesis', Research Report 82–30, C.V. Starr Center for Applied Economics, New York University.
Giles, D.E.A., Goss, B.A. and Chin, O.P.L. (1985) 'Intertemporal allocation in the corn and soybeans markets with rational expectations', *American Journal of Agricultural Economics* 67 (4): 749–60.
Goss, B.A. (ed.) (1986) *Futures Markets: Their Establishment and Performance*, London: Croom Helm.
—— (1987) 'Wool prices and publicly available information', *Australian Economic Papers* 26 (49): 225–36.
—— (1990) 'The forecasting approach to efficiency in the wool market', *Applied Economics* 22: 973–93.
Grossman, S.J. and Stiglitz, J.E. (1976) 'Information and competitive price systems', *American Economic Review* 66: 246–53.
Hall, J.A., Brorsen, B.W. and Irwin, S.H. (1989) 'The distribution of futures prices: a test of the stable Paretian and mixture of normals hypotheses', *Journal of Financial and Quantitative Analysis* 24 (1): 105–16.

Hansen, L.P. and Hodrick, R.J. (1980) 'Forward exchange rates as optimal predictors of future spot rates: an econometric analysis', *Journal of Political Economy* 88: 829–53.
Hirsch, A.A. and Lovell, M.C. (1969) *Sales Anticipations and Inventory Behaviour*, New York: Wiley.
Hsieh, D.A. (1988) 'The statistical properties of daily foreign exchange rates: 1974–1983', *Journal of International Economics* 24: 129–45.
Kawai, M. (1983) 'Spot and futures prices of nonstorable commodities under rational expectations', *Quarterly Journal of Economics* 97: 235–54.
Larson, A.B. (1960) 'Measurement of a random process in futures prices', *Food Research Institute Studies* 1: 313–24.
Lee, C.F. and Leuthold, R.M. (1986) 'An analysis of investment horizon and alternative risk–return measures for commodity futures markets', in B.A. Goss (ed.) *Futures Markets: Their Establishment and Performance*, Chapter 5, pp. 119–36, London: Croom Helm.
LeRoy, S.F. (1989) 'Efficient capital markets and martingales', *Journal of Economic Literature* 27: 1583–621.
Leuthold, R.M. (1972) 'Random walks and price trends: the live cattle futures market', *Journal of Finance* 27: 879–89.
Leuthold, R.M. and Hartmann, P.A. (1979) 'A semi-strong form evaluation of the efficiency of the hog futures market', *American Journal of Agricultural Economics* 61 (3): 482–9.
Lintner, J. (1965) 'Security prices, risk and maximal gains from diversification', *Journal of Finance* 20: 587–615.
McCallum, B.T. (1975) 'Rational expectations and the natural rate hypothesis: some evidence for the United Kingdom', *Manchester School* 43: 56–67.
—— (1979) 'Topics concerning the formulation, estimation and use of macroeconomic models with rational expectations', *Proceedings of the Business and Economic Statistics Section*, pp. 65–72, Washington DC: American Statistical Association.
MacDonald, R. and Taylor, M.P. (1988) 'Testing rational expectations and efficiency in the London Metal Exchange', *Oxford Bulletin of Economics and Statistics* 50 (1): 41–52.
Maddock, R. and Carter, M. (1982) 'A child's guide to rational expectations', *Journal of Economic Literature* 20: 39–51.
Mandelbrot, B. (1963) 'The variation of certain speculative prices', *Journal of Business* 36: 394–419.
Minford, P. and Peel, D. (1986) *Rational Expectations and the New Macroeconomics*, Oxford: Basil Blackwell.
Muth, J. (1961) 'Rational expectations and the theory of price movements', *Econometrica* 29: 315–35.
Pesaran, M.H. (1987) *The Limits to Rational Expectations*, Oxford: Basil Blackwell (corrected edn, 1989).
Plott, C.R. and Sunder, S. (1982) 'Efficiency of experimental security markets with insider information: an application of rational expectations models', *Journal of Political Economy* 90 (4): 663–98.
Praetz, P.D. (1975) 'Testing the efficient markets theory on the Sydney Wool Futures Exchange', *Australian Economic Papers* 14 (25): 240–9.
Rainbow, K. and Praetz, P.D. (1986) 'The distribution of returns in Sydney

Wool Futures', in B.A. Goss (ed.) *Futures Markets: Their Establishment and Performance*, Chapter 9, pp. 191–207, London: Croom Helm.
Rausser, G.C. and Carter, C. (1983) 'Futures market efficiency in the soybean complex', *Review of Economics and Statistics* 65: 469–78.
Robichek, A.A. and Eaker, M.R. (1978) 'Foreign exchange hedging and the capital asset pricing model', *Journal of Finance* 33: 1011–18.
Sephton, P.S. and Cochrane, D.K. (1990) 'A note on the efficiency of the London Metal Exchange', *Economics Letters* 33: 341–5.
Sharpe, W. (1964) 'Capital asset prices: a theory of market equilibrium under conditions of risk', *Journal of Finance* 19: 425–42.
Sheffrin, S.M. (1985) *Rational Expectations*, Cambridge: Cambridge University Press.
Stein, J.L. (1986) *The Economics of Futures Markets*, Oxford: Basil Blackwell.
Stevenson, R.A. and Bear, R.M. (1970) 'Commodity futures: trends or random walks?' *Journal of Finance* 25: 65–81.
Taylor, S.J. (1980) 'Conjectured models for trends in financial prices, tests and forecasts', *Journal of the Royal Statistical Society, Series A* 143: 338–362.
—— (1982) 'Tests of the random walk hypothesis against a price-trend hypothesis', *Journal of Financial and Quantitative Analysis* 17: 37–61.
—— (1985) 'The behaviour of futures prices over time', *Applied Economics* 17: 713–34.
Telser, L.G. and Higinbotham, H.N. (1977) 'Organized futures markets: costs and benefits', *Journal of Political Economy* 85 (5): 969–1000.
Wallis, K.F. (1980) 'Econometric implications of the rational expectations hypothesis', *Econometrica* 48: 49–74.
Wickens, M.R. (1982) 'The efficient estimation of econometric models with rational expectations', *Review of Economic Studies* 44: 55–67.

1 Rational expectations and welfare in financial futures markets

Jerome L. Stein

Futures trading in traditional commodities has been carried on for over a century. Its economic effects have been studied both theoretically and empirically (see Goss and Yamey 1976; Peck 1985). In recent years, the major growth and volume have been in financial futures: treasury bonds, bills and Standard & Poor's 500 Index futures. Their economic roles in the economy are less well understood.

The investment process links three sets of institutions: (a) corporations which undertake capital formation by selling securities to financial intermediaries; (b) financial intermediaries which bid for and then distribute these securities to institutional investors; (c) institutional investors who manage the savings of households and purchase the securities from the intermediaries. The major users of financial futures are the financial intermediaries and institutional investors.

In this chapter we develop a model of the effects of financial futures markets upon the rate of real investment and level of social welfare.

THE SUPPLY OF RISKY ASSETS BY CORPORATIONS

The rate of capital formation is determined by the interaction between the demand for risky assets by the intermediaries and the supply offered by the corporations which want to finance capital formation. The supply function will be derived by using the analysis developed by Keynes (1930), Modigliani and Miller (1958) and Tobin (1969).

The value of the firm is equal to the discounted value of expected profits $F(K)$, where $K = K_0 + \delta K$ is the capital stock and the input of labour is such that the value of its marginal product is equal to the wage. The supply price of capital is 1 dollar and the corporation plans to issue new debt with a face value of s dollars. The value of the corporation is distributed between the value s of the newly issued securities and the equity VE of the existing stockholders:

$$F(K) = \mathrm{VE} + s \tag{1.1}$$

At time t, the newly issued securities are sold to financial intermediaries at price $p(t)$. The corporation uses the proceeds $p(t)s$ to purchase δK of additional capital:

$$\delta K = ps \tag{1.2}$$

The price $p(t)$ offered by the financial intermediary to the corporation is proportional to the Keynes–Tobin Q ratio. The value of the marginal $Q = F'(K)\delta K/s$ is the change $F'(K)\delta K$ in the value to the firm divided by a change s in the debt. From equation (1.2), marginal $Q = pF'(K)$. The higher the intermediary's bid price $p(t)$, the more capital goods can be purchased from the sale of s dollars' worth of face value of newly issued securities and the higher is Q.

The object of the corporation is to select a value of s to maximize the equity of VE of the existing stockholders:

$$\max \mathrm{VE} = F(K_0 + ps) - s \tag{1.3}$$

At the optimum, the equation

$$pF'(K_0 + ps) = 1 \tag{1.4a}$$

is satisfied. The increase in the value of the firm per additional dollar of newly issued debt or equity pF' is equal to 1 dollar. Marginal Q will equal unity at the optimal s.

Specifically, let the production function of the corporation be Cobb–Douglas, where v is the share of the value of output received as profits. Then we can solve (4) for the supply of securities as a function of the price offered by the intermediary:

$$\frac{\mathrm{d}\log p}{\mathrm{d}\log s} = \frac{1 - v}{v} \tag{1.4b}$$

In so far as the share of profits is less than 0.5, the supply curve of risky assets offered by the corporation is convex from below, as shown in Figure 1.1. In general, write the supply curve of risky assets to finance capital formation as (the number of corporations is normalized at unity)

$$p = f(s) \tag{1.4c}$$

We have described the supply side of the market. Next, we

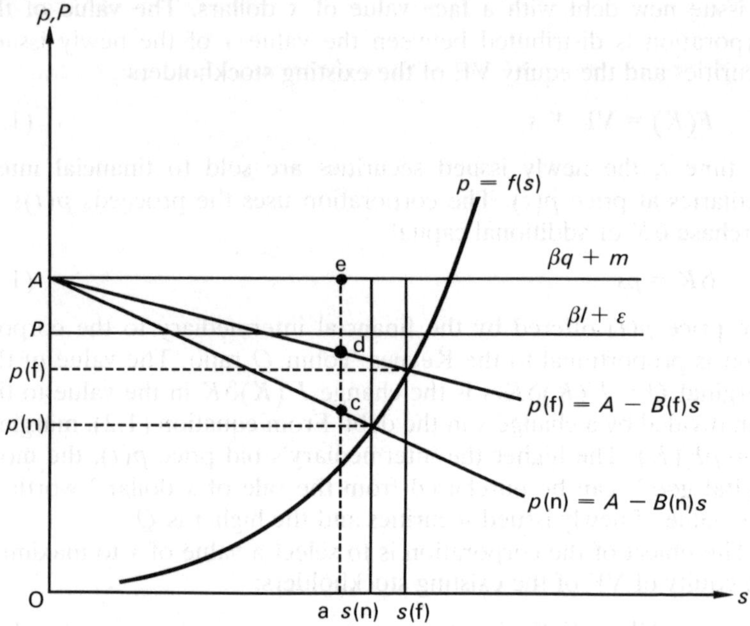

Figure 1.1 Supply of risky assets

describe the demand for these risky assets by financial intermediaries.

FINANCIAL INTERMEDIARIES

The corporation offers to sell *s* dollars' worth of bonds with a face value of 1 dollar per bond to the financial intermediary, and asks for a forward bid price. The profits of the intermediary are described by

$$\pi^*(t) = [P^*(t+1) - p(t)]s + [q(T;t) - q^*(T;t+1)]x(t) \tag{1.5a}$$

The intermediary offers the firm $p(t)s$ for the securities. The carrying cost to the intermediary, from the time t of purchase until time $t+1$ of the sale to the institutional investor, is measured by the short-term interest rate *i*. The total cost per unit to the intermediary is $p(t)(t+1)$, and the total commission is $C(s)$.

The securities will be sold at time $t+1$ to the institutional investors at price $P^*(t+1)$. The securities may be the same as those purchased: for example, high-grade corporate bonds. Alternatively, the intermediary may be the Federal National Mortgage Association which holds these securities as investments and sells s dollars' worth of its own securities to the institutional investors. The Government National Mortgage Association (GNMA) does something similar. In this case, the intermediary substitutes its own credit for that of the corporation, and is able to sell in a broader market at a higher price. In either case, when the intermediary bids $p(t)$, it does not know the price $P^*(t+1)$ at which it will be able to market the securities. The asterisk denotes a stochastic variable.

If the intermediary does not use the futures market, its profit π consists of the first two terms on the right-hand side of

$$\pi^*(t) = [P^*(t+1) - (1+i)p(t)]s + C(s) + [q(T;t) - q^*(T;t+1)]x(t) \qquad (1.5b)$$

The first term is the capital gain or loss, and the second term is the commission. The third term, to be discussed below, refers to transactions in futures. It will simplify matters if we assume that commission $C(s)$ is $ip(t)s$, where i is equal to the normal return on the value of the securities purchased. Then (1.5b) implies (1.5a).

A crucial equation is

$$P(t+1) = \beta I(t+1) + \varepsilon(t+1) \qquad \mathrm{E}(\varepsilon) = m \qquad (1.6a)$$

There is a relation between the price of the corporate bond $P(t+1)$ to be marketed to the institutional investors and the price $I(t+1)$ of a treasury bond. I is referred to as the *absolute* price level of securities, the yield curve or the index. There are two components to the market price $P(t+1)$ of the corporate security. The first part $\beta I(t+1)$ is its relation to the yield curve. The second part $\varepsilon(t+1)$ is the *relative* price of the security, which is constructed to be independent of the absolute price. The price subjectively expected by the intermediary, denoted by E_i, is given by

$$E_i P = \beta \mathrm{E}_i I + m \qquad (1.6b)$$

and the price variance is

$$\mathrm{var}\ P = \beta^2\ \mathrm{var}\ I + \mathrm{var}\ \varepsilon \qquad (1.6c)$$

The fraction of the variance in the price of the security which is attributable to variations in the index is denoted by R^2 and is derived by correlating $P(t+1)$ and $I(t+1)$:

$$R^2 = \frac{\beta^2\ \mathrm{var}\ I}{\mathrm{var}\ P} \qquad (1.6d)$$

The intermediary has confidence in his evaluation of the mean and variance of the relative price (m, var ε). He knows that he does not have expertise in predicting the yield curve – the absolute price. In the period since 1979, there have been very large fluctuations in the yield curve on treasury bonds, and the absolute price risk var I has overwhelmed the relative price risk var ε.

The intermediary can diversify the absolute risk in an inexpensive and flexible way through the use of futures. He sells quantity x of futures contracts. If s consists of high-grade corporate bonds, then x consists of US treasury bonds. If s consists of short-term high-grade corporate securities, then x consists of treasury bills. If s consists of a *portfolio* of securities, then x consists of futures on the S&P 500 Index. The type of future used corresponds to the type of security purchased by the intermediary, as shown in equation (1.12) on p. 18.

Suppose that s consists of high-grade corporate bonds. Then the hedging instrument will be treasury bond futures. The price at time t of a nearby treasury bond future maturing at time T is $q(T; t)$. When the intermediary sells the corporate security at time $t+1$ at price $P(t+1)$, he repurchases the futures contract at price $q(T; t+1)$. Both prices $P(t+1)$ and $q(T; t+1)$ are unknown at time t when the intermediary bids for the corporate bonds. The term $[q(T; t) - q(T; t+1)]\ x(t)$ in equation (1.5a) represents the profits from the transactions in futures.

Hedging with futures is effective if there is a very close relation between the price of the futures $q(T; t+1)$ and the price of the index $I(t+1)$ in equation (1.6a) at the time when the intermediary sells the corporate securities in the market to the institutional investors. The relation between the two prices at time $t+1$ is given by

$$q(T; t+1) = I(t+1)(1+i) + \phi \qquad \mathrm{E}(\phi) = 0 \qquad \text{var}\ \phi > 0 \tag{1.7a}$$

It is often convenient to write (1.7a) as follows:

$$q(T; t+1) = I(t+1) + \phi \tag{1.7b}$$

This would occur if the interest earned on the government bond were equal to the financing costs.

If there were no mispricing, timing problems or problems concerning the deliverability of several different instruments against the futures, then the no-arbitrage condition is that $\phi = 0$. The futures price is equal to the spot price plus the known carrying costs. In many markets, there is a variance to ϕ resulting from the ability to deliver several grades of the spot 'commodity' against the futures contract, the transactions cost, mispricing due to insufficient arbitrage, uncertainty concerning net finance costs between $t + 1$ and T, and restrictions such as those that occurred during the crash of 1987 (when many issues were not traded on the New York Stock Exchange, but the futures exchanges were open). The variance of ϕ is referred to as *basis risk* (see Silber 1985; Stein 1986: 56–9).

The basis risk is given by

$$\text{var } \phi = (1 - r^2) \text{ var } q \qquad (1.7c)$$

It is the fraction of the variation in the futures price that is not explained by variations in the price of the index. The correlation coefficient between $q(T; t + 1)$ and $I(t + 1)$ is 'r'. If we substitute (1.6a) and (1.7a) into (1.5a), we obtain the profit function for the intermediary:

$$\pi^* = [(\beta s - x)I^* + \varepsilon^* s - \phi^* x] + (qx - ps) \qquad (1.8)$$

There are two parts to this equation. The first part in square brackets is stochastic and reflects all the elements of risk. The second part in parentheses is deterministic. The subjective expectation E_i of profits is

$$\text{E}_i\pi = [(\beta s - x)\text{E}_i I + ms] + (qx - ps) \qquad (1.9)$$

Suppose that risk is measured by the variance of profits:

$$\text{var } \pi = (\beta s - x)^2 \text{ var } I + s^2 \text{ var } \varepsilon + x^2 \text{ var } \phi \qquad (1.10)$$

where variables I, ε and ϕ are constructed to be independent of each other. There are three elements of risk to the intermediary. The first is the *absolute* price risk on the uncovered position, $(\beta s - x)^2$ var I. The absolute price risk var I concerns variations in the treasury yield curve (or the S & P 500 Index). This risk became large after 1979 (Figure 1.2) and induced the markets to use financial futures. The second is the *relative* price risk s^2 var ε. This risk has always existed, and the intermediaries specialize in the management of this risk. The third is a *basis* risk var ϕ that occurs when the intermediary uses the futures market. The higher r^2 is, the lower is the basis risk.

The intermediaries are risk averse and act as if they were maximizing the expected utility of profit. Assume that they have the standard mean–variance expected utility function

$$\max \text{E}\,U(\pi) = \text{E}\pi - \frac{\alpha}{2} \text{ var } \pi \qquad (1.11)$$

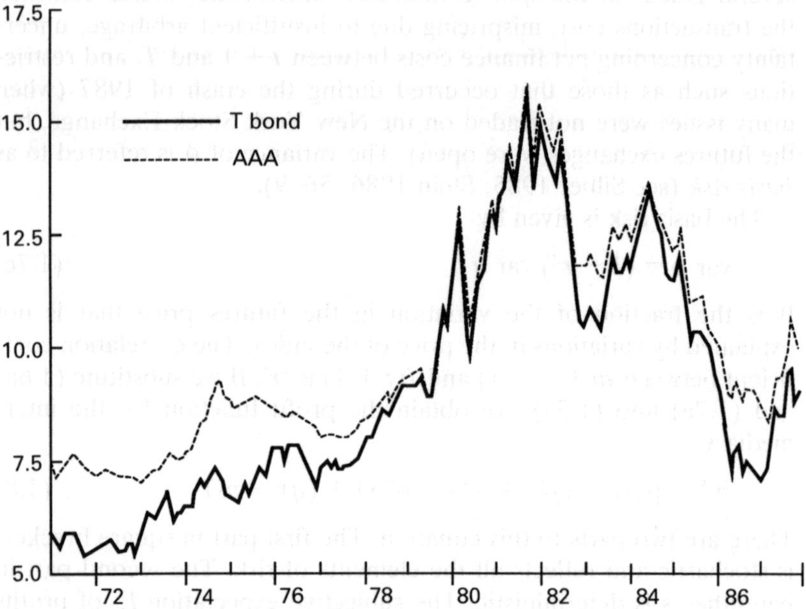

Figure 1.2 Bond yields

where the parameter α reflects the absolute risk aversion. The intermediary operates in a competitive environment where his bid price cannot differ significantly from that of his competitors. In deriving his demand curve for securities, the bid price $p(t)$ is a parameter for any single intermediary. His decision variables are the quantity s of securities to purchase forward from the corporation and the quantity x of futures sold (+) or purchased (−). The market bid price $p(t)$ is determined in the price determination process described below. This will determine the rate of capital formation.

The optimization process implies the equations

$$x = \beta r^2 s + \frac{r^2}{\alpha \text{ var } I}(q - \mathrm{E}_i I) \qquad \text{var } I = r^2 \text{ var } q \tag{1.12}$$

which is the net supply of futures by the intermediary, and

$$p(t) = [\beta(r^2 q + (1 - r^2)\mathrm{E}_i I) + m] - [\alpha(1 - r^2 R^2) \text{ var } P]s \tag{1.13a}$$

which is the demand for securities issued by the corporation.

The supply of futures by the intermediary consists of two parts.

The first term in (1.12) is the hedging element which is proportional to the purchases s of securities from the corporation. The factor of proportionality is βr^2. A unit change in I tends to change P by β. The higher β is, the more futures contracts will be sold for a given value of securities purchased. The r^2 term reflects the closeness of the relation between the futures price q and the price I of the index. The second term in (1.12) is the speculative element. The intermediary will be a short (long) speculator if the futures price exceeds (is below) his subjective expectation of the index. The factor of proportionality $r^2/(\alpha \text{ var } I) = 1/(\alpha \text{ var } q)$ measures the risk tolerance of the intermediary.

Equation (1.13a) is the inverse demand curve of the intermediary for securities offered by the corporation. It relates the forward price bid $p(t)$ to the quantity demanded s. The demand is characterized by an intercept A and a slope B. The letters (n, f) will refer to the cases where either no (n) futures are used or futures (f) are used optimally. Equation (1.13a) abbreviated as

$$p = A - Bs \tag{1.13b}$$

is sufficiently general to cover all cases.

It will facilitate our understanding of (1.13a) if we start with the case where there is no basis risk ($r^2 = 1$). This assumption makes most sense if $t = T + 1$. We then obtain

$$p(\text{f}) = [\beta q(t + 1; t) + m] - (\alpha \text{ var } \varepsilon)s \tag{1.14}$$

The intermediary uses the market-determined futures price $q(t + 1; t)$ on a government security as the certainty equivalent of the price $I(t + 1)$ of the government security. He then takes intercept $A = \beta q + m$ as the expected price of the corporate security at $t + 1$, when it will be sold to the institutional investors. Slope B reflects risk and risk aversion. When there is no basis risk ($r^2 = 1$), there is only the relative price risk $\text{var } \varepsilon = (1 - R^2) \text{ var } P$. The absolute price risk $\beta^2 \text{ var } I$ has been completely diversified away by hedging with treasury bond futures.

If futures cannot be used, the intermediary's demand for the corporate security is given by

$$p(\text{n}) = \text{E}_i P(t + 1; t) - (\alpha \text{ var } P)s \tag{1.15}$$

which is derived from (1.13a) with $r^2 = 0$. The intercept is $\text{E}_i P(t + 1) = \beta \text{E}_i I(t + 1; t) + m$, i.e. the subjective expectation by the intermediary of the price of the security. The slope $\alpha \text{ var } P$ represents the *total* risk involving the price of the security. It is the sum of the absolute and the relative price risks.

Actually, the dichotomy between the no futures and the futures cases is not as extreme as is shown in (1.14) and (1.15). Before there were futures markets in financial instruments, the large intermediaries could engage in 'homemade hedging' (see Stein 1986: 198–9). This was considerably more costly and difficult than hedging via futures. In this chapter, we shall just concentrate on the dichotomy.

THE RATE OF CAPITAL FORMATION

How futures affect the risk premium

The supply of securities offered by firms is given by equation (1.4c). The higher is the intermediary's bid price (which is proportional to the Tobin Q ratio), the greater is the rate of capital formation. Normalize the number of intermediaries at unity. Then, in general, the aggregate demand curve of the intermediaries is given by equation (1.13a). When there are no futures markets in financial instruments, the intermediary demand curve is (1.15), denoted by $p(\mathrm{n}) = A(\mathrm{n}) - B(\mathrm{n})s$. When there is a well-developed futures market in financial instruments, the intermediary demand curve is denoted $p(\mathrm{f}) = A(\mathrm{f}) - B(\mathrm{f})s$.

The total risk premium is Bs. The intermediary demand curve is flatter when there are well-developed futures markets because the absolute price risk has been diversified away. When there is an optimal amount of hedging, a relative price risk and a basis risk exist. When there are no futures markets, an absolute and a relative price risk exist. The value of $B(\mathrm{f})$ is less than that of $B(\mathrm{n})$ because the absolute price risk β^2 var I exceeds the basis risk var ϕ.

The percentage risk reduction premium is $[1 - B(\mathrm{f})/B(\mathrm{n})] = (rR)^2$ when futures markets are used optimally. This is derived from equations (1.13a)–(1.15). In figure 1.1, suppose that Oa of securities were offered to the intermediary. Without futures, the bid price would be ac. With futures, the bid price would be ad. The percentage risk reduction is cd/ce = $(rR)^2$.

Suppose for the moment that $A(\mathrm{f}) = A(\mathrm{n})$, i.e. the intercept of the intermediary is the same with or without futures markets. Then, the equilibrium bid price is $p(\mathrm{n})$ when there are no financial futures, and the rate of capital formation is $s(\mathrm{n})$ in terms of the value of newly issued securities. When there are financial futures, the equilibrium bid price is $p(\mathrm{f})$, and the value of newly issued securities is $s(\mathrm{f})$.

In the case where the intercepts are the same, the existence of financial futures unambiguously raises the rate of capital formation by lowering the risk premium and raising the bid price (the Q ratio). Formally, the equilibrium forward bid price is determined by

$$p = cs \tag{1.16}$$

and (1.13a). Equation (1.16) is the linearized version of supply curve equation (1.4c) for the corporations. The equilibrium forward bid price is given by

$$p = \frac{Ac}{B + c} \tag{1.17}$$

and the equilibrium quantity of risky assets sold to finance capital formation is given by

$$s = \frac{A}{B + c} \tag{1.18}$$

In so far as the risk premium B(f) is less than B(n), the equilibrium values of s(f) and p(f) with futures are greater than s(n) and p(n) without futures (see Figure 1.1). There is a higher Tobin Q ratio and rate of capital formation when the intermediary uses futures optimally.

Futures markets and price discovery

The next question is: what is the informational content of the futures price? The anticipated price at which the risky security will be sold to the institutional investors is A(n) or A(f), derived from equations (1.15) and (1.14) respectively.

The intercept of the intermediary demand curve when there are no financial futures is A(n). It is the subjectively expected sales price $E_i P(t+1;\, t)$ held by the intermediary. When there are futures markets (and no basis risk), the intercept A(f) is equal to $\beta q + m$. The intermediary uses the futures price q as its estimate of the absolute price level and adds to βq the mean value m of the differential between the price I of the index and the price P of the security.

The futures price is determined by the condition that Σx, the excess supply of futures by commercial firms, is equal to the excess demand for futures by non-commercial firms. The commercial firms that are short hedgers have output price uncertainty and their supply of futures is the sum of equations similar to (1.12). Intermediaries are in the set of commercial firms. There are also commercial firms that have input price uncertainty. For example, an institutional investor may expect an inflow of pension fund money, and may want to buy GNMA securities in a few months. He may ask an intermediary for a forward ask price $p(t)$ for these securities. When the intermediary quotes the price $p(t)$, he does not know what he will have to pay for the GNMA securities. In this case, the intermediary is a long hedger, and his equations are the negatives of (1.12) and (1.13a); his x and s are negative.

Therefore, aggregating equation (1.12) over the intermediaries facing both output price uncertainty and input price uncertainty, the net supply of futures by commercials ($X = \Sigma x$) is given by

$$X = w_1(q - \mathrm{E}_1 I) \tag{1.19}$$

The total spot position $S = \Sigma s$ may be positive, zero or negative. We shall work with the case where $S = 0$, but could just as easily assume that it is a stochastic variable. The w_1 in (1.19) measures the average risk tolerance $1/\alpha$ var I multiplied by the number of commercials, and E_1 measures their average subjective expectation.

The low cost of speculating in futures induces the entry of non-commercials (denoted by 2). They are the pure futures speculators. Their excess demand Z for futures is given by

$$Z = w_2(\mathrm{E}_2 I - q) \tag{1.20}$$

It is proportional to the expected profit per unit $\mathrm{E}_2 I - q$, where $\mathrm{E}_2 I$ is the average subjective expectation and w_2 is the average risk tolerance multiplied by the number of commercials.

Equilibrium in the futures market is given by

$$X = Z \tag{1.21}$$

which states that the excess supply of futures by the commercials is equal to the excess demand from the non-commercials. The resulting futures price $q(t + 1; t)$ is given by

$$q(t + 1; t) = \frac{\Sigma w_i \mathrm{E}_i I(t + 1; t)}{\Sigma w_i} \tag{1.22}$$

which is a weighted average of the subjectively expected prices of the commercial and non-commercials. The stochastic variables are $I(t + 1)$ and $\varepsilon(t + 1)$. There is an objective mean of the absolute price (for example, of a treasury bond). This mean, which is denoted by $\mathrm{E}I$ (without a subscript), is the price of the treasury bond at time $t + 1$ that would result from productivity, thrift and monetary/fiscal policies at home and abroad in a world without speculation. It is the price (interest rate) that is determined in open-economy macro-models. In fact, there will be factors determining $I(t+1)$ other than those discussed in those models. Hence $I(t+1)$ is a stochastic variable with an objective mean EI and a variance var I.

In the Muth rational expectations (MRE) hypothesis it is assumed that the market always knows the objective means of distributions. In the asymptotically rational expectations (ARE) hypothesis it is argued that market participants learn the true mean in a Bayesian manner (Stein 1986: 69–76). At any time, each agent has a prior estimate of the mean, denoted by $y(t)$. He takes a sample from the information set and obtains a sample mean which is an unbiased estimate of the objective mean EI. The Bayesian error is E$I - y(t)$, i.e. the difference between the objective mean and the prior estimate.

The posterior estimate can be expressed in several ways. First, it is a linear combination of the prior $y(t)$ and the sample mean, which is an unbiased estimate of EI. The weight assigned to the sample mean is $\tau(t)$, and the weight assigned to the prior is $1 - \tau(t)$. Second, the posterior estimate is equal to the prior $y(t)$ plus the fraction $\tau(t)$ times the difference between the observed sample mean and the prior, i.e. $\tau(t)[\mathrm{E}I - y(t)]$.

When the distribution of I is stationary, then with repeated sampling the prior converges to the objective expectation and the variance of the Bayesian error converges to zero. (The proofs are given by Stein (1986).)

This ARE Bayesian analysis is formalized in the following equations (ARE are more general than MRE in so far as the ARE hypothesis converges to the MRE hypothesis when the distributions are stationary):

$$q(t+1;\, t) = \frac{\Sigma w_i E_i(t+1;\, t)}{\Sigma w_i}$$

$$= \mathrm{E}I - [1 - \tau(t)][\mathrm{E}I - y(t)] \qquad (1.23a)$$

$$\operatorname{plim} \tau(t) = 1 \qquad (1.23b)$$

$$\operatorname{plim} \operatorname{var}\, [\mathrm{E}I - y(t)] = 0 \qquad (1.23c)$$

$$\mathrm{E}[\mathrm{E}I - y(t)] = 0 \qquad (1.23d)$$

Equation (1.23d) states that, on average, there is no Bayesian error but that Bayesian errors may exist at any time. Equation (1.23c) states that the variance of the Bayesian error eventually converges to zero. Equation (1.23a) is not adaptive expectations, because the weight $\tau(t)$ is not constant but converges (at a specified rate) to unity.

The price discovery process can be viewed as the process whereby $A(\mathrm{f}) = \beta q + m$ reflects the realized price $P(t+1) = \beta I(t+1) + \varepsilon(t+1)$ that the security will sell for at time $t+1$. The crucial variable describing the price discovery process is $P(t+1) - A(\mathrm{f})$. This difference is given by

$$P - A = \beta(I - q) + (\varepsilon - m) \tag{1.24}$$

which is shown graphically in Figure 1.1 (a special case). Equations (1.23) and (1.24) are used to derive the following equation:

$$P - A = U + \mathrm{BE} \tag{1.25a}$$

where the terms U and BE are defined as

$$U = P(t+1) - \mathrm{E}P = [\beta I(t+1) + \varepsilon(t+1)] - [\beta \mathrm{E}I + m] \tag{1.25b}$$

and

$$\mathrm{BE} = \mathrm{E}P - A = \beta[1 - \tau(t)][\mathrm{E}I - y(t)] \tag{1.25c}$$

For simplicity, we assume that the agents know the objective mean m of the relative price but must learn EI of the absolute price. The variable $U = P(t+1) - \mathrm{E}P$ is random, and is the difference between the actual price of the security and its objective expectation. It will be referred to as an unavoidable error. The variable $\mathrm{BE} = \mathrm{E}P - A$ is a multiple of the Bayesian error, and is the deviation between the objective expectation of the price EP and $\beta q + m$.

On average, $P - A$ will be zero because on average U and BE are zero. However, $P - A$ will have a variance defined by

$$\mathrm{var}(P - A) = \mathrm{var}\ U + \mathrm{var\ BE} + 2\ \mathrm{cov}(U, \mathrm{BE}) \tag{1.26}$$

This expression measures the efficiency of the price discovery process. If there were MRE, there would be no Bayesian error: $y = \mathrm{E}I$. The difference between the actual price $P(t+1)$ and its objective mean EP would just result from variations of $I(t+1)$ around its objective mean EI and $\varepsilon(t+1)$ around m. We call $U = P(t+1) - \mathrm{E}P$ an unavoidable error.

We have assumed that, on average, the Bayesian error $\mathrm{E}I - y$ is zero. The variance of the Bayesian error arises from the failure of the agents' prior estimate of the mean to converge to the objective mean.

The price discovery process concerns the issue of whether the existence of futures markets reduces or increases the variance of the Bayesian error var BE in equation (1.26). This issue has not, as yet, been resolved.

WELFARE AND EFFICIENCY

A question of great social importance is: what contribution does a futures market make to society? Several different attempts have been made to answer this question.

One group asks whether futures trading increases or decreases the variance of the spot price. Empirical studies have tried to estimate what the price variance would have been if there were no futures markets, and they then compare it with the actual price variance. These studies fail to ask whether the actual price variance differs from the optimal price variance, and a standard of optimal price variance must be ascertained.

A second group asks whether the futures market passes the 'efficiency' tests used in the finance literature. The efficient market hypothesis (EMH) states that the futures price is the best and unbiased estimator of the subsequent spot price. The statistical tests examine whether (a) the futures price is an unbiased estimate, and (b) other variables add significantly to the prediction of the subsequent spot price. The deficiency of the EMH tests is that they cannot rank markets in terms of performance or welfare. They cannot answer the elementary question: which markets are operating well and which are operating badly?

A quantitative welfare measure of market performance

In this section we derive a quantitative measure of welfare performance which permits us to measure the benefits of futures markets, compare speculative markets and evaluate the consequences of proposed regulation. (See Stein 1986 ch. 6, 1990.)

The intermediary's bid price $p(t) = \delta K/s$ is equal to the value of the capital goods purchased per dollar of securities issued. Thus $p(t)$ is equal to the marginal utility of consumption lost by using the resources for capital formation. The supply curve $p = f(s) = cs$ in Figure 1.3 is the marginal cost curve of capital formation, which is equal to the marginal utility of the consumer goods sacrificed to produce the capital goods.

At time $t + 1$ the securities are sold in the market at price $P(t + 1)$. This price is equal to the marginal utility of consumption

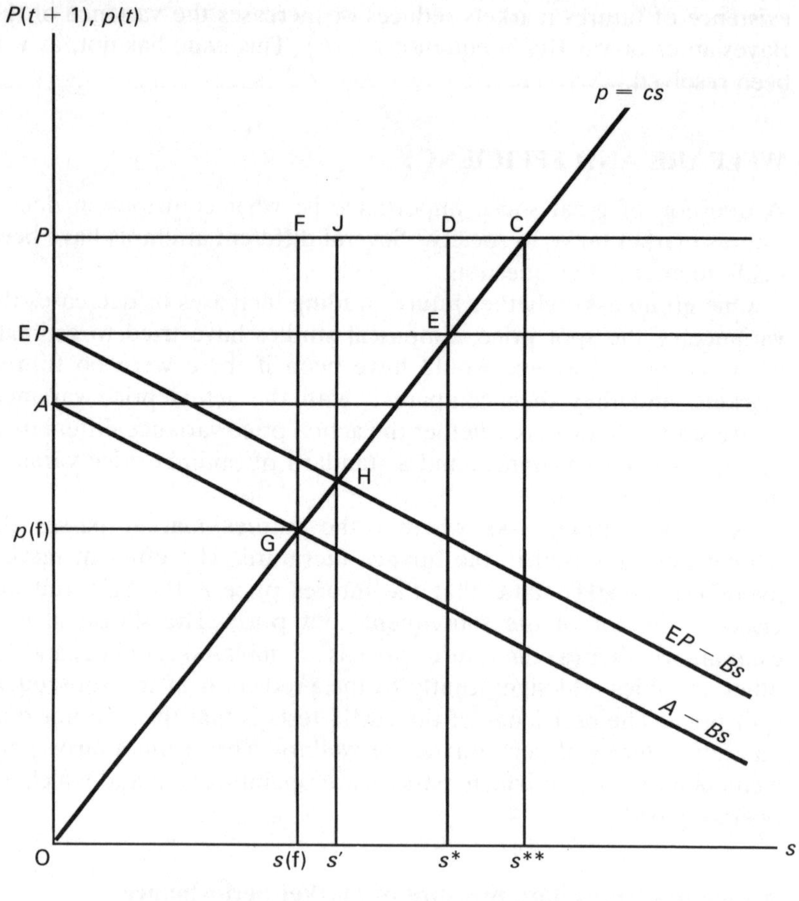

Figure 1.3 Futures markets and welfare

sacrificed to purchase the securities. The demand curve for securities by the institutional investors at time $t + 1$ drawn in Figure 1.3 is the marginal utility of the securities. In so far as price $P(t + 1) = \beta I(t + 1) + \varepsilon$ is independent of s, the demand is perfectly elastic, or the marginal utility derived from the purchase of the securities is constant. (This is merely a simplifying assumption.)

The use of resources at time t and the subsequent sale of securities at time $t + 1$ changes welfare by the vertical distance between $P(t + 1)$ and $p(t) = cs$ in Figure 1.3. Marginal welfare is

$$w'(s) = P(t + 1) - p(t) = P(t + 1) - cs \tag{1.27}$$

If there is perfect foresight, then optimal welfare occurs when the rate of investment $s = s^{**}$ such that marginal welfare is zero: $w'(s^{**}) = 0$. Maximal welfare is $w(s^{**})$. The measure of welfare loss $L(s)$ is the difference between the maximal welfare $w(s^{**})$ and the welfare $w(s)$ that results from rate s of capital formation.

In figure 1.3, the maximal welfare is triangle OPC. If the rate of investment is s(f), then the welfare loss is triangle FGC. Formally, the welfare loss $L(s)$ is the integral of $w'(s)$ from s to s^{**}. $L(s)$, the area of the triangle, is given by

$$L(s) = w(s^{**}) - w(s) = [P(t+1) - p(t)]\frac{(s^{**} - s)}{2} \qquad (1.28)$$

We know the actual rate of capital formation s but we do not know the optimum s^{**}. Since we know that the slope of the marginal cost curve is c, we can express $L(s)$ in terms of measurable variables. This loss is given by

$$L(s) = \frac{[P(t+1) - p(t)]^2}{2c} \qquad (1.29)$$

The most important thing to notice is that the welfare loss involves a square, since it is the area of a triangle. The loss can be decomposed into the components discussed in the previous section:

$$L(s) = \frac{[(P-A) + (A-p)]^2}{2c} \qquad (1.30)$$

where the first term $P - A$ is the price discovery term and the second term $A - p$ is the risk premium.

In terms of Figure 1.3, suppose that the actual rate of investment is s(f). The welfare loss is triangle GFC. The price discovery component is distance PA. The risk premium component is distance Ap(f). These components are discussed above.

The price discovery component $P - A = (P - \mathrm{E}P) + (\mathrm{E}P - A)$ was derived in equation (1.25a). It is the sum of two stochastic variables: an unavoidable error $U = P - \mathrm{E}P$ and a Bayesian error $\mathrm{BE} = \mathrm{E}P - A$. The expected value of the welfare loss $\mathrm{E}L(s)$, taken over these two variables, is given by

$$\mathrm{E}L(s) = \frac{\mathrm{E}[(P - \mathrm{E}P) + (\mathrm{E}P - A) + (A - p)]^2}{2c}$$

$$= \frac{\mathrm{E}[U + \mathrm{BE} + \mathrm{RP}]^2}{2c} \qquad (1.31)$$

The expected welfare loss measures the deviation from a perfect foresight situation. This is an unrealistic standard. It would make more sense to use the MRE condition as the standard of comparison.

If there were MRE, at time t people would know the objective mean EI of the price of the government bond (the index) that will prevail at $t + 1$. There is no Bayesian error, and $A = \mathrm{E}P = \beta \mathrm{E}I + m$ is the intercept of the demand curve of the intermediary. The equilibrium quantity of investment would be s' such that $p(t) = \mathrm{E}P - Bs' = cs'$. Then the only components of the marginal loss are (a) the unavoidable error U due to random variations of $P(t + 1)$ around EP and (b) the risk premium RP.

There is also a good reason to argue, as do Arrow and Lind (1970), that there should not be a social risk premium. In social investment, the risk is allocated among all the taxpayers. When there are many taxpayers, each absorbs a small part of the loss and there is no social risk premium.

When the MRE assumption is combined with the Arrow–Lind argument, the optimal allocation of resources should involve no Bayesian error or risk premium. The optimal rate of investment is $s = s^*$, where the bid price $p(t)$ is equal to EP. Then the expected welfare loss will be E$L(s^*)$ as described by

$$\mathrm{E}L(s^*) = \frac{\mathrm{var}\ U}{2c} \tag{1.32}$$

which is the minimum expected loss. The measure of social loss SL is given by the ratio of (1.31) to (1.32):

$$\mathrm{SL} = \frac{\mathrm{E}[P(t + 1) - p(t)]^2}{\mathrm{var}\ U} \tag{1.33}$$

This ratio can be understood from Figure 1.3. If there were MRE and no risk premium, the investment rate would be s^*. The marginal cost would be equal to the MRE price: $p(t) = cs = \mathrm{E}P$. The welfare loss arises when the actual price $P(t + 1)$ differs from the MRE price EP. If the actual price is P, then the welfare loss is triangle CDE. The expectation of these triangles is E$L(s^*)$ in (1.32).

Suppose that there is both a Bayesian error $\mathrm{E}P - A$ and a risk premium $A - p$. Then investment is s(f) and the welfare loss is triangle CFG. This triangle is the sum of three components.

1 The unavoidable welfare loss resulting from U is given by triangle CDE.
2 If there were MRE and a risk premium, then investment would be

at point s' where $EP - Bs' = cs'$. The loss that results from a risk premium and MRE is trapezoid EDJH.

3 If there is also a Bayesian error $EP - A > 0$, then investment is $s(f)$ where $A - Bs = cs$. This produces an additional welfare loss equal to trapezoid JFGH.

When $s = s(f)$, then

$$SL = \frac{CFG}{CDE} = \frac{CDE + DEHJ + JFGH}{CDE}$$

During any period, the welfare loss triangle can be smaller than CDE because of the covariance term in the following equation:

$$\begin{aligned} SL &= \frac{E[(P - EP) + (EP - p)]^2}{E(P - EP)^2} \\ &= 1 + \frac{E(EP - p)^2 + 2E(P - EP, EP - p)}{\text{var } P} \\ &= 1 + \frac{E(BE + RP)^2 + 2E(U, BE + RP)}{\text{var } P} \end{aligned} \tag{1.34}$$

If, during a given period, the Bayesian error BE and the unavoidable error U are negatively correlated, the social loss triangle can be less than CDE. For example, if A exceeds EP when P exceeds EP, then more investment would be produced than would exist if there were MRE and a risk premium. That case would be serendipitous, because we would expect U and BE to be independent.

We can now obtain a quantitative measure of market performance in terms of the SL statistic. The numerator is a mean square $E[P(t + 1) - p(t)]^2$ between the price $P(t + 1)$ paid by the institutional investor and the intermediary's bid price $p(t)$. The denominator is the variance of the price of the security in the market. Each term is measurable. Therefore, we can obtain SL(f) and SL(n) for the cases when there are and when there are not futures markets. The greater price volatility that leads to the introduction of a futures market is explicitly taken into account in the denominator. Moreover, we can rank speculative markets in terms of their SL statistics. The higher the SL is, the worse is the performance.

CONCLUSION

We know that futures markets reduce the risk premium and increase welfare. *A priori*, we do not know whether futures markets improve or adversely affect the price discovery process. However, when we examine the SL statistics we can answer the question of whether futures improve or decrease the efficiency of the price discovery process.

The two aims of this chapter have been (a) to develop a theory of the effects of financial futures upon the rate of real investment and (b) to devise a welfare measure of market performance. The first aim was achieved in the first three sections, and the second was achieved in the fourth section.

REFERENCES

Arrow, K. and Lind, R. C. (1970) 'Uncertainty and the evaluation of public investment', *American Economic Review* 60: 364–78.

Goss, B. A. and Yamey, B. (1976) *The Economics of Futures Trading*, London: Macmillan.

Keynes, J. M. (1930) *A Treatise on Money*, London: Macmillan.

Modigliani, F. and Miller, M. (1958) 'The cost of capital, corporation finance, and the theory of investment', *American Economic Review* 48: 261–97.

Peck, A. E. (1985) 'The economic role of traditional commodity futures markets', in A. E. Peck (ed.) *Futures Markets: Their Economic Role*, Washington, DC: American Enterprise Institute.

Silber, W. (1985) 'The economic role of financial futures', in A. E. Peck (ed.) *Futures Markets: Their Economic Role*, Washington, DC: American Enterprise Institute.

Stein, J. L. (1986) *The Economics of Futures Markets*, New York: Basil Blackwell.

—— (1990) 'An evaluation of the performances of speculative markets', in L. Phlips (ed.) *Commodity, Futures and Financial Markets*, Kluwer Academic Publishers, 153–78.

Tobin, J. (1969) 'A general equilibrium approach to monetary theory', *Journal of Money, Credit and Banking* 1: 15–29.

2 Foreign currency futures spreads and risk premiums

Thomas H. McCurdy and Ieuan G. Morgan

INTRODUCTION

The intertemporal asset pricing model was extended a few years ago to price nominal assets in an international setting (for example, Lucas 1982). Many applications of the model to financial forward markets followed, including those by Hansen and Hodrick (1983), Hodrick and Srivastava (1984) and Mark (1985). However, it is only recently that the work of Cox *et al.* (1981) and Richard and Sundaresan (1981) on futures has been adapted for financial futures. Applications to foreign currency futures include those by Hodrick and Srivastava (1987) and McCurdy and Morgan (1987, 1988a).

In these analyses, emphasis has been placed on testing for the potential time-varying risk premiums implied by the intertemporal asset pricing model. However, the applications to financial futures markets are very recent, and their results with respect to risk premiums are inconclusive. Hodrick (1987: 140–50) reviewed some of the evidence and concluded that more work was needed to resolve the issues raised by conflicting inferences drawn in different analyses. The aim of this chapter is to provide some new evidence concerning the temporal behaviour of risk premiums in foreign currency futures prices. This new evidence is derived from the study of spreads in the futures market in which a long position in one contract is offset by a short position in another contract for the same commodity but a different maturity.

Futures market analysis favours the use of high-frequency data. For example, tests of the time series behaviour of the basis, or difference between futures and spot prices, proposed by McCurdy and Morgan (1988b) require the use of daily data since cash flows are generated daily by the institutional practice of marking to market and overnight interest rates are stochastic. Direct testing of the martingale hypothesis for futures prices themselves is less restrictive in this respect, but it seems reasonable to assume that, if an interval of observation longer than one day is chosen for examining the rate of change of futures prices, the resulting loss of information may reduce the power of the tests to reject the hypothesis. It might be possible to reconcile some of the different inferences for weekly as opposed to daily data in this way, but a serious limitation of the published work to date has been the indirect nature of the testing for the risk premium hypothesis as the alternative to the martingale hypothesis. On the one hand, measurement of consumption and the general price level at a daily frequency is not feasible, and so testing for consumption and nominal (or purchasing power) risk in an intertemporal model must be indirect. On the other hand, the wealth-based single-period theory of the capital asset pricing model was adapted to futures pricing by Dusak (1973) and Black (1976), and it provides an observable measure for risk in the form of the daily excess returns from the market portfolio. Use of this measure in a multi-period consumption setting can be supported by a conditional capital asset pricing model or by the recent work of Epstein and Zin (1987) in which the standard additive expected utility specification is generalized.

Use of daily data also presents some potential problems. Test results rejecting a null hypothesis of no risk premium with daily data have been ambiguous because of the confounding influence of day of the week periodicity in futures prices. Even though the null hypothesis may have been rejected in these instances, the specific alternative of a risk premium was not being tested. In a futures spread formed from contracts of different maturities for the same commodity, the periodicity in the futures price of one contract may be offset by similar periodicity in the futures price of the other contract.

McCurdy and Morgan (1988c) found significant time-varying systematic or market risk in foreign currency futures prices. In this chapter we present evidence of small but significant systematic or market risk estimates in foreign currency futures spreads, and therefore of a systematic risk in futures prices related to the length of maturity of the contract. Our results indicate that the shorter maturity futures contract has the greater systematic risk.

Breeden (1980) estimated market risks as well as consumption betas for various real commodities and contract maturities with annual and quarterly futures data. His paper included the following remarks:

> Due to the very high correlations between spot and futures prices for most commodities, the determinants of futures' consumption betas are likely to be explained in large part by the same factors as the spots are. In applying the theory ... to the analysis of futures an important consideration is of the dependence of elasticities upon the time to maturity ... A possible result, which is seen in some commodities in the subsequent empirical estimates of consumption-betas, is that consumption-betas decline as the time to maturity increases, due to supply responses.

Breeden expressed his findings in this way:

> Note that, contrary to the generally negative quarterly market beta estimates ... verified here for many contract maturities, the consumption beta estimates show that several futures contracts have positive systematic risks as defined by the intertemporal CAPM [Capital asset pricing model]. For these contracts normal backwardation is predicted by the intertemporal CAPM, whereas the single period CAPM predicts contango.

Since we find positive estimates of systematic or market risk in foreign currency futures prices (McCurdy and Morgan 1988c) and negative estimates in spreads in which there is a long position in the longer maturity contract and a short position in the shorter maturity contract, our daily data analyses of market risks in foreign currency futures appear to be consistent with the pattern suggested by Breeden's work on consumption risks rather than market risks. However, our analyses of futures contracts deal with financial assets as opposed to real commodities, use daily as opposed to quarterly or annual data and explicitly model the time-varying variance of the futures prices as conditional heteroscedasticity.

In this chapter we use the intertemporal asset pricing paradigm to value a hedged position consisting of a futures spread. We present the univariate test equation for futures spreads risk premiums and the associated conditional variance function, and the bivariate test equation for time-varying spreads risk premiums. Issues related to the data are discussed, and univariate and bivariate results are summarized. Brief concluding comments are given in the final section.

THEORETICAL BACKGROUND

Let C_t be the number of units of the good consumed at t, p_t be the price per unit of the (consumption) good at t and $M_{t,\,t-1}$ be the intertemporal marginal rate of substitution of domestic currency between time t and time $t-1$. For the special case of a constant time preference factor δ and an additively time-separable multi-period utility function,

$$M_{t,\,t-1} \equiv \delta \frac{u'(C_t)}{u'(C_{t-1})} \quad \frac{p_{t-1}}{p_t}$$

$F_{T,t}$ is the price at t of a futures contract to deliver one unit of the foreign currency at T and R_{t-1} is 1 plus the US riskless rate of interest from $t-1$ to t.

Given that a futures contract has zero present value because the investment outlay is zero, and that we have a long position in futures initiated at t and offset by a short position taken at $t+1$, Theorem 1 of Richard and Sundaresan (1981), adapted for pricing nominal assets, implies that

$$0 = \mathrm{E}_t\left[\delta \frac{u'(C_{t+1})}{u'(C_t)} \frac{p_t}{p_{t+1}} (F_{T,\,t+1} - F_{T,t}) R_t\right]$$

Covariance decomposition gives

$$F_{T,t} = \mathrm{E}_t F_{T,t+1} + \mathrm{cov}_t\left[\delta \frac{u'(C_{t+1})}{u'(C_t)} \frac{p_t}{p_{t+1}} R_t,\, F_{T,t+1}\right] \tag{2.1}$$

A direct implication of (2.1) for futures contracts with two different expiration dates, $T = 1$ and $T = 2$, is

$$\frac{F_{2,t-1} - F_{1,t-1}}{F_{1,t-1}} = \frac{\mathrm{E}_{t-1}(F_{2,t} - F_{1,t})}{F_{1,\,t-1}} +$$

$$\mathrm{cov}_{t-1}\left(M_{t,t-1}R_{t-1},\, \frac{F_{2,t} - F_{1,t}}{F_{1,t-1}}\right) \tag{2.2}$$

which defines the value of a futures spread at $t-1$ in terms of quantities expected for t. In (2.2) all quantities corresponding to those in (2.1) have been divided by $F_{1,\,t-1}$, the value of the futures price for the contract with the shorter time to maturity, to make them independent of scale. The price $F_{1,\,t-1}$ is, of course, known at $t-1$.

The conditional covariance in (2.2) can be interpreted as a one-period risk premium for the spread. For example, for simplicity let $\mathrm{E}_{t-1}(F_{2,t} - F_{1,t})$ be zero. Then the left hand side of (2.2) has the same sign as that of $\text{cov}_{t-1}(M_{t,t-1}, F_{2,t} - F_{1,t})$. If the marginal utility of consumption is declining in C_t, then $F_{2,t-1} < F_{1,t-1}$ if the shorter maturity futures contract is a better hedge against variation in consumption at t than the longer maturity contract or, equivalently, $\text{cov}_{t-1}(M_{t,t-1}, F_{1,t}) > \text{cov}_{t-1}(M_{t,t-1}, F_{2,t})$. A sufficient condition for the conditional covariance term in (2.2) to be zero is that the prices for the two futures contracts in the spread have the same covariation with the marginal utility from a dollar's worth of consumption.

The risk premium in (2.2) was derived from the intertemporal asset pricing model and, as indicated in the introduction, is not in a directly testable form in applications using daily data. Hansen *et al.* (1982) and Hansen and Hodrick (1983), building on an idea due to Breeden (1979), assumed the existence of a benchmark portfolio b with nominal return $R_{b,t}$ perfectly conditionally correlated with $M_{t,t-1}$, to derive a conditional capital asset pricing model. As in Campbell (1987), the perfect correlation assumption establishes that this portfolio must be efficient, i.e. on the minimum variance frontier; the existence of any asset assumed to have the same expected return but lower variance would require that the conditional correlation coefficient of the portfolio $\text{corr}_{t-1}(M_{t,t-1}, R_{b,t})$ is greater than unity.

Let z be the minimum variance portfolio orthogonal to portfolio b. Since $\text{E}_{t-1}(M_{t,t-1}, R_{z,t}) = 1$ and $\text{cov}_{t-1}(M_{t,t-1}, R_{z,t}) = 0$, then $\text{E}_{t-1} R_{z,t} = 1/\text{E}_{t-1} M_{t,t-1}$. Given the assumption of a riskless nominal asset, for which $\text{E}_{t-1}(M_{t,t-1} R_{t-1}) = 1$, $\text{E}_{t-1} R_{z,t} = R_{t-1}$. In other words by Corollary 3A of Roll (1977), portfolio b with return perfectly conditionally correlated with $M_{t,t-1}$ must be the portfolio at the point of tangency between the efficient set and a straight line through the riskless rate in mean standard deviation space. In this model, the tangent portfolio is on the negatively sloped portion of the minimum variance frontier. Because portfolio b is efficient, corollary 3 of Roll (1977) establishes that returns on individual assets can be expressed as exact linear functions of its returns and those of its unique minimum variance orthogonal portfolio z. Then (2.2) can be rewritten in terms of the expected excess returns $\text{E}_{t-1}(R_{b,t} - R_{t-1})$ in a conditional capital asset pricing model. That is, with the notation

$$R^*_{b,t} \equiv R_{b,t} - R_{t-1}$$

for the tangent portfolio return in excess of the riskless rate of interest and

$$b_{t-1} \equiv \frac{\mathrm{cov}_{t-1}[(F_{2,t} - F_{1,t})/F_{1,t-1}, R^*_{b,t}]}{\mathrm{var}_{t-1}(R^*_{b,t})},$$

for the conditional risk, (2.2) becomes

$$\frac{\mathrm{E}_{t-1}(F_{2,t} - F_{1,t})}{F_{1,t-1}} = \frac{F_{2,t-1} - F_{1,t-1}}{F_{1,t-1}} + b_{t-1}\mathrm{E}_{t-1}R^*_{b,t} \quad (2.3)$$

THE UNIVARIATE TEST EQUATION FOR FUTURES SPREADS RISK PREMIUMS

In the univariate analyses, tests for risk premiums associated with futures spreads must proceed under the assumption that the systematic risk is constant (i.e. the conditional and unconditional moments are equal). We obtain indirect tests for the existence of time-varying risk premiums by examining the behaviour of the test equation with respect to omitted variables that are potentially relevant *a priori.* Direct estimates of time-varying systematic risk premiums with a bivariate model will be described in the next section.

A link between theory and data for empirical work depends on $\mathrm{E}_{t-1}R_{z,t} = R_{t-1}$, with $R_{b,t}$ being the return from the tangent portfolio. To obtain a test equation from (2.3), we identify the tangent portfolio with the market portfolio, with excess return $R^*_{\mathrm{m},t}$, replace the rational expectation of the scaled spread by its realized value minus a forecast error with a conditional mean of zero, allow for a first-order moving-average error process in the time series behaviour of the test equation residuals and add indicator variables to capture any significant day of the week periodicity. Then, except for any indicator variables,

$$\frac{F_{2,t} - F_{1,t}}{F_{1,t-1}} - \frac{F_{2,t-1} - F_{1,t-1}}{F_{1,t-1}} = \gamma_0 + \gamma_1 R^*_{\mathrm{m},t} + \psi\varepsilon_{t-1} + \varepsilon_t \quad (2.4a)$$

We shall continue to refer to the quantity given by the dependent variable in (2.4a) as the spread.

For the conditional variance h_t of the error term

$$\varepsilon_t | I_{t-1} \sim \mathrm{N}(0, h_t)$$

we use an integrated generalized autoregressive conditional heteroscedasticity (IGARCH) model introduced by Engle and Bollerslev

(1986). Let g_{it-1} represent an $n \times 1$ vector of variables in the information set at $t-1$. Then the IGARCH model for the conditional variance is

$$h_t = \alpha_0 + (1-\beta)\varepsilon_{t-1}^2 + \beta h_{t-1} + \sum_{i=1}^{n} \phi_i g_{it-1} \tag{2.4b}$$

THE BIVARIATE TEST EQUATION FOR FUTURES SPREADS RISK PREMIUMS

Baillie and Bollerslev (1987) and Bollerslev (1987) have proposed a multivariate model for analysing vectors of rates of change of spot and forward prices of foreign currencies. Their model achieved a parsimonious specification by the assumption of constant conditional correlation between any pair of currencies. We use a bivariate version of this model, pairing each currency in turn with the market portfolio excess returns to analyse futures spreads while letting the systematic risk of the spread vary through time. One reason for doing this is to represent a possible effect of time to maturity of the contract on conditional systematic risk.

The bivariate test equation for the futures spread is similar to equation (2.3) but with the systematic risk specified to be the conditional covariance defined to be the product of the constant conditional correlation between the spread and the excess return from the market portfolio and the time-varying conditional standard deviations of these variables. The behaviour of the excess returns from the market portfolio itself is modelled as IGARCH with an MA(1) error term, as in Chou (1987).

Our application of the bivariate model suffers from one conceptual difficulty. The market portfolio represents an important part of world aggregate wealth but futures market contracts represent zero net wealth. Marcus (1984) has emphasized this point. Letting the futures data reflect the contemporaneous market portfolio behaviour makes sense, but any potential dependence in the other direction, stemming from the symmetric influence of the constant correlation coefficient on the conditional variances in the model, can make sense only if the futures market data are interpreted as representing components of wealth not included in the prices of New York Stock Exchange and American Exchange common stocks.

With the notation $R^*_{\mathrm{m},t} = R_{\mathrm{m},t} - R_{t-1}$ for the excess return from the market portfolio, $h_{\mathrm{m},t}$ for its conditional variance, $h_{\mathrm{f},t}$ for the conditional variance of the spread, ρ for the constant correlation between the two and $h_{\mathrm{f,m},t} = \rho h_{\mathrm{f},t}^{1/2} h_{\mathrm{m},f}^{1/2}$ for the corresponding conditional covariance, the bivariate model system of equations is

$$\frac{F_{2,t} - F_{1,t}}{F_{1,t-1}} - \frac{F_{2,t-1} - F_{1,t-1}}{F_{1,t-1}} =$$

$$\gamma_{0,\mathrm{f}} + \frac{h_{\mathrm{f,m},t}}{h_{\mathrm{m},t}} (\gamma_{0,\mathrm{m}} + \psi_{\mathrm{m}} \varepsilon_{\mathrm{m},t-1}) + \psi_{\mathrm{f}} \varepsilon_{\mathrm{f},t-1} + \varepsilon_{\mathrm{f},t} \tag{2.5a}$$

$$h_{\mathrm{f},t} = \alpha_{0,\mathrm{f}} + (1 - \beta_{\mathrm{f}}) \varepsilon_{\mathrm{f},t-1}^{2} + \beta_{\mathrm{f}} h_{\mathrm{f},t-1} + \sum_{i=1}^{n} \phi_i g_{i,t-1} \tag{2.5b}$$

$$R_{\mathrm{m},t}^{*} = \gamma_{0,\mathrm{m}} + \psi_{\mathrm{m}} \varepsilon_{\mathrm{m},t-1} + \varepsilon_{\mathrm{m},t} \tag{2.6a}$$

$$h_{\mathrm{m},t} = \alpha_{0,\mathrm{m}} + (1 - \beta_{\mathrm{m}}) \varepsilon_{\mathrm{m},t-1}^{2} + \beta_{\mathrm{m}} h_{\mathrm{m},t-1} \tag{2.6b}$$

This basic structure is augmented by the addition of an indicator variable with the value of unity on Monday or on a Tuesday following a holiday on Monday, and zero otherwise, to the regression equation for the market portfolio excess return. Similarly, for the British pound spread, an indicator variable with the value of unity on Friday and zero otherwise is added to the regression equation. These additions were indicated by our specification tests discussed below.

DATA

Futures prices for the British pound, the Canadian dollar, the Deutschmark, the Japanese yen and the Swiss franc (BP, CD, DM, JY and SF respectively) were taken from the 1985 version of the file provided by the Center for Research in Futures Markets (CRFM) of the University of Chicago. We used futures settlement prices for the contracts with the shortest and next to shortest maturities available at any time up to and including the Friday before the end of the life of the shortest contract. The data start on 1 October 1981 and end on 31 December 1985. Until 1 October 1981, US dollar cheques written to purchase spot foreign exchange for delivery on a given business day cleared for federal funds the following business day. The resulting artificially high demand for foreign currency before the weekend was described by Levi (1978); very closely related day of the week patterns in changes in futures prices for five currencies have been described by McCurdy and Morgan (1987). By starting our sample period on 1 October 1981, we avoid the market imperfection that originated in the spot market and spilled over into the futures markets for foreign currencies. The series of 1,075 observations gives an effective sample size of 1,074 because the first observation is used in the start of the estimation.

In some of our tests for omitted variables we used short-term interest rates to compute a relative interest rate differential. The shortest debt maturity for which rates were quoted in readily available sources was two days for most actively traded foreign currencies, but overnight Eurocurrency interest rates were available for the United States and Japan. The Eurocurrency rate for Canada switched from being call to two-day notice part way through our sample period on 21 November 1983. On and after this date we used the 'most often quoted' call rate quoted by the Bank of Canada. When one or both interest rates were unavailable because of holidays we substituted both rates for the previous day.

For the market return in (2.4a), and in the bivariate analyses, we used the value-weighted market portfolio return in excess of the overnight rate of interest. The market portfolio return was taken from the daily data file of the Center for Research in Security Prices of the University of Chicago.

Futures prices are subject to rules specifying the maximum price change that can occur in one day. In the sample period, the limits were not tight for these five currencies and they were removed entirely on 22 February 1985. There were no occasions at all on which there were limit moves in BP and SF, six days in CD, two in DM and three in JY. When a limit move occurs for a given futures contract, the settlement price for that contract is clearly not an equilibrium price. When both contracts involved in a spread have limit moves on the same day, the resulting distortion in the dependent variable is probably not severe because the deviations from the equilibrium prices tend to cancel each other. A potentially serious problem occurs when one contract has a limit move but the other does not, as could happen towards the end of the life of the contract with shorter maturity. Under the rules in effect the limits did not apply in the 'spot' month beginning on the last day of trading of the month before the month in which the contact matured. In other words, except for most of the last year of the sample period, spreads were potentially awkward quantities to work with in the last three weeks or so of a contract's life because the near futures price was free but the far futures price was subject to the limit rules. For example, in

JY on 2 March 1984 there was a limit move on the June 1984 contract but not on the March 1984 contract, although the price change for this contract was greater. We treated this type of event by defining an indicator variable with the value of unity if on a given day the settlement price was a limit move for one contract in the spread but free for the other.

UNIVARIATE RESULTS

We present the estimates of equation (2.4) for each currency in Table 2.1. Table 2.2 reports the results of some diagnostic test statistics on

Table 2.1 Univariate model estimates of futures spreads

		BP	*CD*	*DM*	*JY*	*SF*
Constant	$\hat{\gamma}_0$	−0.0198	−0.0015	−0.0018	−0.0235	−0.0052
		(0.0126)	(0.0059)	(0.0107)	(0.0096)	(0.0108)
$R_{m,t} - R_{t-1}$	$\hat{\gamma}_1$	−0.0075	−0.0011	−0.0040	−0.0097	−0.0026
		(0.0016)	(0.0010)	(0.0016)	(0.0016)	(0.0018)
F	$\hat{\gamma}_2$	−0.079				
		(0.033)				
ε_{t-1}	$\hat{\psi}$	−0.062	−0.191	−0.178	−0.244	−0.236
		(0.038)	(0.035)	(0.035)	(0.032)	(0.031)
Constant	$\hat{\alpha}_0$	0.0	0.0029	0.0061	0.0	−0.0080
			(0.0007)	(0.0016)		
IGARCH	$\hat{\beta}$	0.759	0.787	0.844	0.764	0.905
		(0.028)	(0.030)	(0.020)	(0.032)	(0.022)
F	$\hat{\phi}_1$	0.060				0.056
		(0.014)				(0.007)
N	$\hat{\phi}_2$				0.260	
					(0.090)	
$\lvert R_{t-1}/Z_{t-1} - 1\rvert$	$\hat{\phi}_3$				0.0091	
					(0.0024)	
Limit	$\hat{\phi}_4$				1.467	
					(0.590)	

Notes: Standard errors are shown in parenthesis.

F is an indicator variable for Friday, N is an indicator for the first day of trading of a spread with a new futures contract and 'Limit' is an indicator for the event that only one futures price of the two in the spread was restricted by the limit rules.

For the lower bound restrictions on α_0 the OPG LM test statistic p values were 0.22 for the BP, 0.99 for the JY and 0.46 for the SF.

Table 2.2 Diagnostic tests for the models in Table 2.1

	BP	*CD*	*DM*	*JY*	*SF*
R	−1.85 (0.06)	−4.83 (0.00)	−2.74 (0.01)	−0.79 (0.43)	−3.05 (0.00)
$Q(10)$	6.37 (0.78)	14.43 (0.15)	4.11 (0.94)	10.30 (0.41)	5.17 (0.88)
$Q^2(10)$	6.33 (0.79)	10.17 (0.43)	5.25 (0.87)	15.08 (0.13)	9.31 (0.50)
S	4.44 (0.04)	1.30 (0.25)	0.09 (0.76)	4.21 (0.04)	0.70 (0.40)
K	19.16 (0.00)	10.51 (0.00)	15.61 (0.00)	23.23 (0.00)	9.32 (0.00)

Notes: *R* is the test statistic for runs above the mean, $Q(10)$ is the Ljung–Box form of the portmanteau statistic for autocorrelation in the first ten lags of the standardized residuals, $Q^2(10)$ is the same statistic for the squared standardized residuals, and *S* and *K* are the conditional moment test statistics for skewness and kurtosis respectively. The *p* values, shown in parenthesis, are for the χ^2 distribution.

the standardized residuals $\varepsilon_t / h_t^{1/2}$ as well as conditional moment tests (Newey 1985; Tauchen 1985) for skewness and excess kurtosis. Outer product of the gradient Lagrange multiplier (OPG LM) test statistics for omitted variables (Godfrey and Wickens 1982; Davidson and MacKinnon 1988) are presented in Table 2.3. In all analyses, the spread, the relative interest rate differential and the excess market return values are scaled by multiplication by 1,000.

Table 2.1 shows very small but significantly negative values of the estimates of the coefficient γ_t for the constant systematic risk of the futures spread in three currencies: BP, DM and JY. The equation estimated is not the same for every currency. CD and DM have particularly simple equations. BP is slightly more complicated because the Friday indicator variable is included in both the regression and the conditional variance. The conditional variance function for JY is complicated: it includes an indicator variable with a value of unity on the first day of the changeover to a new pair of contracts in the spread and zero otherwise, the absolute value of the relative interest rate differential and an indicator variable with the value of unity if, at *t*, only one of the futures prices of the pair in the spread was constrained by the limit move rules of the exchange. The conditional variance function of SF was problematic until its constant term was allowed to assume a negative value. The constrained value

Table 2.3 Outer product of the gradient Lagrange multiplier tests for omitted variables

	BP		*CD*		*DM*		*JY*		*SF*	
	Mean	*Variance*	*Mean*	*Variance*	*Mean*	*Variance*	*Mean*	*Variance*	*Mean*	*Variance*
d.f.	1	2	1	1	1	1	1	2	1	2
$R_{t-1}/Z_{t-1} - 1$	1.22	1.55	2.53	0.71	1.44	0.07	2.02		0.35	3.49
	(0.27)	(0.46)	(0.11)	(0.40)	(0.23)	(0.79)	(0.16)		(0.55)	(0.17)
$\|R_{t-1}/Z_{t-1} - 1\|^{1/2}$	2.87	1.96	1.75	0.36	1.90	1.14	0.03	4.39	0.22	3.24
	(0.09)	(0.38)	(0.19)	(0.55)	(0.17)	(0.71)	(0.86)	(0.11)	(0.64)	(0.20)
M	2.07	1.50	0.01	0.30	2.25	1.08	0.41	0.00	0.14	0.57
	(0.15)	(0.47)	(0.92)	(0.58)	(0.13)	(0.30)	(0.52)	(0.99)	(0.71)	(0.75)
T	0.03	1.49	0.46	1.35	1.75	0.06	0.38	4.75	2.26	0.60
	(0.86)	(0.47)	(0.50)	(0.25)	(0.19)	(0.81)	(0.54)	(0.09)	(0.13)	(0.74)
W	0.05	4.84	0.25	2.80	0.00	3.51	0.04	0.13	0.02	0.57
	(0.82)	(0.09)	(0.62)	(0.09)	(0.99)	(0.06)	(0.84)	(0.94)	(0.89)	(0.75)
Th	1.83	2.79	0.38	0.06	1.49	1.25	0.32	3.85	0.23	1.07
	(0.18)	(0.25)	(0.54)	(0.81)	(0.22)	(0.26)	(0.57)	(0.15)	(0.63)	(0.59)
F			0.26	0.32	1.14	0.70	1.13	0.20	0.64	
			(0.61)	(0.57)	(0.29)	(0.40)	(0.29)	(0.90)	(0.42)	
N	0.99	2.78	0.11	0.00	0.46	3.28			0.10	0.84
	(0.32)	(0.25)	(0.74)	(0.99)	(0.50)	(0.07)			(0.75)	(0.66)
$T - t$	1.63	6.01	1.53	0.50	2.85	0.56	1.15	0.26	0.35	9.43
	(0.20)	(0.05)	(0.22)	(0.48)	(0.09)	(0.45)	(0.28)	(0.88)	(0.55)	(0.01)

$(T-t)^{1/2}$	1.17	5.13	1.21	0.93	2.60	0.90	1.49	0.51	0.29	6.94
	(0.28)	(0.08)	(0.27)	(0.33)	(0.11)	(0.34)	(0.22)	(0.77)	(0.59)	(0.03)
$(T-t)^{-1/2}$	0.26	2.95	0.18	1.77	1.16	0.98	1.32	0.40	0.01	1.89
	(0.61)	(0.23)	(0.67)	(0.18)	(0.28)	(0.32)	(0.25)	(0.82)	(0.92)	(0.39)

Notes: p values, for the χ^2 distribution with d.f. degrees of freedom are shown in parenthesis. For the time to contract expiration variables the square of the variable is tested in the variance, but for $R_{t-1}/Z_{t-1} - 1$ the absolute value is tested in the variance. For the other interest rate differential variable, the day of the week indicators and the indicator N for the first day of trading of a spread with a new futures contract, the same form is tested in the variance and the mean.

(a lower bound of −0.008) for the constant term, reported in Table 2.1, had a *p* value of 0.46, indicating that the constraint did not conflict with the data.

Significantly negative coefficient estimates of the MA(1) term were obtained in all currencies except BP. It is not clear what feature of the settlement prices of futures contracts for the same commodity induces the moving-average structure in the futures spread since the settlement prices are determined simultaneously. A known source of negative first-order autocorrelation in common stock returns, particularly where the minimum price fluctuation allowed by the exchange is large relative to the price, is the bid–ask spread (Roll 1984). Even if there were a counterpart in futures markets, it would be difficult to explain why the currency with the least noticeable moving-average structure in the spread is BP. The currency has a minimum price fluctuation of US$ 0.0005, five times that for the other major currencies (with the exception of JY), but its value in the sample period was only two or three times the value of the currencies with lower minimum price fluctuation.

A second possibility is that the longer-term contract of the spread, because it is typically less frequently traded than the nearer-term contract, has a settlement price that may have been determined by its last trade made earlier in the day than the last trade for the more actively traded contract. Even if the settlement prices are fixed simultaneously, the prices on which they were based would not have been for simultaneous trades. As shown by McCurdy and Morgan (1988b) for the basis, a first-order moving-average structure is then induced. The possibility that the moving-average term is induced by non-simultaneous trades, in turn related to less active trading of the longer-term contract, may also be consistent with the negative estimates obtained for the systematic risk of the spread. Scholes and Williams (1977), in a similar context, have shown how infrequent trading leads to a downward bias in the estimate of systematic risk of a security. A sufficiently strong bias of this kind could produce the observed negative systematic risk estimates for the spread even if the true risk for each of the futures is equal. Since we can offer no direct evidence to evaluate these possibilities, which depend on critical assumptions about the way that settlement prices are determined, we shall ignore them except to recognize their potential contribution to the moving-average structure and/or the systematic risk estimate for spreads.

Table 2.2 shows that there is some evidence of dependence in the standardized residuals, corresponding to positive autocorrelation, since the number of runs above the mean is significantly smaller than expected in CD, DM, and SF. Neither the portmanteau test for the first ten lags of the autocorrelation function nor the estimated first-order autocorrelation coefficient itself (not shown) confirms this evidence. The portmanteau test for the first ten lags of the autocorrelation function for the squared standardized residuals does not detect any remaining heteroscedasticity. In other words, the IGARCH representation of the conditional variance seems to be satisfactory. Our choice of the more parsimonious model IGARCH, as opposed to generalized autoregressive conditional heteroscedasticity (GARCH), was based on log likelihood ratio tests of the restriction $\alpha_1 + \beta = 1$ (Bollerslev 1988). The choice was supported by the absence of a noticeable advantage, according to the residual diagnostic statistics, of GARCH over IGARCH in this application. Since the likelihood ratio statistics for the restriction had *p* values of 0.51, 0.35, 0.46, 0.00 and 0.05 for the five currencies, only JY indicated a possible advantage of GARCH. The final row of Table 2.2 reveals excess kurtosis in every currency.

Table 2.3 presents the OPG LM tests for missing variables. Evidence of a missing variable in the regression equation (or mean) would be important because it would indicate a possible inadequacy of the systematic risk term as a surrogate for the conditional covariance term in (2.2). No evidence of this kind is found in Table 2.3, although, of course, the BP spread regression equation was augmented by the inclusion of the Friday indicator variable when such tests detected the need for it.

The OPG LM tests for variables omitted from the conditional variance function are also generally satisfactory. Only in SF is there an indication of a potential problem; low *p* values are shown for the statistics for the time to maturity and one of its transformations – the square of the time to maturity. Attempts to include this variable or its square in the variance function would fail because its coefficient would be sufficiently negative to result in a negative conditional variance for some days.

We infer that Tables 2.2 and 2.3 have revealed only relatively minor faults with the univariate model. An unexpected feature of the analysis was that the day of the week patterns in price in the futures prices themselves, recorded by McCurdy and Morgan (1988c), were not entirely eliminated in the spreads. It also seems fair to conclude that representing the risk premium or conditional covariance term in (2.2) by a specification of constant systematic risk for the futures spread is reasonable. The bivariate estimates of the next section provide further evidence about the risk premium under a different specification.

BIVARIATE RESULTS

In the bivariate analyses we were generally able to fit the exact equivalents of the univariate models described in the previous section. Table 2.4 shows the estimates for the bivariate system of equations, and Table 2.5 shows the diagnostic checks and conditional moment tests on the standardized residuals. Where the bivariate and univariate models differ, as for BP and JY, the bivariate model is the simpler of the two. In BP, the MA(1) term for the futures spread was dropped because it added negligible explanatory power; the *p* value for the likelihood ratio test statistic of 1.40 was 0.24. In JY, the estimated coefficient for the absolute value of the relative interest rate differential in the conditional variance function fell to an insignificantly small positive value; the *p* value for the likelihood ratio test statistic of 1.16 was 0.28. At the same time, the estimated value of the IGARCH parameter β_f for JY increased from 0.764 in the univariate analysis to 0.919 in the bivariate analysis.

A major feature of Table 2.4 is the set of estimated constant conditional correlation coefficient values. The correlation coefficient estimate is significantly negative in the futures spreads for three of the five currencies (BP, DM and JY), and these are the same three currencies as those with significantly negative estimates of systematic risk for the spreads in the univariate analyses in Table 2.1. In other words, the inferences that can be drawn from the univariate and bivariate analyses with regard to systematic risk are quite similar. Again, the correlations are small: a coefficient of −0.1 can be interpreted roughly as implying that 1 per cent of the variation of the futures spread is accounted for by the market portfolio excess returns. The time series of the spread consists of observations from the two shortest term futures contracts for a given foreign currency. On the Friday before the expiration of one contract the spread relates to the difference between the expected spot prices at, typically, 96 days later and five days later. On the following Monday, data from a new contract are taken and the spread relates to expected spot prices 184 days and 93 days later. The difference in the maturities is constant at 91 days. If the relationship between the systematic risk of the futures and the time to maturity of the contract is not markedly non-linear over this range, the constant difference of 91 days may help to explain why the inferences from the univariate (constant systematic

Table 2.4 Bivariate model estimates of futures spreads

		BP	*CD*	*DM*	*JY*	*SF*
Constant	$\hat{\gamma}_{0,f}$	−0.016 (0.014)	−0.001 (0.006)	−0.001 (0.011)	−0.023 (0.011)	−0.005 (0.011)
F	$\hat{\gamma}_{1,f}$	−0.071 (0.032)				
$\varepsilon_{f,t-1}$	$\hat{\psi}_{1,f}$		−0.186 (0.035)	−0.184 (0.034)	−0.216 (0.031)	−0.233 (0.032)
Constant	$\hat{\alpha}_{0,f}$	0.0	0.0029 (0.0007)	0.0037 (0.0013)	−0.0006 (0.0010)	−0.008
IGARCH	$\hat{\beta}_{1,f}$	0.835 (0.032)	0.785 (0.028)	0.881 (0.021)	0.932 (0.024)	0.918 (0.025)
F	$\hat{\phi}_{1,f}$	0.029 (0.011)				0.053 (0.007)
N	$\hat{\phi}_{2,f}$				0.142 (0.038)	
Limit	$\hat{\phi}_{3,f}$				0.512 (0.245)	
$\frac{h_{f,t}^{1/2}}{h_{m,t}^{1/2}}(\gamma_{0,m}+\psi_m\varepsilon_{m,t-1})$	$\hat{\rho}$	−0.113 (0.029)	−0.018 (0.031)	−0.069 (0.030)	−0.140 (0.031)	−0.045 (0.032)
Constant	$\hat{\gamma}_{0,m}$	0.076 (0.026)	0.073 (0.028)	0.078 (0.029)	0.080 (0.026)	0.077 (0.024)
M	$\hat{\gamma}_{1,m}$	−0.203 (0.048)	−0.206 (0.052)	−0.209 (0.052)	−0.203 (0.052)	−0.202 (0.046)
$\varepsilon_{m,t-1}$	$\hat{\psi}_{1,m}$	0.148 (0.033)	0.151 (0.032)	0.153 (0.033)	0.152 (0.033)	0.152 (0.032)
Constant	$\hat{\alpha}_{0,m}$	0.0014 (0.0011)	0.0014 (0.0011)	0.0014 (0.0011)	0.0014 (0.0012)	0.0014 (0.0011)
IGARCH	$\hat{\beta}_{1,m}$	0.960 (0.010)	0.960 (0.010)	0.960 (0.010)	0.960 (0.010)	0.960 (0.010)

Notes: Standard errors are shown in parentheses

M is an indicator taking the value of unity on Monday or on a Tuesday following a holiday Monday, *F* is an indicator variable for Friday, *N* is an indicator for the first day of trading of a spread with a new futures contract and 'limit' is an indicator for the event that only one futures price of the two in the spread was restricted by the limit rules.

Table 2.5 Diagnostic tests for the models in Table 2.4

	BP	*CD*	*DM*	*JY*	*SF*
R_f	−0.95	−4.77	−4.70	−2.29	−4.15
	(0.34)	(0.00)	(0.00)	(0.02)	(0.00)
$Q_f(10)$	5.29	14.24	6.86	12.47	5.80
	(0.87)	(0.15)	(0.74)	(0.25)	(0.83)
$Q_f^2(10)$	8.09	9.35	4.08	17.40	10.12
	(0.62)	(0.50)	(0.94)	(0.07)	(0.43)
$Q_{f,m}(10)$	3.38	9.39	8.81	5.50	4.45
	(0.97)	(0.50)	(0.55)	(0.86)	(0.92)
R_m	1.24	1.38	1.49	1.84	1.36
	(0.22)	(0.17)	(0.14)	(0.07)	(0.17)
$Q_m(10)$	4.90	4.76	4.75	4.51	4.76
	(0.90)	(0.91)	(0.91)	(0.92)	(0.91)
$Q_m^2(10)$	2.94	2.87	3.03	3.29	2.97
	(0.98)	(0.98)	(0.98)	(0.97)	(0.98)

Notes: See notes to Table 2.2. Subscript f refers to futures spread, and subscript m to the market portfolio excess returns. $Q_{f,m}$ is the portmanteau statistic for the autocorrelation function for the cross-products of the standardized residuals of the two series.

risk) and bivariate (varying systematic risk) specifications are so similar.

The diagnostic test statistics for the standardized residuals from the bivariate analyses in Table 2.5 are also similar to those for the univariate analyses. There is an unexpectedly small number of runs of observations above the mean in the runs test for all spreads except BP. The portmanteau tests on the first ten lags do not detect this persistence, nor do the equivalent tests of the squared standardized residuals detect any remaining heteroscedasticity. Similarly, the autocorrelation function for the cross-products of the standardized residuals from the futures spreads and the market portfolio excess returns reveals no evidence of interaction that would suggest the need for a more complicated model of the joint evolution of the time series. The specification of constant correlation but time-varying covariance appears to be adequate.

An informal evaluation of the adequacy of the constant correlation model can be obtained by a comparison of the five sets of estimates for the market portfolio excess returns in Tables 2.4 and 2.5. Marked differences between the estimates for the market portfolio equations in the bivariate analyses of the various currencies would be cause for concern. There do not seem to be important differences of this kind; the coefficient estimates for the market portfolio excess return equations in Table 2.4 do not change much when one currency is replaced by the next, nor are the *p* values for the diagnostic test statistics for the market portfolio returns sensitive to the choice of currency in Table 2.5. This robustness of the estimation of the market portfolio component is fortunate given the conceptual difficulty, discussed on p. 37, arising from the fact that the foreign currency spread position is not a component of net wealth. The results suggest that there is no serious difficulty with this particular empirical application of the bivariate model.

CONCLUSION

In this chapter we have provided new evidence about the temporal behaviour of risk premiums in foreign currency futures data. The evidence was found from the study of futures spreads in which a long position in one contract is offset by a short position in another contract for the same commodity. Very small but significant systematic or market risk estimates were found in three foreign currencies, indicating that the systematic risk in futures prices may be related to the length of maturity of the contract. Our results correspond to the shorter maturity futures contract's having the greater systematic risk. These conclusions hold for both the univariate and the bivariate sets of estimates and therefore are not sensitive to the specification of systematic risk as constant in the former or time varying in the latter. This suggests that the relationship between systematic risk and time to maturity of the futures contract is approximately linear over the range of times examined. The spread maintains a constant difference of 91 days between the times of maturity of the two contracts in the position: if the relationship is approximately linear it does not matter whether, for example, the shorter maturity contract has 91 days or only one day to expiration.

The conclusion that the shorter maturity contract has greater systematic risk should be qualified because it is not necessarily true that the analysis has controlled for all relevant factors. For example, it is apparent that the open interest and trading frequency of foreign currency futures contracts is much larger in the shorter-term than the longer-term contract. Until further more detailed evidence is obtained, our results suggest that the sensitivity of systematic risk to the time to maturity of the contract is slight enough for the relationship to have little quantitative economic importance.

NOTE

We thank the Social Sciences and Humanities Research Council of Canada for financial support.

REFERENCES

Baillie, R.T. and Bollerslev, T. (1987) 'A multivariate generalized ARCH approach to modelling risk premia in forward foreign exchange rate markets', unpublished manuscript.

Black, F. (1976) 'The pricing of commodity contracts', *Journal of Financial Economics* 3: 167–79.

Bollerslev, T. (1987) 'Modelling the coherence in short run nominal exchange rates: a multivariate generalized ARCH model,' unpublished manuscript, Northwestern University.

—— (1988) 'Integrated ARCH and cointegration in variance,' unpublished manuscript, Northwestern University.

Breeden, D.T. (1979) 'An intertemporal asset pricing model with stochastic consumption and investment opportunities,' *Journal of Financial Economics* 7: 265–96.

—— (1980) 'Consumption risk in futures markets,' *Journal of Finance* 35: 503–20.

Campbell, J.Y., (1987) 'Stock returns and the term structure', *Journal of Financial Economics* 18: 373–99.

Chou, R.Y. (1987) 'Persistent volatility and stock returns – some empirical evidence using GARCH, unpublished manuscript, University of California at San Diego.

Cox, J., Ingersoll, J. and Ross, S. (1981) 'The relation between forward prices and futures prices', *Journal of Financial Economics* 9: 321–46.

Davidson, R. and MacKinnon, J.G. (1988) 'Specification tests based on artificial regressions', unpublished manuscript, Queen's University, Kingston, Ontario.

Dusak, K. (1973) 'Futures trading and investor returns: an investigation of commodity market risk premiums', *Journal of Political Economy* 81: 1387–406.

Engle, R.F. and Bollerslev, T. (1986) 'Modelling the persistence of conditional variances,' *Econometric Reviews* 5 (1): 1–50.

Epstein, L. and Zin, S.E. (1987) 'Substitution, risk aversion and the temporal behaviour of consumption and asset returns I: A theoretical framework,' IER Discussion Paper 699, Queen's University, Kingston , Ontario.

Godfrey, L.G. and Wickens, M.R. (1982) 'Tests of misspecification using locally equivalent alternative models', in G.C. Chow and P. Corsi (eds) *Evaluating the Reliability of Macro-economic Models*, New York: Wiley.

Hansen, L.P. and Hodrick, R.J. (1983) 'Risk averse speculation in the forward foreign exchange market: an economic analysis of linear models,' in J.A. Frenkel (ed.) *Exchange Rates and International Macroeconomics*, Chicago Il: University of Chicago Press for the National Bureau of Economic Research.

Hansen, L.P. Richard, S.F. and Singleton, K.J. (1982) 'Econometric implications of the intertemporal capital asset pricing model', unpublished manuscript, Carnegie-Mellon University.

Hodrick, R.J. (1987) *The Empirical Evidence on the Efficiency of Forward and Futures Foreign Exchange Markets*, Chur: Harwood.

Hodrick, R.J. and Srivastava, S. (1984) 'An investigation of risk and return in forward foreign exchange', *Journal of International Money and Finance* 3: 1–29.

—— (1987) 'Foreign currency futures,' *Journal of International Economics* 22: 1–24.

Levi, M.D. (1978) 'The weekend game: clearing house vs. federal funds', *Canadian Journal of Economics* 11: 750–7.

Lucas, R.E., Jr (1982) 'Interest rates and currency prices in a two-country world', *Journal of Monetary Economics* 10: 335–60.

Marcus, A.J. (1984) 'Efficient asset portfolios and the theory of normal backwardation: a comment', *Journal of Political Economy* 92: 162–4.

Mark, N.C. (1985) 'On time varying risk premia in the foreign exchange market: an econometric analysis', *Journal of Monetary Economics* 16: 3–18.

McCurdy, T.H. and Morgan, I.G. (1987) 'Tests of the martingale hypothesis for foreign currency futures with time-varying volatility', *International Journal of Forecasting* 3: 131–48.

—— (1988a) 'Testing the martingale hypothesis in Deutsche mark futures with models specifying the form of heteroscedasticity', *Journal of Applied Econometrics* 3: 187–202.

—— (1988b) 'The behaviour of the basis in foreign currency futures markets', unpublished manuscript, Queen's University, Kingston, Ontario.

—— (1988c) 'Evidence of risk premia in foreign currency futures markets', unpublished manuscript, Queen's University, Kingston, Ontario.

Newey, W.K. (1985) 'Maximum likelihood specification testing and conditional moment tests,' *Econometrica* 53: 1047–70.

Richard, S.F. and Sundaresan, M. (1981) 'A continuous time equilibrium model of forward prices and futures prices in a multigood economy', *Journal of Financial Economics* 9: 347–72.

Roll, R. (1977) 'A critique of the asset pricing theory's tests; Part 1: On past and potential testability of the theory', *Journal of Financial Economics* 4: 129–76.

—— (1984) 'A simple implicit measure of the effective bid–ask spread in an efficient market', *Journal of Finance* 39: 1127–39.

Scholes, M. and Williams, J. (1977) 'Estimating betas from nonsynchronous data,' *Journal of Financial Economics* 5: 309–27.

Tauchen, G.E. (1985) 'Diagnostic testing and evaluation of maximum likelihood models,' *Journal of Econometrics* 30: 415–43.

3 Assessing market performance

An examination of livestock futures markets

Raymond M. Leuthold and Philip Garcia

INTRODUCTION

Futures markets perform several roles or functions, and the list varies marginally from author to author. Goss (1981) identified four roles: (a) facilitate stockholding; (b) facilitate the shifting of risk; (c) provide a mechanism for the collection and dissemination of information; (d) provide forward prices. Central to any list, regardless of the type of commodity or instrument, is the formation of forward prices. Accurate forward prices from the futures market are critical, since many market participants use these prices for production, processing, pricing and marketing decisions (Gardner 1976; Hurt and Garcia 1982). Inaccurate forward prices can lead to erroneous price signals, and consequently to a misallocation of resources.[1] This problem is particularly relevant to livestock production and marketing.

Inaccurate forward prices can result from markets that are inefficient, usually in the sense of not efficiently utilizing information.[2] Numerous investigators of futures markets have attempted to assess the degree of sources of market inefficiencies using a variety of analytical techniques (Kamara 1982). Results have been mixed (Goss 1983). Weak form tests assess whether futures markets fully utilize the information available in previous prices. Unfortunately, these tests do not directly establish whether the source of market inefficiency is uncertainty and the lack of market information, or whether the information is available but a market imperfection exists.

A more conventional and rigorous approach for assessing forward pricing efficiency is a semi-strong form analysis where the forecasting ability of the futures market is compared with that of alternative forecasters. This is a test of whether futures prices more fully reflect all publicly available information. The pricing efficiency of the market is then usually tested within a mean squared error (MSE) framework, which is a necessary condition. Relative MSEs, however, provide only an indication of the potential for market inefficiency. A sufficient condition for market inefficiency is whether the forecasting method can generate risk-adjusted profits which exceed the cost of usage. In addition, the performance of the futures market can be assessed, or confirmed, by measuring the social welfare loss. The social welfare loss also relates to efficient forecasting ability, and examines differences in MSE of a futures market at different forecasting horizons to approximate relative losses in producer and consumer surplus.

In this chapter we assess the forward pricing performance of the live cattle and hog futures markets by examining both the necessary and sufficient conditions of the markets and by measuring their social welfare loss. The predictive accuracy of the two markets is first evaluated relative to out-of-sample econometric, autoregressive integrated moving-average (ARIMA) and composite forecasts through a comparison of MSEs. Then the sufficient condition for market inefficiency is examined by assessing the returns generated from trading strategies which implement the most accurate forecasts. The relative performance results of these two markets are confirmed by measuring their social welfare loss.[3]

The conventional approach for assessing futures market efficiency begins with the premise that a market is efficient relative to an information set if the price correctly reflects the information in the relevant set (Fama 1970). In a forecasting sense, an efficient futures market provides the most accurate representation of subsequent spot prices. In this framework, finding a more accurate forecasting model than the futures market leads to the conclusion that the market is not processing information as effectively as might be expected and therefore is relatively inefficient. Failure to incorporate all 'available' information in the pricing process also leads to a social welfare loss.

This method of efficient market evaluation can be limited by its failure to take into consideration factors which may explain why futures prices are biased expectations of subsequent spot prices. Risk aversion, irrational market behaviour, imperfect capital markets and transactions costs lead to discrepancies between current futures prices and subsequent spot prices. Further, even in a world which is perfect in all respects except that information is costly to obtain, futures market prices may not accurately reflect all available information (Grossman and Stiglitz 1980). If the market price reveals all information for free, it does not pay anyone to invest in individual information gathering. Hence, the market price does not reveal all information as traders who buy the information earn a higher return. However, in equilibrium the extra returns earned are just sufficient to offset the cost of the information.

Thus, even if a particular model's forecast is more accurate than the forecasts of the futures markets, inefficiency does not necessarily follow owing to risk and information costs. Joerding (1986) has recently shown that, in an efficient market in which agents have rational expectations, market forecasts do not necessarily have a smaller MSE than every individual forecast. Even with zero information costs, the discovery of a forecasting method with lower MSE than the futures market does not indicate market inefficiency unless an agent can earn abnormal profits. Rausser and Carter (1983) argue that evaluation of the MSE is only a necessary condition, and that a sufficient condition for inefficiency requires an examination of the risk-adjusted profits relative to the modelling, information and implementation costs.[4]

Although literature exists on developing and estimating models for forecasting cash cattle and hog prices, less work has been done on evaluating the out-of-sample forecasting accuracy of the futures markets for these two livestock commodities. Just and Rausser (1981) examined the quarterly forecasting accuracy of both the cattle and hog futures markets for the period from December 1976 to December 1978. They found that the ability of live cattle futures prices to forecast subsequent spot prices improved as the contract approached maturity, and that these short-term forecasts outperformed some commercially available forecasting services. Similarly, the hog futures market outperformed commercial forecasts one quarter forward, but they found just the opposite for four quarters forward for hogs. Leuthold and Hartmann (1979, 1981) examined the forecasting accuracy of the live hog futures market on a monthly basis, and both the live hog and cattle futures markets on a quarterly basis, utilizing separate econometric models in each case. While some periods existed where the futures market outperformed the econometric model, and other periods with just the opposite performance, their results suggested on balance that the hog econometric representations were superior to the hog futures market, but that for live cattle the futures market was a marginally superior forecaster. Using a time series approach, Shonkwiler (1986) suggests that hog futures prices more than two months from maturity do not represent rational forecasts.[5]

ECONOMIC EFFICIENCY AND WELFARE LOSS

Alternative approaches exist for measuring the forward pricing efficiency of futures markets. Early empirical work utilized the weak form test procedure which focused on whether futures prices followed a random walk or the more general martingale properties. Various authors (see Rausser and Carter 1983) have indicated that market inefficiency does not necessarily follow from failure of the martingale property. Stein (1980) showed that even if prices are a martingale, avoidable welfare losses can occur.

A common procedure for implementing weak form tests is to regress the final realized cash price on the previous corresponding futures prices and test whether the constant equals zero and the slope equals unity. Acceptance of these hypotheses is a sign of an efficient market. However, it is known that this regression may suffer from statistical problems, and Stein (1986) again argues that social loss can occur even if this efficient market hypothesis test is accepted.

Research on efficient markets has moved towards the more rigorous semi-strong form tests which utilize publicly available information.[6] These models generate forecasts to compare their performance with that of futures markets. The common method of evaluation is to compare across models the MSEs, defined as

$$\text{MSE} = \frac{\Sigma(P - A)^2}{n}$$

where P and A are predicted and actual values respectively and n is the number of forecasts. An indirect test developed by Ashley *et al.* (1980) can be used to examine whether the MSEs of the futures market forecasts are significantly different from the MSEs of the alternative forecasting models.[7] This procedure and test will be performed here.

Comparing MSEs is a test of the necessary condition, but not the sufficient condition, of an efficient market. The latter condition is a test of whether a trade can utilize the forecasts to generate risk-adjusted profits. Specifically, a simulation procedure can be designed to buy a futures contract if the forecast exceeds the basis-adjusted futures, and to sell if the forecast is below the adjusted futures. Profits and losses are then summarized over several trades, a procedure followed in this study.

Stein (1986) argues that the traditional approaches to examining the efficient market hypothesis do not provide a quantitative measure of the relative performance of markets, and ignore any social welfare loss associated with producer and consumer surplus relative to inherent noise in the system. He suggests a measure of welfare loss which may be free of the usual statistical problems, and we shall use this in conjunction with our semi-strong form tests.

Stein's measure of *ex post* welfare loss is proportional to the square of the price deviation between the subsequent realized cash price and the futures price. The proportion is directly related to the slopes of the underlying demand and supply curves. The loss in utility from an incorrect futures price is the area under the realized demand curve and above the existing marginal cost (supply) curve, and between the actual output and the perfect foresight competitive equilibrium output. The loss (price deviation) is the sum of unavoidable error, risk premium and the difference between subjective and objective expectations (Bayesian error).[8]

Markets based on rational expectations in the Muth sense would have no Bayesian error since agents would know the true expectations. All markets have unavoidable loss because of noise in the system, and so Stein's measure of *ex post* welfare loss is that loss beyond the unavoidable loss which would result from risk premium and differences in expectations. Risk premiums would come from net hedging pressure and inadequate speculation, while Bayesian error results because participants do not know the objective mean of the distribution of demand.

To provide an empirical measure of social loss Stein assumes that the nearby or delivery contract has a risk premium of near zero and that market participants know the true mean of the distribution of prices.[9] Hence any error remaining is unavoidable error. Thus, an approach to approximating the social loss (SL) of the contract K months before delivery is to compare relative MSEs:

$$\mathrm{SL}(K) = \frac{\mathrm{MSE}(K)}{\mathrm{MSE}(1)}$$

Under Stein's assumptions, the minimum value of this measure is $\mathrm{SL} = 1$.

In this chapter we use both the semi-strong form efficiency test and the social welfare loss concept to examine market performance. With the efficiency test we examine both the necessary and sufficient conditions.

LIVESTOCK MODEL SPECIFICATION AND ESTIMATION

Separate econometric models are formulated for both the live hog and live cattle markets as performance norms. Each is a farm level recursive demand–supply model based on monthly data. The cattle model utilized data from July 1976 to December 1981, while the hog model incorporates data from 1976 to 1982. The objective is to portray each market accurately while keeping the model parsimonious for ease of forecasting. Supply in month t for each model, represented by slaughter, is hypothesized to be a function of expected output price and prices of inputs to $t-6$. The lagged specification corresponds to the approximate feeding and finishing times for feeding operations. Input prices considered are the price of feeder animals, the price of corn and interest rates. Previous research for hogs demonstrates the importance of including sow farrowings from multiple previous quarters along with the input prices. To avoid complications in forecasting, the actual price of the commodity in $t-6$ represents the expected output price in each case. Dummy variables are added for seasonality.

Since the primary purpose of each model is to forecast farm level prices, the demand side of the system is modelled as a price-dependent equation. Independent variables in each equation include cattle slaughter, hog slaughter, broiler slaughter, per capita income and seasonal monthly dummy variables. The addition of multiple slaughter variables in each equation allows for substitutability in meat consumption.

The theoretical models are specified as follows:

$$\mathrm{CS}_t = f_1(\mathrm{PC}_{t-6}, \mathrm{PFDS}_{t-6}, \mathrm{PCN}_{t-6}, \mathrm{PR}_{t-6}, \mathrm{DV}_k)$$

$$\mathrm{PC}_t = f_2(\mathrm{CS}_t, \mathrm{HS}_t, \mathrm{BS}_t, I/N_t, \mathrm{DV}_k)$$

for cattle and

$$\mathrm{HS}'_t = f_3(\mathrm{PH}_{t-6}, \mathrm{PCN}_{t-6}, \mathrm{PR}_{t-6}, \mathrm{FAR}_{t-6,9}, \mathrm{DV}_k)$$

$$\mathrm{PH}_t = f_4(\mathrm{HS}'_t, \mathrm{CS}_t, \mathrm{BS}_t, I/N_t, \mathrm{DV}_k)$$

for hogs, where CS is cattle slaughter (US, 1,000 head), PC is the average price of slaughter steers (choice, 1,100–1,300 pounds, Omaha, dollars per hundredweight), PFDS is the average price of feeder steers (eight markets, dollars per hundredweight), PCN is the price of corn (US, dollars per bushel), PR is prime interest rate (US), HS is hog slaughter (US, 1,000 head), BS is broiler slaughter (US, million pounds), I/N is personal income per capita (US dollars), HS′

is hog slaughter (US, million pounds), PH is the price of barrows and gilts (seven markets, dollars per hundredweight), FAR is sow farrowings (ten states, 1,000 head), DV_k represents dummy variables for eleven months of the year and $t-6$ denotes variables lagged six months. Sow farrowings are the averages of the previous second and third quarters. Prices and income are not deflated since the goal is to evaluate the performance of actual price level forecasts. The data were collected from standard public (government) sources. These simplified recursive models with finite lags portray the relevant characteristics of both the hog and cattle markets. They avoid the need to generate predictions for a large number of exogenous variables which can create additional forecast errors.

The cattle model was first estimated as a recursive system using Zellner's seemingly unrelated regressions. Normal goodness-of-fit tests were conducted on the coefficients and regressions, and the model was adjusted accordingly. That is, several insignificant variables were dropped, and a slope dummy variable DINCAP, which interacts with income, was added to the demand equation because of an apparent structural shift in the demand for beef, especially with regard to income elasticity (Hudson and Vertin 1985).[10] The data also revealed a hypothesized structural shift in slaughter rates; thus an intercept dummy variable DM was added to the supply equation. Both dummy variables take a value of zero from July 1976 to November 1978, and a value of unity from December 1978 to December 1981.

For the purposes of forecasting, a reduced form equation was formulated by substituting the supply equation into the demand equation and expressing the price of cattle as a function of all the exogenous variables. All the variables on the right-hand side were entered directly as regressors. Because of first-order autocorrelation in the residuals, a maximum likelihood procedure which corrects for autocorrelation in the presence of a lagged dependent variable was employed. The results for July 1976 to December 1981 were (t values are in parentheses)

$$\begin{aligned}\mathrm{PC}_t = {} & \underset{(-3.38)}{-68.42} + \underset{(4.90)}{15.40 I/N_t} - \underset{(-4.48)}{14.68\mathrm{DINCAP}} - \underset{(-1.01)}{0.43\mathrm{PC}_{t-6}} \\ & + \underset{(1.41)}{0.45\mathrm{PFDS}_{t-6}} + \underset{(0.05)}{0.05\mathrm{FEB}} + \underset{(1.05)}{1.44\mathrm{MAR}} + \underset{(1.40)}{2.51\mathrm{APR}} \\ & + \underset{(2.80)}{4.78\mathrm{MAY}} + \underset{(2.01)}{3.47\mathrm{JUN}} - \underset{(-1.39)}{2.81\mathrm{JUL}} + \underset{(0.21)}{0.49\mathrm{AUG}}\end{aligned}$$

$$+ \underset{(0.65)}{1.34\text{SEP}} - \underset{(-0.20)}{0.34\text{OCT}} - \underset{(-0.50)}{0.73\text{NOV}} - \underset{(-1.03)}{1.15\text{DEC}}$$

$$+ \underset{(0.68)}{1.76\text{DM}}$$

The $\bar{R}^2$ before adjusting for autocorrelation was 0.95 with a standard error of estimate of 2.08 and a mean of \$56.54 for PC.

The signs of the coefficients are generally as expected. Income per capita is positive, but the income dummy variable is strongly negative, suggesting a possible structural change in beef demand (Frank 1984). Lagged price of cattle and lagged price of feeder steers would be positive and negative respectively in a supply equation, but change signs in the reduced form model as expected. The monthly dummy variables are strongest in the spring and early summer.

The hog model was first estimated using least squares. Examination of the residuals indicated a high degree of autocorrelation. The two-step full transform method described by Gallant and Goebel (1976) was used to obtain efficient and unbiased estimates of the coefficients. In effect, an autoregressive (AR) process of order p was fitted to the least-squares residuals which were used to transform the data and obtain generalized least squares (GLS) estimates.[11] The order of the AR process was determined by examination of the autocorrelations and partial autocorrelations. AR models were fitted and Q statistics were calculated to examine the adequacy of the specifications. Normal goodness-of-fit tests were conducted on the coefficients and regressions, and the model was adjusted accordingly. That is, several insignificant variables were dropped and an income per capita squared term $(I/N)^2$ was added in the demand equation to reflect the changing nature of pork consumption relative to income (Brandt 1985).[12] Once the models were finally specified the cross-correlation coefficient of the error terms was small (0.05) and insignificant, indicating that estimating the equations separately is appropriate for this recursive system.

The fitted model and accompanying statistics are presented below (t values are in parentheses):

$$\text{HS}'_t = \underset{(-3.45)}{-636.17} + \underset{(18.33)}{0.11\text{FAR}_{t-6,9}} + \underset{(2.68)}{5.30\text{PH}_{t-6}} - \underset{(-2.77)}{143.33\text{FEB}}$$

$$+ \underset{(5.69)}{280.53\text{MAR}} + \underset{(5.98)}{229.44\text{APR}} + \underset{(3.13)}{171.38\text{MAY}}$$

$$+ \underset{(3.63)}{190.12}\text{JUN} + \underset{(1.71)}{78.04}\text{JUL} + \underset{(3.94)}{206.42}\text{AUG}$$

$$+ \underset{(2.66)}{140.01}\text{SEP} + \underset{(7.73)}{309.11}\text{OCT} + \underset{(5.65)}{283.56}\text{NOV}$$

$$+ \underset{(2.02)}{102.97}\text{DEC}$$

$$\bar{R}^2 = 0.90 \qquad Q(24) = 22.85$$

$$\text{PH}_t = \underset{(2.49)}{38.39} - \underset{(-6.67)}{0.02}\text{HS}'_t + \underset{(2.05)}{8.70}I/N_t - \underset{(-1.56)}{0.36}(I/N)^2_t - \underset{(-1.44)}{2.34}\text{FEB}$$

$$+ \underset{(1.40)}{2.31}\text{MAR} + \underset{(0.16)}{0.20}\text{APR} - \underset{(-0.38)}{0.67}\text{MAY} - \underset{(-0.56)}{0.98}\text{JUN}$$

$$- \underset{(-1.55)}{2.50}\text{JUL} + \underset{(0.59)}{1.03}\text{AUG} + \underset{(1.26)}{2.17}\text{SEP} + \underset{(3.01)}{4.10}\text{OCT}$$

$$+ \underset{(0.41)}{0.68}\text{NOV} + \underset{(0.81)}{1.27}\text{DEC}$$

$$\bar{R}^2 = 0.86 \qquad Q(24) = 31.45$$

The residual AR processes differed across equations; the supply and demand equations exhibited significant AR parameters at three, four and thirteen lags, and at one, three, four and thirteen lags respectively. The $\bar{R}^2$ values calculated on the original data and the transformed predictions from the estimated models are reasonable. The signs of the coefficients are generally as expected. Supply is positively related to lagged farrowings and own expected price for $t + 6$. Demand is negatively related to consumption in period t. Income per capita is positive but its square is negative, suggesting a curvilinear relationship between income and price. The monthly dummy variables are most prominent in the supply equation reflecting the seasonality in output.

In addition to the econometric models, ARIMA models were developed for both live cattle and live hog prices for forecasting purposes. Identification efforts led to the specification of an ARIMA model (2, 1, 2) for live cattle prices as follows (t values are in parentheses);

$$(1 - \underset{(10.93)}{1.49}\beta + \underset{(6.18)}{0.85}\beta^2)(1 - \beta)\text{PC}_t$$

$$= 0.39 + (1 - 1.24\beta + 0.55\beta^2)\varepsilon_t$$
$$\quad (1.59) \qquad (-6.06)\ (2.68)$$

$$Q(24) = 25.97$$

This model is first differenced with second-order AR and moving-average components where the β act as lag operators.

Examination of live hog prices led to the specification of the following ARIMA (2, 0, 0) model:

$$(1 - 1.30\beta + 0.49\beta^2)\mathrm{PH}_t = 8.11$$
$$\quad (13.40)\ (5.05) \qquad (3.77)$$

$$Q(22) = 24.21$$

This model is a second-order AR model. The Ljung and Box (1978) Q statistic did not detect significant autocorrelation in the residuals of the estimated ARIMA processes of either model.[13]

FORECASTING PROCEDURE

In order to utilize potentially useful new information about market relationships, all the models are re-estimated each period incorporating new observations in the data set. The procedure followed in this study is to drop the oldest observation as each new observation is added, keeping constant the number of observations in each estimation.[14] This procedure limits the memory of the system by totally discounting the most distant information (Harvey 1981: 194), and permits the estimates of the structure to respond more quickly to fundamental structural changes than when old observations are retained.[15]

Each month new out-of-sample forecasts are obtained for horizons of one to six months for each model. This updating, re-estimating and subsequent forecasting procedure continues from January 1982 to December 1985 for cattle, and from January 1983 to December 1986 for hogs. In the econometric model, only the unlagged income variables need to be forecast exogenously. This is done using a straightforward time series model.

Prior to generating the forecasts, all the models (and the error structure of the econometric models) were checked for appropriate specification at each time period. The specification for the hog ARIMA model changed twice during the forecasting period, while the specification of the cattle ARIMA model was different for only one period. The error structure of the hog econometric model changed frequently during updating. For cattle, after correcting for first-order autocorrelation no additional serial correlation existed. The econometric model forecasts for each commodity are combined with their ARIMA forecasts with equal weight to generate composite forecasts.

The purpose of forecasting is to compare the performance of these models with the respective futures markets using the MSE procedure. The MSEs reported contain only the forecasting errors for those months of the year when there exists a corresponding futures contract (six months for cattle and seven months for hogs). Forecasts for those months without a delivery contract are ignored in the evaluation process.

Direct comparison of the MSEs of the models and futures prices can be complicated by a maturity basis. For cattle, calculated differences between monthly average cash and future prices in the maturity month were not significantly different from zero, and so direct comparison of MSEs is permitted without a basis adjustment. For hogs, however, a significant positive basis exists, so that an adjustment is necessary for a direct comparison. Following the procedure in Holt and Brandt (1985), the expected basis for each contract is a simple average of the actual delivery month basis for that corresponding month for the most recent years. In all cases, the futures market forecasts are based on the monthly average of daily closes for the contract during the last month of the data set used in the econometric and ARIMA forecasting models.

EVALUATION OF PERFORMANCE

Necessary condition

Tables 3.1 and 3.2 present the MSEs of the three forecast models for six time horizons for cattle and hogs respectively. Also listed for comparison are the MSEs for the respective futures contracts indicating their error in forecasting maturity month prices. The MSEs are based on cumulative observations, so that the number of observations increases with each subsequent forecast. Although MSEs are available after each monthly update, only those through the first year and the fourth year of forecasts are shown as examples. These two are representative of the intervening MSEs.

For each horizon and forecast period there is always one model which has a lower MSE than the futures market for the same horizon

Table 3.1 Mean square errors for various cattle forecasting models and futures for horizons of one to six months ahead

Forecast technique	*Horizon (months ahead)*	*1982*	*1982–5*
ARIMA	1	3.57	6.19
	2	9.00	11.69
	3	18.15	22.48
	4	34.11	27.81
	5	43.96	34.34
	6	43.96	38.63
Econometric	1	3.88	10.64
	2	6.50	15.70
	3	8.29	20.90
	4	11.56	24.44
	5	11.36	27.65
	6	12.46	27.76
Econometric–ARIMA composite	1	2.40	4.60
	2	6.81	11.26
	3	9.86	17.93
	4	18.58	22.61
	5	22.37	26.75
	6	23.14	28.70
Futures	1	5.86	12.88
	2	20.98	22.45
	3	28.20	26.85
	4	45.43	34.83
	5	39.82	30.50
	6	41.22	29.40

for both cattle and hogs. Sometimes all forecast models have smaller MSEs than the futures market.

Regarding relative abilities, the results vary by commodity, period and forecast horizon. For cattle, through the first year of forecasts (1982), the composite model was the most accurate for the one-month horizon, while the econometric model performed the best for the two-month to six-month horizons. By the end of the fourth forecast year (1985), the composite model was the most accurate for the one-month to five-month horizons, while the econometric model was marginally superior for the six-month horizon. Overall, the composite model outperformed the econometric and ARIMA models.

Table 3.2 Mean square errors for various hog forecasting models and futures for horizons of one to six months ahead

Forecast technique	*Horizon (months ahead)*	*1983*	*1983–6*
ARIMA	1	11.90	10.08
	2	46.16	36.65
	3	17.82	37.26
	4	10.64	39.51
	5	12.51	40.56
	6	6.70	40.07
Econometric	1	3.67	17.92
	2	5.65	31.62
	3	3.75	36.53
	4	5.02	42.15
	5	4.59	41.53
	6	3.95	40.57
Econometric–ARIMA composite	1	5.63	11.01
	2	20.79	29.56
	3	9.12	32.97
	4	5.62	35.28
	5	7.10	36.71
	6	4.86	35.99
Basis-adjusted futures	1	23.84	18.01
	2	27.69	37.34
	3	31.47	49.64
	4	25.56	60.39
	5	41.35	61.86
	6	38.14	62.62

For hogs, the econometric model begins in 1983 as the most accurate forecaster of the three models for all horizons. By the end of the fourth year (1986), however, the time series model is the most accurate for the one-month horizon. For time horizons of two to six months, the composite model eventually becomes the best performer during the forecast period in each case. Composite models incorporate information from multiple sources, and it is not uncommon for them to provide more accurate forecasts than individual models (Brandt and Bessler 1981).

The magnitude of the reduction and the statistical difference of the MSEs between the most accurate model and the futures market forecasts vary by forecast horizon and the forecasting method. For cattle, the largest reductions in the MSEs for forecasts up to 1985 were in the first two horizons. There the MSEs generated from the composite model were 64 per cent and 50 per cent smaller respectively than the MSEs for the futures forecasts. Both these MSEs from the composite model were statistically smaller than the corresponding MSE from the futures market at the 0.05 level of significance. Smaller and less dramatic reductions were evidenced in the three- to six-month horizons. Using the most accurate forecast model, reductions of 33 per cent, 35 per cent, 12 per cent and 6 per cent occurred for the four most distant horizons respectively. The four- and five-month horizons yielded statistically significant differences in the MSEs at the 0.05 level, and the three-month horizon was significant at the 0.10 level. Only at the six-month horizon is the hypothesis of equal MSEs not rejected.[16]

For hogs, the reduction in MSEs for the most accurate forecasts up to 1986 relative to the futures markets ranged from 21 per cent for the two-month horizon to 44 per cent for the one-month horizon. The reductions at the one-, four-, five- and six-month horizons all exceed 40 per cent, and each is statistically smaller than the respective futures MSE at the conventional 0.05 level of significance. Differences in the MSEs for the other two horizons are significant at the 10 per cent level.

According to the traditional MSE method of evaluation, these results suggest that both the cattle and hog futures markets are relatively inefficient in a semi-strong form sense. Specifically, for the one- to five-month horizons for cattle and for all horizons for hogs, the futures market does not seem to incorporate all publicly available information at the time of forecast since alternative models demonstrate significantly smaller forecast errors. Inefficiency is less certain at the three-month horizon for cattle and at the two- and three-month horizons for hogs, and is non-existent for the six-month horizon for cattle.

The typical evaluation procedure in the literature of forward pricing efficiency of the futures markets, as discussed earlier, may not be sufficiently rigorous, however. A model can demonstrate smaller MSEs than the futures market, but that does not necessarily mean that a trader can turn such information into profitable trading opportunities. Rausser and Carter (1983) argue that the sufficiency condition depends on an evaluation of the risk-adjusted benefits and costs. To obtain a measure of the benefits directly, trading in the futures market is simulated using the forecast information from the models. Since futures contracts exist for alternate months, forecasts with horizons of two, four and six months are used.[17]

Sufficient condition

The simulation procedure was designed to buy a futures contract if the forecast exceeds the (adjusted) futures, and to sell if the forecast is below the (adjusted) futures. Specifically, starting with the two-month forecasts, if the most accurate forecast for the next delivery month is more than $0.15 per hundredweight (the approximate commission costs) above (below) the average corresponding futures price during the forecasting month, a futures contract is purchased (sold) at the closing price of the next trading day and held until the close of either the first or the tenth day of the delivery month.[18] If the forecast is within $0.15 of the futures,[19] no action takes place. For example, at the end of December, forecasts become available for February. If the forecast is more than $0.15 above or below the average of the February closing prices during the month of December, a trade occurs with a contract being initiated on the first trading day of January and liquidated on 1 February or 10 February (or the nearest trading day).[20] The profit or loss of this trade is recorded after deducting a commission cost of $0.15.

The forecast from the model with the lowest MSE up to the date of the market decision is used in the analysis. Specifically, the MSEs based on the first year's forecast errors are used to begin the first set of trading exercises for 1983 (cattle) or 1984 (hogs). Updated MSEs are calculated after each forecast and are used to select the most accurate model which is then used for the next set of forecasts and trading decisions. The above procedure is followed for all the contracts maturing during the period 1983–5 for cattle and the period 1984–6 for hogs.

The same procedure and signals are followed for the four-month forecasts. The forecast for the most accurate model (lowest MSE) at the time of the market decision is compared with the average price of the futures contract four months forward for a potential trading signal. However, here there are two alternative procedures for liquidation. In the first procedure, the contract position based on the initial signal is held until the maturity month, a period of more than three months, ignoring any new information. This procedure is called the 'fixed-market strategy'. In the second procedure, the initial position is held until the two-month forecasts are available, at which time the most accurate forecast at that time is compared with the then existing average futures price. If the signal remains the same, no new action occurs. However, if the signal is different, then the original position is liquidated and a new one is established on the first trading

Table 3.3 Results of simulated market activities for cattle, 1983–1985

Horizon	*Profitable trades* Number	*Range of returns ($/cwt)*	*Average return per contract ($)*	*Unprofitable trades* Number	*Range of returns ($/cwt)*	*Average return per contract ($)*	*Total returns ($)*
Trade liquidated on the tenth day of the delivery month							
Two month	10	(0.20, 8.45)	1,228[a]	8	(−0.45, −6.95)	1,004[a]	4,248
Four month							
Fixed strategy	11	(1.00, 13.02)	1,975	6	(−0.62, −9.07)	−1,718	11,412
Flexible strategy	9	(1.00, 13.02)	2,046	8	(−0.62, −12.38)	−1,856	3,568
Six month							
Fixed strategy	8	(0.23, 8.95)	1,790	8	(−0.05, −10.95)	−1,406	3,080
Flexible strategy	8	(0.23, 8.95)	1,730	8	(−1.01, −15.88)	−2,364	−5,080
Trade liquidated on the first day of the delivery month							
Two month	11	(0.05, 5.03)	959	7	(−0.40, −3.02)	−757	5,244
Four month							
Fixed strategy	11	(0.22, 10.73)	1,826	6	(−0.45, −12.40)	−1,782	9,392
Flexible strategy	10	(0.25, 10.73)	1,642	7	(−1.53, −9.05)	−1,604	5,188
Six month							
Fixed strategy	10	(0.08, 9.48)	1,593	6	(−0.55, −13.23)	−2,110	3,268
Flexible strategy	7	(0.08, 9.13)	1,883	9	(−0.10, −12.55)	−1,705	−2,164

Note: [a] Average returns per hundredweight can be found by dividing by 400.

Table 3.4 Results of simulated market activities for hogs, 1984–1986

	Profitable trades			*Unprofitable trades*			
Horizon	*Number*	*Range of returns ($/cwt)*	*Average return per contract ($)*	*Number*	*Range of returns ($/cwt)*	*Average return per contract ($)*	*Total returns ($)*
Trade liquidated on the tenth day of the delivery month							
Two month	11	(0.30, 9.95)	1,075[a]	6	(−1.63, −4.90)	−992[a]	5,873
Four month							
Fixed strategy	10	(0.37, 17.20)	1,859	6	(−0.05, −5.97)	−571	15,164
Flexible strategy	13	(0.37, 12.08)	1,425	4	(−0.05, −5.97)	−688	15,773
Six month							
Fixed strategy	9	(0.80, 18.88)	2,460	7	(−0.30, −6.97)	−743	16,939
Flexible strategy	10	(3.53, 21.47)	2,191	6	(−0.30, −3.07)	−520	18,790
Trade liquidated on the first day of the delivery month							
Two month	10	(1.90, 6.82)	1,057	7	(−0.05, −5.12)	−887	4,361
Four month							
Fixed strategy	9	(0.55, 17.35)	1,994	7	(−0.05, −6.57)	−580	13,886
Flexible strategy	12	(0.46, 12.02)	1,547	5	(−0.27, −6.57)	−664	15,244
Six month							
Fixed strategy	9	(0.15, 19.03)	2,340	7	(−0.80, −6.60)	−852	15,096
Flexible strategy	11	(0.15, 22.52)	1,984	5	(−0.88, −5.23)	−744	18,104

Note: [a]Average returns per hundredweight can be found by dividing by 300.

day following the two-month forecast. Of course, it is possible that the old position is liquidated and no new position is taken if the futures price and forecast are within $0.15 of each other, or a new position may be established if none was held from four months to two months for the same reason. This procedure is called the 'flexible-market strategy'. It is designed to take advantage of the most recent information.

The procedures for the six-month forecasts are the same as for the four-month forecasts. Both the fixed-market strategy and the flexible-market strategy situations are examined. However, under the latter situation we could update and change positions at four months and at two months prior to maturity.

Tables 3.3 and 3.4 show the results of the simulated trading activities for cattle and hogs respectively. These results are separated into profitable and unprofitable trades, and whether the trades liquidate on the first or tenth day of the month. The last column gives the total returns.

For cattle in Table 3.3, returns for the six-months flexible strategy are negative, but the other four strategies indicate positive profits from the trading simulation for both liquidation dates. Only the four-month fixed strategy shows large returns. Most of the time the number of profitable trades exceeds the number of unprofitable trades for a strategy, but the chances of having a very large losing trade seem substantial. In our judgement, the variability across trades is very large, indicating high risk. The four-month fixed strategy shows promise, but on balance the results across strategies and horizons are not very attractive from a trading standpoint. Even the flexible-market strategy does not improve the simulation results. For the four-month and six-month forecasts the flexible strategy returns decline dramatically relative to the fixed market strategy.

None of the models tracked the data very well in 1985, when the monthly cattle price in Omaha fell from $57.30 in June to $52.28 in August and then rebounded to $64.41 in November. The MSEs for all models, including the futures, are considerably larger in 1985 than for the previous two years. Similarly, the simulation results reflect the inability of the models to detect this sudden shift in price. Large trading losses were experienced in 1985 under all strategies, wiping out some reasonable gains accumulated during 1983 and 1984, and increasing the variances markedly. Although not explicitly tested, the models would probably have performed poorly in 1986 as well, when cattle prices dropped rapidly owing to the announced dairy buy out programme.[21]

Thus, although the cattle models had MSEs lower than the futures market on balance, large profits across all strategies and horizons, especially when considered in the light of their variability, could not be generated from trading simulations in the cattle market. This is not a complete test of the sufficiency conditions. While it does provide a measure of the trading benefits and the risk associated with the use of various forecasting models, the costs of model building and updating are not considered. Including these would reduce the net benefits.

For hogs (Table 3.4), all total returns are positive, reflecting both that the number of profitable trades exceeds the number of unprofitable trades and that the average return per contract on profitable trades exceeds the average loss per contract on unprofitable trades. In addition, the range of returns on profitable trades usually exceeds the range of losses on unprofitable trades, indicating that the models are capable of generating large gains on individual trades without corresponding large losses on other trades. Thus, on balance, the models are capable of generating substantial profits over the three-year simulation period.

The four- and six-month forecasts generate the largest profits, while the two-month strategy does the poorest. The flexible-strategy results usually exceed the fixed-strategy results, indicating the need to incorporate the most recent information. Finally, returns are higher if trades are held until the tenth day of the month instead of the first, indicating that prices in the spot month generally moved in the direction forecast. In contrast with the cattle results, hog returns are much higher across the group of strategies, and individual returns are more skewed to profitable results.

In sum, from our perspective, these results suggest that the live hog futures market is semi-strong form inefficient, especially at more distant horizons, as judged by both forecasting accuracy and simulated trading activity results. That is, econometric, time series and composite models based on existing and available public information can be formulated which have smaller MSEs than the futures market and which also generate positive trading profits. It appears that the trading results for more distant horizons could be quite attractive to many risk-averse traders; the benefits from market activities may be substantial.

While the analysis provides insight into the benefits of using alternative forecasting methods, it is not a complete test of the sufficiency condition. As mentioned above, a full test of the sufficiency condition would require a more complete delineation of the costs and the sources of the returns. Additional informational costs (personnel and computing) in building the above models were not trivial.[22] Incorporation of these outlays would make the benefits relatively less attractive. Nevertheless, the cost of future model upkeep is considerably less than the initial costs. Also, the benefits could reflect a risk premium as well as informational inefficiency. It is not clear how to identify these specific sources of the returns.[23] However, it seems that the returns generated for hogs are too large to be associated solely with a risk premium. On balance, the results suggest to us that informational inefficiency exists in the hog futures market.

Social loss

Social loss from futures markets can be approximated by the ratio of the MSE K months before delivery relative to the MSE during the delivery month. This assumes that any error during the last month of trading is unavoidable error, and that no Bayesian error nor risk premium remains. Thus, if the social loss for a contract exceeds unity, then there is loss to society from the market because either participants do not know the objective mean of the distribution of demand (or irrational expectations) or there is net hedging pressure and inadequate speculation (risk premium), or both.[24] There is no clear way of separating and identifying these two potential sources of loss.

Table 3.5 presents the social loss measure for cattle and hogs. These comparative results show that the relatively more inefficient market (hogs) is associated with larger welfare loss. Even where markets are judged efficient, welfare loss is still positive (cattle). However, this additional measure of performance, while limited, confirms the semi-strong form empirical results and demonstrates the potential for improved performance if a futures market is efficient and utilizes all publicly available information.

Table 3.5 Social loss measure for cattle and hog futures markets

	Social loss	
Horizon	*Cattle*	*Hogs*
2	1.74	2.07
3	2.08	2.76
4	2.70	3.35
5	2.37	3.43
6	2.28	3.48

SUMMARY AND CONCLUSIONS

Previous research on the performance of futures markets in a semi-strong form forecasting framework has resulted in inconclusive results. In this chapter, structural econometric and ARIMA models were developed to forecast monthly cattle and hog prices. A mean square prediction error criterion was employed to compare forecasts from these models and their composites with the futures market. The sufficiency condition of the efficiency test was examined by simulating trading results based on the most accurate forecast for horizons of two, four and six months.

The results demonstrate, particularly for cattle, that utilizing only the MSE in examining the forward pricing efficiency of a futures market versus other forecasting models is not a sufficiently rigorous criterion. For both cattle and hogs, at least one model, and sometimes all of them, forecasts more accurately in an MSE sense than does the futures market. In accordance with the necessary condition, the MSEs (except for the six-month horizon for cattle) of forecasting models suggest that the cattle and hog futures markets are not incorporating all the latest public information.

The simulation results for hogs corroborated the market analysis based on the MSE criterion. For the distant horizons the most accurate forecaster demonstrates ability to generate substantial positive profits. Profitable trades exceed unprofitable trades; returns are skewed as gains are more likely than losses of similar size. Many risk-averse traders would probably act on the signals provided here if they expected returns of the magnitude shown. For two-month horizons, where the MSE test indicated a difference only at higher levels of significance, simulation returns were relatively lower.

For cattle, however, examination of the sufficiency condition fails to support this conclusion. Simulation results based on the most accurate forecast generate in aggregate low but extremely variable profits. It is difficult to imagine a risk-averse trader using these models for trading signals with such large risk–return trade-offs.

The market performance results are confirmed by Stein's measure of social welfare loss which shows larger losses in the hog market than in the cattle market.

These results do not provide a complete assessment of market performance. However, they do permit comparative assessment of market efficiency and the social welfare loss associated with the inaccurate forecasting ability of these markets. The results are not a complete test of market efficiency because total costs have not been itemized, nor the sources of benefits identified. Market efficiency can never be proved; it can only fail to be disproved. For cattle, an undiscovered model or set of market strategies could lead to the conclusion that the market is semi-strong form inefficient. However, based on this study the trading returns do not show strong evidence for inefficiency in the live cattle futures market while the benefits in the hog market are quite large and attractive, indicating that, at least for the distant horizons, informational inefficiencies do exist. Also, in a comparative sense these results suggest larger welfare loss in the hog market than in the cattle market.

The results of this study raise several interesting issues and suggest a research agenda. A primary question emerges regarding the reasons for the differential forecasting ability of hogs and cattle futures markets. While it may be easier to model the cyclical and biological patterns for hogs relative to cattle, this does not explain why the market has not incorporated this information in establishing prices. Perhaps, up to this point, the uncertain returns have limited the willingness of individual market participants to invest time and resources to generate forecasts. Alternatively, as suggested by earlier researchers, the market may be more concerned with short-term price relationships as opposed to long-term trends and price movements. From our perspective, neither of these arguments is very convincing, and the explanation for the differential forecasting ability of these markets merits additional attention. Another related issue which arises in studies of this nature is the difficulty in identifying the sources of market inefficiency. Is the forecast inaccuracy primarily a function of differences in information assimilation? Or does a systematic risk premium which influences the results exist? In our assessment of the speculative returns on the hog market, we indicate that their magnitude appears to be too large to be explained only as a function of a risk premium. Yet it would be of value to differentiate more definitively between risk premium and ineffective information assimilation. This requires the development of a more complete theory of risk premium behaviour which would permit a varying risk premium and empirical assessment of its existence. Finally, it is important to recall that the futures market performs a variety of roles and functions. Here, we examined only one aspect of the pricing function – the ability effectively to incorporate information in establishing forward prices. Clearly, a complete assessment of the performance of hog and cattle futures markets requires an examination of all the identified functions in a consistent economic framework.

NOTES

1 Inaccurate forward prices for financial instruments lead to trader arbitrage opportunities and profits, which are sometimes riskless.
2 The hypothesis of unbiased forward prices relates to rational expectations in the economics literature, and to market efficiency in the finance and agricultural economics literature. We emphasize the latter approach.
3 An alternative explanation for informationally inefficient futures markets is that a risk premium exists. Unfortunately, there is no clear way to distinguish empirically between these competing hypotheses. In the case of hogs, we argue later that the out-of-sample trading returns appear too large to be associated solely with a risk premium, an argument also used by Bilson (1981) with foreign exchange rates.
4 This approach does not consider the correlation between fluctuations in profit levels from the use of futures contracts and the value of other assets that a market participant may hold (Bond and Thompson 1986). Expansion of the analysis to incorporate this possibility is beyond the scope of this study.
5 Others, such as Koppenhaver (1983), have examined forward pricing efficiency, but not by utilizing a structural model or by assessing out-of-sample forecasts.
6 Examples include Leuthold and Hartmann (1979, 1981), Goss (1983) and Rausser and Carter (1983).
7 Brandt and Bessler (1982) also provide details of this test and its procedure. Several authors recommend decomposing the MSEs into their bias, regression and disturbance components. However, this decomposition is subject to criticism, especially for forecasts of more than one step ahead (Granger and Newbold 1977: 284–8).
8 Stein's measure is a very limited evaluation of the futures market. He assumes that the market already exists and measures losses relative to a futures market which has perfect foresight. The perfect market has no risk premium and no basis risk, and the futures price is equal to the subsequent realized cash price. This measure ignores any gains which accrue to the establishment of futures trading.
9 This assumption is made despite some empirical evidence by Paul (1986) that a small liquidation bias may exist in maturing futures contracts.
10 The insignificance of variables resulted, in part, from multicollinearity in the data. For example, the simple correlation coefficient between income per capita and broiler slaughter exceeded 0.90. Somewhat surprisingly, the price of corn was not a significant explanatory variable in the final model. During initial estimation other variables (for example, cattle and calves on feed), other structural relationships (seemingly unrelated specification of beef and hog systems together) and other finite lags on the independent variables were examined. These efforts did not improve the performance of the model.
11 Maximum likelihood (ML) provides an alternative approach for estimating the model. Both methods have similar asymptotic properties but may behave differently in small samples. Monte Carlo studies suggest that the two-step full transform method appears to be as efficient as ML (Harvey 1981). ML tends to do better when the autoregressive parameters are

large. The two-step full transform procedure is presented here as it outforecasts the ML estimator in the out-of-sample 1983 pre-simulation period discussed later.

12 As with the cattle model, the insignificance of variables was, in part, a function of collinearity in the data. Again, the price of corn was not a significant explanatory variable. Experiments with other variables, other structural relationships and other finite lags on the independent variables did not improve the performance of the model.

13 The adequacy of the hog model was further examined using the Lagrange multiplier (LM) test proposed by Godfrey (1979). Examination of the LM results and visual examination of the autocorrelations and partial autocorrelations suggested the existence of higher-order autocorrelation. A restricted AR process of order 1, 2, 11 and 13 was estimated. This model did not perform as well as the simple model for out-of-sample forecasts in the 1983 pre-simulation period.

14 An exception to this is the ARIMA for cattle. Since its process seemed to be consistent, old observations were not dropped as new ones were added.

15 In the last fifteen years the hog cycle has been changing from its previously regular four-year pattern, as documented by Shonkwiler and Spreen (1982).

16 While subject to the limitations noted above, the MSEs for cattle were also decomposed into their bias, regression and disturbance components. For futures and all the forecast techniques, most of the error was contained in the disturbance component. Further examination of the sources of error across alternative models and forecast horizons failed to demonstrate any clearly interpretable patterns.

17 For this simulation the July hog futures contract is ignored for the convenience of constant forecasting and trading horizons.

18 Two alternative liquidation dates are examined. First, the models forecast the monthly price, and so the trading day closest to the tenth of the month is selected as a representative of the monthly average. This is midway between the first day of the month and the last trading day. A single day is selected because market participants cannot trade the monthly average. For comparison, results are also generated assuming that trades are liquidated on the first day of the delivery month. This day is selected because many traders view holding speculative positions into the spot month as risky and leave the market at this time.

19 All units are on a per hundredweight basis.

20 Trading results were not sensitive to representing the futures price by the average monthly price, the average price for the last week or the price on the last day of the month.

21 Results were also generated allowing for a $0.30 interval between the forecast and futures before a trade could be triggered. No systematic difference in the results appeared.

22 A partial examination of the daily interest costs associated with margin calls for hogs revealed them to be small (even for large adverse price movements) and partially offset by interest earned on unrealized profits. Hence, these costs are not included in our results.

23 Recent attempts to identify time-varying risk premium parameters are

controversial owing to the lack of an empirically tractable economic model of risk premium (Stein 1986: 177).

24 Remember that this particular measure examines only losses, and does not attempt to identify gains from the establishment of a futures market. Also, the measure implicitly assumes that the unavoidable error does not increase at more distant horizons.

REFERENCES

Ashley, R., Granger, C.W.J. and Schmalensee, R. (1980) 'Advertising and aggregate consumption: an analysis of causality', *Econometrica* 48: 1149–67.

Bilson, J.F.O. (1981) 'The "speculative efficiency" hypothesis', *Journal of Business* 54: 435–51.

Bond, G.E. and Thompson, S.R. (1986) 'Optimal commodity hedging within the capital asset pricing model', *Journal of Futures Markets* 6: 421–31.

Brandt, J.A. (1985) 'Forecasting and hedging: an illustration of risk reduction in the hog industry', *American Journal of Agricultural Economics* 67: 24–31.

Brandt, J.A. and Bessler, D.A. (1981) 'Composite forecasting: an application with U.S. hog prices', *American Journal of Agricultural Economics* 63: 135–40.

—— (1982) 'Forecasting with a dynamic regression model: a heuristic approach', *North Central Journal of Agricultural Economics* 4: 27–33.

Fama, E.F. (1970) 'Efficient capital markets: a review of theory and empirical work', *Journal of Finance* 25: 383–417.

Frank, M.D. (1984) 'Structural change in the retail demand for beef, chicken, and pork: an application of gradual switching regression', Ph.D. Dissertation, University of Illinois, Urbana-Champaign.

Gallant, A.R. and Goebel, J.J. (1976) 'Nonlinear regression with autocorrelated errors', *Journal of the American Statistical Association* 71: 961–7.

Gardner, B.L. (1976) 'Futures prices in supply analysis', *American Journal of Agricultural Economics* 58: 81–5.

Godfrey, L.G. (1979) 'Testing the adequacy of a time series model', *Biometrika* 66: 67–72.

Goss, B.A. (1981) 'The forward pricing function of the London Metal Exchange', *Applied Economics* 13: 133–50.

—— (1983) 'The semi-strong form efficiency of the London Metal Exchange', *Applied Economics* 15: 681–98.

Granger, C.W.J. and Newbold, P. (1977) *Forecasting Economic Time Series*, New York: Academic Press.

Grossman, S.J. and Stiglitz, J.E. (1980) 'On the impossibility of informationally efficient markets', *American Economic Review* 70: 393–408.

Harvey, A.C. (1981) *Time Series Models*, Oxford: Philip Allan.

Holt, M.T. and Brandt, J.A. (1985) 'Combining price forecasting with hedging of hogs: an evaluation using alternative measures of risk', *Journal of Futures Markets* 5: 297–309.

Hudson, M.A. and Vertin, J.P. (1985) 'Income elasticities for beef, pork, and poultry: changes and implications', *Journal of Food Distribution Research* 16: 25–31.

Hurt, C.A. and Garcia, P. (1982) 'The impact of price risk on sow farrowings, 1967–78', *American Journal of Agricultural Economics* 64: 565–8.

Joerding, W. (1986) 'The model dependence of relative mean-square error tests for market efficiency', *Journal of Economics and Business* 38: 227–36.

Just, R.E. and Rausser, G.C. 'Commodity price forecasting with large-scale econometric models and the futures market', *American Journal of Agricultural Economics* 63: 197–208.

Kamara, A. (1982) 'Issues in futures markets: a survey', *Journal of Futures Markets* 2: 261–94.

Koppenhaver, G.D. (1983) 'The forward pricing efficiency of the live cattle futures market', *Journal of Futures Markets* 3: 307–19.

Leuthold, R.M. and Hartmann, P.A. (1979) 'A semi-strong form evaluation of the efficiency of the hog futures market', *American Journal of Agricultural Economics* 63: 482–9.

—— (1981) 'An evaluation of the forward-pricing efficiency of livestock futures markets', *North Central Journal of Agricultural Economics* 3: 71–80.

Ljung, G.M. and Box, G.E.P. (1978) 'On a measure of lack of fit in time series models', *Biometrika* 65: 297–303.

Paul, A.B. (1986) 'Liquidation bias in futures price spreads', *American Journal of Agricultural Economics* 68: 313–21.

Rausser, G.C. and Carter, C. (1983) 'Futures market efficiency in the soybean complex', *Review of Economics and Statistics* 65: 469–78.

Shonkwiler, J.S. (1986) 'Are livestock futures prices rational forecasts?', *Western Journal of Agricultural Economics* 11: 123–8.

Shonkwiler, J.S. and Spreen, T.H. (1982) 'A dynamic regression model of the U.S. hog market', *Canadian Journal of Agricultural Economics* 30: 37–48.

Stein, J.L. (1980) 'The dynamics of spot and forward prices in an efficient foreign exchange market', *American Economic Review* 70: 565–83.

—— (1986) *The Economics of Futures Markets*, New York: Basil Blackwell.

4 Rational expectations and experimental methods

Glenn W. Harrison

Recent developments in economic theory and experimental economics have significantly broadened the concept of 'rational expectations'. In this chapter we review and evaluate these developments, arguing that they have important methodological implications.

One theme of this review is that there are many senses in which it can be said that an economic agent's expectations about the behaviour of others are 'rational'. This is not merely a semantic issue. It will be shown that being explicit about the meaning of 'rational behaviour' can be crucial to an understanding of behaviour in many experiments. Moreover, it is *only* in an experiment, in which the 'true model' is known to the investigator independently of the observed behavioural outcomes, that the operational importance of the distinctions that are proposed can be fully appreciated.

Three notions of expectations that are 'rational' in some useful sense are proposed. The first is what are called rationalizable expectations (RAE), following Bernheim (1984, 1986) and Pearce (1984). In this case we ask what the minimal requirements on behaviour are implied by the assumption that agents are Bayesian expected utility maximizers. This assumption is about as minimal, in terms of the degree of rationality it requires of individual behaviour, as possible.

The second notion is called realizable expectations (REE) and is implied by the game-theoretical notion of Nash equilibrium (NE) due to Nash (1951), which requires that expectations be consistent in the sense that they are mutually realizable and stable *ex post.* When the expectations of all agents are realized, no agent has any desire to change his component expectation. This assumption represents a significant strengthening of the notion of RAE.

The final notion is Muthian rational expectations (MRE), following Muth (1961). In this case it is required that the expectations of agents be consistent with the true model that is being evaluated. Whereas REE require only that behaviour conditioned on expectations be reinforced by observed outcomes, MRE further require that these observed outcomes be consistent with the model (or, at least, 'some model'). The importance of this distinction for understanding experimental behaviour was first noted by Smith *et al.* (1988).

These concepts are explained in more detail in the next three sections. At the same time, some experimental evidence is evaluated illustrating the operational, as distinct from semantic, importance of the concepts. In order to avoid semantic confusion the use of the generic expression rational expectations (RE) will be reserved for instances in which the theorist or experimentalist does not explicitly say which of the three classes (RAE, REE or MRE) is intended.

A second theme of this review is the relationship between 'common information', or 'common priors', and equilibrium behaviour. This relationship is implicitly quite different in economic theory and experimental economics. In economic theory common information is virtually always synonymous with common knowledge; although a firm distinction is made between the two, this distinction is rarely invoked in the construction of theoretical models. In experiments, the link between common information and equilibrium behaviour is typically the result of 'learning behaviour' and 'subject experience'. One question explored in this review is to what extent 'learning by doing' in an experimental situation can bring about a situation of '(as if) common knowledge'? When we observe what seems to be an equilibrium outcome in an experiment, is it because subjects have been able to transform common information into common knowledge by means of observing the outcomes of early periods? Moreover, how does the particular institution being studied affect this process?

This theme is related to the first. It might be argued in some environments that only MRE are consistent with 'long-run' equilibrium behaviour. If expectations are not consistent with the underlying model of the environment, then the system cannot be in 'full' equilibrium until those expectations have somehow adjusted to match the solution values of the model. None the less we might observe that behaviour in the interim is perfectly consistent with either or both of the weaker notions of 'rational expectations'. The process by which expectations become 'tighter and tighter' around those sustained by theory, if indeed they do, is in evidence in many of the experiments reviewed. However, the theoretical modelling of this process is not well advanced. An attempt is made to identify the experimental evidence for this learning process.

RATIONALIZABLE EXPECTATIONS

Theory

Expectations arise when the pay-offs to one player depend on the outcome of some uncertain event. That event could be determined by a roll of a die by Nature, or it could be determined by the actions of some other human player. The first player must form some belief about the likelihood of each of the possible outcomes of the event. Given these beliefs, in the form of a proper probability distribution, the player can select an action that maximizes his expected utility.

In a game against Nature the beliefs that the player is presumed to employ are 'objective', in the sense that the player has some prior distribution (possibly diffuse) over the actions that Nature will take, and that prior is independent of the choice set of the agent. One rationalization of this presumption could be that Nature is literally operationalized by some mechanical randomizing device with these properties.

In a game against human opponents the player forms his prior distribution by applying assumed rules of behaviour to his opponents. For example, I might conjecture that you will make one move instead of another because I can see that that move is in your best interest *whatever I do.* Even in making a statement as innocuous as this several things are presumed.

First, I assume that you see the game as I see it. This is known as 'common knowledge' of the game (especially the pay-offs).

Second, I am assuming that you are going to maximize your own expected utility given *your* assessment of the game. Apart from your knowledge of the pay-offs and the moves that I can make, this includes your beliefs about my actions. However, in the example given you did not need to form any beliefs about my actions, since you had a dominant strategy to play.

What if you did not have a dominant strategy to play? Assume that we are playing a simple game of co-ordination. If we take the same action we each receive a good pay-off; if we take different actions we each receive a bad pay-off. Assume that the pay-offs for co-ordinating are all the same, and the pay-offs for not co-ordinating are all the same (thus there does not arise any question as to which co-ordinated outcome is best). Crucially, assume that we must each take our actions without knowing what the other has chosen. This defines a simple normal form game.

You do not care which strategy I choose, but only that we choose the same strategy. Which strategy do you expect me to choose?

Without further information[1] you do not have any idea as to which strategy I might play. A Good Bayesian would therefore adopt a diffuse prior over all choices, assigning equal weight to each possible strategy. If I expect you to have these beliefs about my choice, what choice do I expect you to make? Again, I have no information to guide me to make one choice over another. If you have a diffuse prior as to my choice, it does not matter to you which strategy you choose. Thus I am also forced to have a diffuse prior over your strategy choices.

What are the possible outcomes of this game? Clearly, *any strategy combination is possible* given the restrictions that we have placed on the way in which each player forms his beliefs about the other player. Specifically, I could easily 'rationalize' *my* playing strategy i by asking if you could possibly have beliefs about me that could lead you to play strategy i. The answer us 'yes', since if you have a diffuse prior over my choices then you can do no better than picking a choice at random (you do no worse by picking one that matches your birthday). A similar argument allows *me* to rationalize *your* choice of strategy i. Thus co-ordinated outcomes are rationalizable.

The more interesting possibility is to ask whether any other outcomes are rationalizable. Assume that I have rationalized the playing of strategy i by the above logic. The question is then whether or not *you* could rationalize the playing of any strategy j, $j \neq i$. Clearly the answer is 'yes', since you have a diffuse prior over my choices and do not know that I have in fact chosen strategy i when you must make your choice. Thus non-coordinated actions are also rationalizable.

Indeed, it is possible to show that in any two-person game in normal form the only strategy combinations that are *not* rationalizable are those that include dominated pure strategies (see Pearce 1984: 1035). There are no dominated strategies in the co-ordination game outlined above; hence it follows that every strategy combination is rationalizable. Note that the set of rationalizable strategy combinations is larger than the set of NE: in the co-ordination game only co-ordinated strategy outcomes are NE. Thus the notion of RAE is weaker than the notion of an NE – recall that NE is identical with a certain form of rational expectations we denote as REE.

It is apparent that the NE of a game are also the RAE of a game. Indeed, we could argue that the NE of a game are 'focal' RAE in the sense that they satisfy a certain *ex post* consistency requirement that the RAE do not: no player would wish to defect unilaterally from an NE, even after learning what strategies his opponents chose. It is crucial to note, however, that this additional consistency requirement does not follow from the simple presumptions about agent rationality that underlie the RAE concept. Moreover, there may well be other criteria that make one set of RAE outcomes more or less 'focal'.

Experiments

What can we learn from laboratory experiments about the behavioural validity of the notion of RAE? The evidence is in two parts. The first type of evidence concerns the validity of the minimal rationality requirement of RAE: do people behave as if they follow the axioms of expected utility theory (EUT)? If not, we might not attach much weight to a solution concept that presumes that they do.

The second type of evidence asks directly whether observed outcomes of experimental games are RAE. We examine this type of evidence in the next section.

There appears to be a received wisdom among many economists that the postulates of EUT provide inadequate foundations for a positive model of choice under uncertainty (see, for example, Tversky and Kahneman 1986; Machina 1987). It is claimed that experimentalists have demonstrated that virtually any tenet of EUT can be shown to be violated. Indeed, one commentator proposes that for 'any rational choice, the behaviouralists (e.g. Amos Tversky) can produce a laboratory counterexample' (Zeckhauser 1986: 254).

Consider an example of these experiments. Tversky and Kahneman (1986: 80–1) posed a simple stochastic choice question to 124 undergraduate students, announcing that one-tenth of them would have the chance to play their chosen gamble. The subjects were asked to choose between two prospects, which are 'described by the percentage of marbles of different colors in each box and the amount of money you win or lose depending on the color of a randomly drawn marble'. The prospects were as follows:

A	90 per cent white $0	6 per cent red win $45	1 per cent green win $30	3 per cent yellow lose $15
B	90 per cent white $0	7 per cent red win $45	1 per cent green lose $10	2 per cent yellow lose $15

Option A is dominated by option B, but was chosen by 58 per cent of the subjects.

Shocking as this outcome may seem from an EUT perspective, assume that the subjects were (locally) risk neutral. Options A and B have expected values of \$2.55 and \$2.75 respectively. Given the *one-in-ten chance of actually playing the gamble*, a subject forgoes only \$(2.75 2.55)/10 = \$0.02 by selecting the dominated option. This expected value calculation might seem too onerous to perform correctly without a calculator.

Harrison (1989, 1990a, b) demonstrates that the evidence from a wide range of experiments that are claimed to violate EUT does not satisfy the 'pay-off' dominance requirement of a valid microeconomic experiment. This requirement, a sufficient condition[2] proposed by Smith (1982), requires that agents be adequately motivated to make good, rather than bad, decisions. That is, the financial incentives that an agent faces must be more than enough to overcome the (subjective) costs of making better decisions. The 'preference reversal' experiment of Grether and Plott (1979), which is a widely cited piece of evidence that EUT is not a good predictor of individual choice, fails to satisfy this condition.

It should also be noted that much of the experimental literature that shows violations of EUT does not satisfy the 'pay-off saliency' condition of Smith (1982). This condition requires that the alternative choices that agents face have different pay-offs in terms of some reward medium that has utility to the agent; that is, the agent perceives a link between alternative choices and alternative pay-offs. All the hypothetical questionnaires conducted by Kahneman and Tversky (1979), for example, fail to meet this requirement.

The conclusion that the received wisdom that 'EUT is dead at the hands of experimentalists' involves an uncritical reading of the experimental literature.

NASH EQUILIBRIUM AND REALIZABLE EXPECTATIONS

Theory

A stronger notion of RE can be derived from the concept of an NE of a non-cooperative game. An NE is a set of (possibly mixed) strategies for each player such that each player's strategy choice is a best response in expected utility terms *given* that all *other* players in fact use the strategies specified for them in the NE. Alternatively, an NE is a set of strategies that satisfies the following stability condition: no agent would want to deviate *unilaterally* from this strategy, *and* this is true for all agents. Note that this does not imply that an agent might not do *equally* well by using another strategy, just that he has no expected *gain* from deviating from the strategy prescribed for him in the NE.

The concept of NE has been popular in game theory. It has also been subject to the criticism that it is too 'weak', in the sense that there may be many NE in any given game. If a theory predicts only that the outcome will be an NE, and there exist many NE, the theory is said to be 'weak' (in a positivist sense). It should be noted again that *all NE are rationalizable*, but that *all rationalizable strategy combinations need not be NE*. Thus the concept of NE, which defines the notion of REE, is stronger than the notion of a rationalizable strategy set defining the notion of RAE.

Experiments

The Nash (1950) theory of bargaining characterizes an environment in which bargaining occurs. It does not characterize any particular process of bargaining. The environment consists of a set of feasible expected utility pay-offs to each agent and a 'disagreement' outcome, along with mild regularity conditions on these. The process of bargaining is not explicitly modelled, in the sense that no specific logistics of offer and counter-offer are proposed. Instead, the process is characterized by specifying that its outcome satisfy a certain set of axioms. There is a unique element of the feasible set of pay-offs that satisfies the axioms proposed by Nash (1950); see Roth (1979) for a review of the axiom selection game that has been played out in the subsequent literature. The Nash (1950) solution (NS) is the cornerstone of traditional 'co-operative bargaining theory'.

In a series of laboratory experiments, Roth and Malouf (1979), Roth *et al.* (1981), Roth and Murnighan (1982) and Roth and Schoumaker (1983a) (hereafter R1, R2, R3 and R4 respectively) have tested the NS as a predictive model of behaviour. Their experiments employ an explicit bargaining process, which is described below. They find that the NS is *not* an adequate model of behaviour in these experiments.

Subjects in these experiments respond systematically to the provision of information about their opponent's monetary prizes, even though such information is not predicted to influence behaviour according to the NS (i.e. the information is superfluous to the characterization of the environment to which the NS applies). Specifically, observed agreements tend to be bimodally distributed around two focal points: the NS in which the product of the expected *utility* gains (relative to the disagreement outcome) is maximized, and an equal monetary gain agreement in which each agent expects to receive the same *monetary* gain as the other agent. When these two focal points are identical, observed agreements tend to be distributed unimodally about them with very little variance. When they are distinct, however, the first anomaly of these experiments emerges: *efficient agreements other than the NS are observed.*

A second anomaly from these experiments is the *observed incidence of disagreements.* In the basic 'control' experiments of Roth and Schoumaker (1983a: Tables 3 and 4) 23 per cent of the sessions in trials 11–25 ended in disagreement. Although some theories admit the possibility of disagreement (see Chatterjee (1985) for a review), such outcomes are at odds with co-operative game theory.

Binmore *et al.* argue that this line of experimental research

> confirms a view that is common among social psychologists: namely, that subjects tend to seek a 'fair' outcome to bargaining problems. The thrust of the enquiry is then to determine what the subjects will regard as fair in a given situation.
>
> A tension exists between this work and the theoretical approach revitalized by Ariel Rubinstein (1982).... This new approach involves modelling the process of offer and counteroffer by means of which agreement can be reached, as a formal non-cooperative game; and studying agreements that can be sustained as equilibria of this game.
>
> (Binmore *et al.* 1985: 1178)

Binmore *et al.* report on a bargaining experiment with an explicit and simple process. They find that subjects that have some experience with the strategic structure of their game behave 'like a game theorist' rather than 'play fair'. The interpretation of the experiments of R1–R4 as inconsistent with economic theory is spreading. Kahneman *et al.*, for example, claim in reference to R2, *inter alia,* that it ' is a mild embarrassment to the standard [economic] model that experimental studies often produce fair behaviour even in the absence of enforcement' (Kahneman *et al.* 1986: 736–7).[3]

The implications of these important results for the earlier experiments of R1–R4 are threefold: (a) the subjects in the earlier experiments did not fully appreciate the strategic structure of the game they were in; (b) the subjects behaved as predicted by non-cooperative game theory rather than co-operative game theory; (c) the subjects did not behave as predicted by co-operative *or* non-cooperative game theory. Implication (a) is not particularly plausible

– the basic binary lottery game of R1–R4 is exceedingly simple to understand, even though some of the treatments employed ('chips' in R2 and combinations of complete and common knowledge in R3) could conceivably have bewildered some subjects.

It is argued here, however, that implication (b) is correct. Using non-cooperative game theory, it is possible to explain the apparent 'misbehaviour' of the subjects in R1–R4 – misbehaviour from the perspective of co-operative NS theory – as rational. The first anomaly can be explained as NE outcomes of the bargaining game employed in R4. Both anomalies can be explained as outcomes supportable by rationalizable strategies.

We can therefore say that there is nothing irrational about the expectations and behaviour of these subjects *vis-à-vis* the minimalist RAE notion. Similarly, there is nothing irrational about these subjects choosing (efficient) outcomes other than the NS if we use the more restrictive REE notion. On the other hand, the observed disagreements are inconsistent with REE. To the extent that the NS provides a 'true model' around which expectations might form, the observed behaviour is irrational from the strict MRE perspective. These experiments therefore provide an excellent illustration of our distinctions between RAE, REE and MRE.

In each of R1–R4 two subjects were bargaining over the division of 100 lottery tickets. Every extra lottery ticket that a subject received in the game gave him a 0.01 higher probability of winning a subsequent lottery. Thus, if one subject received all 100 lottery tickets, that subject would win his lottery with certainty. Even without knowledge of the monetary prizes that each player could win, the expected utility of each lottery ticket allocation to each player is determined. The disagreement outcome was for both players to receive no lottery tickets at all. We refer to games of this form as 'binary lottery games'.

In the experiments of R1–R3 the bargaining process was relatively unstructured. Interacting via computer terminals, each player could send messages or proposals to his opponent. A message was non-binding and could consist of virtually anything that could be typed in the time allowed (exceptions were physical threats and references to the agent's own monetary prize, which were blocked from transmission by the experimenter). A proposal was binding and consisted of a proposed allocation of the 100 lottery tickets. If the same proposal was sent back by the other player, it was deemed to be accepted. Any number of proposals and messages could be sent by either player in the time allowed. Thus the timing and content of the strategy space open to agents was, in principle, infinite.

In the experiment reported in R4, however, considerable structure was imposed on the bargaining process. Messages, as defined above, could not be sent at all. Proposals could still be sent, but only in two stages. In the first stage each agent could privately send a proposal without knowing what the other agent was proposing. A player's stage 1 'demand' is the number of tickets he proposes for himself. If the two proposals requested allocations for each of the senders that summed to 100 lottery tickets or less, this was the 'agreed outcome' of the game. If not, the two players proceeded to stage 2.

In stage 2 the players could either repeat their stage 1 demand or accept their opponent's offer. If they both repeated their demands, the disagreement outcome applied. If player 1 (2) repeats his demand and player 2 (1) accepts the stage 1 offer of 1 (2), the agreement is that offer. If each accepts the stage 1 offer of the other, then player 1 (2) receives what was offered him by player 2 (1) in stage 1.

This two-stage bargaining game is straightforward to analyse. We can show that every efficient division of tickets is supported by a non-cooperative NE. Let α be player 1's demand and β be player 2's demand such that $\alpha + \beta = 100$. Then each player's strategy to play α (or β) and repeat their offer whenever the second stage is reached is an NE. If $\alpha + \beta < 100$ then either player can do better by increasing his demand until $\alpha + \beta = 100$. Thus inefficient outcomes that do not fully divide the pie are not NE. Nash (1953), of course, drew the same conclusion from a similar non-cooperative demand game (before applying his own 'imaginative' refinement procedure).

Next we consider subgame perfect NE in pure strategies. If $\alpha + \beta > 100$ and stage 2 is reached, then subjects play the game shown in Figure 4.1. Each player has only two pure strategies: to repeat his demand or to accept the other offer. If both players repeat their stage 1 offers, then both receive the disagreement outcome (zero for each

		Player 2	
		Accept	Repeat
Player 1	Accept	$100-\beta$; $100-\alpha$	$100-\beta$; β
	Repeat	α ; $100-\alpha$	0 ; 0

Figure 4.1 Normal form of bargaining experiment subgame

player). If both players accept the other's offer then we have a strictly inefficient outcome. Finally, if one player 'repeats' and the other 'accepts', we have an efficient outcome in which the 'repeating player' receives his stage 1 demand and the other player receives the rest of the pie.

Given that $\alpha + \beta > 100$ and $\alpha, \beta > 0$ it follows that $100 - \beta < \alpha$ and $100 - \alpha < \beta$. Therefore the two efficient outcomes are supported by the NE (Accept, Repeat) and (Repeat, Accept). It is obvious that these are the only pure strategy NE.

From our analysis of the subgames of the bargaining game it is now easy to find subgame perfect NE for the bargaining game. For example, 'demand $\alpha = 100$ and always repeat' for player 1 and 'demand $\beta = 0$ and always accept' for player 2 is subgame perfect. (The symmetric pair of strategies with $\alpha = 0$ and $\beta = 100$ also form a subgame perfect NE.) Indeed, all efficient outcomes can be supported by subgame perfect NE; although subgame perfection as a refinement principle does reduce the set of *NE strategies*, it does not eliminate any of the *outcomes* supported as NE.[4]

Although it is not possible to write down an extensive form game corresponding to the permitted bargaining process in R1–R3, it is strongly arguable that the above two-stage process is applicable to those experiments as well. In particular, it is plausible that any messages sent in R1–R3 were deemed incredible and uninformative and were ignored by both sides. Similarly, the two-stage demand game of R4 could have been played using the proposals permitted in R1–R3. The point is that there clearly *exists* a feasible bargaining process that *can* explain the outcomes of R1–R4 as rational behaviour in a non-cooperative game.[5]

Another implication of our analysis concerns the interpretation of the experimental treatment in R4: the effect of *artificially* inducing expectations about the bargaining strength of one's opponent. This was done by having each subject play for fifteen periods against computer-simulated opponents, in the belief that they were human. These simulated opponents followed strategies that led them to foster agreements that were either NS or the equal monetary gains outcome (as found in R1–R3). At the beginning of period 16 the humans were told the outcomes from periods 11–15 of their future human opponents. Thus, if I had been accustomed to playing against simulated 'wimps' I would see the recent history of several unfortunates that had played against simulated 'bullies'. In this way the experimenters modified any 'home-grown' expectations that I might have brought to the experiment.

In brief, R4 found that the outcomes between human bargainers in periods 16–25 broadly reflected the expected outcomes which had been induced. Thus, in the above example, I would tend to have extracted significantly more than my NS share of the lottery tickets.

These experiments are important in showing that the subjective expectations of bargainers can play a crucial role in determining outcomes. However, they do *not* address the hypothesis that those expectations 'can be manipulated *independently* of the strategic possibilities and feasible outcomes of the bargaining situation' (Roth and Schoumaker 1983a: 365, emphasis added). The reason that they do not address this hypothesis is that the induced expectations were NE of the non-cooperative game involved in the experiments.

Designing an experiment that addresses this hypothesis is not easy without imposing a quite different structure on the bargaining process. To the extent that all Pareto optimal outcomes are pure strategy NE for the bargaining process of R4, they are rationalizable outcomes. It is not surprising at all, then, that two of these NE happen to be focal points even in the absence of artificial encouragement. As noted by Bernheim (1984: 1009), if 'agents share the common belief that Nash equilibrium is normally realized, they no longer entertain the rationally admissible doubt that an opponent will fail to conform.' This line of analysis nicely formalizes the claim of Roth and Schoumaker (1983b: 1339) that the behaviour observed in their experiments 'seems consistent with utility maximization, and we do not see any justification for calling that behaviour irrational'. To say that I was 'perfectly justified' in writing down a demand in excess of my NS expectation, in the example given above, is just to say that this is a rationalizable strategy for me.[6]

Finally, consider the implications of imposing a requirement of rationalizability on the behaviour of subjects. We see that any feasible outcome, efficient or not, is rationalizable in this game. If the second-stage subgame is reached, we know that $0 \leq 100 - \alpha < \beta$ and $0 \leq 100 - \beta < \alpha$. Hence, in Figure 4.1 no pure strategy is strictly dominated, and every strategy is therefore rationalizable. Thus every outcome, including disagreement, can be supported by rationalizable conjectures.[7] Similarly, there exist rationalizable conjectures that will support either player's forcing the subgame by demanding enough in stage 1.

In conclusion, it should be emphasized that the bargaining experiments of R1–R4 are excellent vehicles for testing the NS concept of co-operative game theory, the purpose for which they were designed.[8] The fact that the subjects in those experiments lead one to reject that concept, and hence MRE, should not be taken to imply that their behaviour is inconsistent with other solution concepts of (non-cooperative) game theory and the associated notions of RAE and REE.

MARKET EQUILIBRIUM AND MUTHIAN RATIONAL EXPECTATIONS

Competitive market experiments place a great strain on the plausibility of MRE models. In this section we present experimental evidence which supports the following redirection of MRE. First, we must be able to model the fact that subjects use institutions as active guides to their decision-making. In particular, we must model the way in which the institution shapes an individual's opportunity cost assessment of specific messages by responding to these messages in particular ways. Second, we must be able to distinguish between general and agent-specific knowledge which exists at a behavioural equilibrium. If a change in an individual's environment leads to new behaviour, this can be explained in one of two ways. Either the individual has already estimated the opportunity costs of particular actions in the new environment, perhaps by analogy with the old environment, or the individual's behaviour can be viewed as a process of systematic learning in the new environment. A reasonable model of expectations should be able to predict when an institution will lead to learning by analogy and when it will lead to learning by trial and error.

In the remainder of this section we examine the behaviour of a particular market institution, the double auction (DA), in different experimental environments. We shall assume that the reader is broadly familiar with the experimental procedures used in DA markets; Plott (1982) provides an excellent introduction.

Smith (1982) reviews a long series of laboratory experiments designed to examine a competitive institution which is based on field DA. He finds that: 'Strict privacy together with the trading rules of a market institution are sufficient to produce competitive market incomes at or near 100% efficiency' (Smith 1982: 176). This result is most striking when we observe that the markets studied in this research programme were for discrete units of a single homogeneous good with only a few buyers (with strictly private reservation prices) and sellers (with strictly private cost information). Furthermore, the DA institution was forced to arrive at an allocation with no allowance for retrading or recontracting.

Price forecasts

Williams (1987) studied the formation of price expectations in DA. Using his notation, let F_t denote an individual's forecast of mean price for period t, P_t denote the actual mean price at time t and ε_t denote a random variable with mean zero. Williams noted that the RE hypothesis implies that mean forecasts will be distributed around actual mean prices:

$$F_t = P_t + \varepsilon_t \tag{4.1}$$

An alternative adaptive expectations hypothesis can be written as

$$F_t = F_{t-1} + \beta(P_{t-1} - F_{t-1}) + \varepsilon_t \tag{4.2}$$

Note that if mean prices are stationary, i.e. $P_t = P$ for all t, then the special case of $\beta = 1$ in (4.2) is the RE hypothesis (4.1).

It is important to note that the RE hypothesis represented by (4.1) does not require that mean observed prices equal the predicted prices according to competitive equilibrium (CE) theory. As such, hypothesis (4.1) tests what we have termed REE, which is weaker than MRE. This is not to say that (4.1) does not test the generic notion of RE, but just to be precise as to what is required of the data before we reject or accept the generic RE hypothesis on the basis of equation (4.1).

The data to test these hypotheses come from twelve experiments with six buyers and six sellers, and one experiment with seven buyers and seven sellers. Eight of the twelve experiments used 'inexperienced' subjects, while the other four used 'once experienced' subjects. The CE trading volume was twenty-four units.

Asking subjects for forecasts introduces a methodological complication. In order to make forecast data salient, subjects must be rewarded on their accuracy. However, rewarding forecasts changes each subject's pay-offs and introduces a new strategic element. A subject must decide if he/she could make more money by trying to manipulate market outcomes so that his/her forecast is 'good'. The difficulty here is that there are actually 'two games in town': the game in which agents influence market prices by means of trading activity, and the game in which they guess what those prices will be. The agent may choose to do poorly in the first game, say by buying at higher prices than he would otherwise, so as to be able to do better on the second game.

To address this problem Williams (1987) kept the reward for forecasting quite low relative to the rewards from trading at CE prices. However, this in turn raises the question of whether agents had any incentive to take the forecasting game seriously.[9]

In these experiments the subject with the smallest cumulative absolute forecast error was paid an additional dollar. During the experiment subjects did not know how well they were forecasting relative to others. This procedure for inducing subjects to make accurate forecasts raises two further problems.

First, the expected pay-off for one agent from making a particular forecast (as distinct from some other forecast) depends on what he conjectures that the other subjects will forecast. Without knowing what each player conjectures about the forecasts of every other player we cannot therefore determine precisely what the incentives were for the player to forecast well.

Second, the fact that there was only one pay-off for all twelve agents means that the expected pay-offs for any one agent are only a fraction of the total (presuming that no subject had any prior that he was a better or worse forecaster than any other). Thus each player might expect to earn 100/12 = 8.33 cents from the forecasting game. Note that the game refers to forecasts for four trading periods, implying that the expected return in each period is only 8.33/4 = 2.08 cents. It is far from obvious that these incentives satisfy the dominance precept of experimental economics (see p. 83). A simple way of avoiding these two problems would be to reward each player as a function of his own forecast performance, without reference to the forecasts of other players.

We have taken care to be precise as to the incentive structure of the forecasting experiments of Williams (1987) because such experiments are potentially important sources of information on expectations. When Smith *et al.* (1988: 1136) claim that 'Williams (1987) provided evidence that $1 is sufficient incentive for serious forecasting, but not so large as to motivate strategic manipulation of the mean price in an effort to win the forecasting prize', it is not apparent what evidence they have in mind. The treatments indicated above (having agents forecast the observed market behaviour of a distinct set of agents, and having forecasting rewards for one player depend only on that player's forecast performance) could test this claim.

Williams (1987) tested the RE and adaptive expectations models using pooled cross-sectional forecast data from the twelve experiments. The models were rewritten for estimation purposes as follows:

$$F_t = \alpha + \beta P_t + \mu_t \qquad (4.1')$$

$$F_t - F_{t-1} = \alpha + \beta(P_{t-1} - F_{t-1}) + \mu_t \qquad (4.2')$$

where, for simplicity, individual subscripts and experiment subscripts have been removed. Williams also ran (4.1′) and (4.2′) on samples from different repetitions to investigate whether estimates improve with subjects' experience.

If subjects' forecasts satisfy the RE model (4.1), then $\alpha = 0$, $\beta = 1$ and μ_t will be serially uncorrelated in (4.1′). Williams (1987: Tables 1 and 2) rejects both of these null hypotheses at the 99 per cent level; the estimated β is around 0.5 in all his equations. If forecasts satisfy the adaptive expectations model (4.2), then $\alpha = 0$ and $0 < \beta < 1$ in equation (4.2′). Williams (1987: Table 3) finds that this equation fits well with estimates of β from 0.79 to 0.88 and R^2 between 0.49 and 0.79. However, α was estimated to be slightly, but significantly, less than zero.

In conclusion, an intriguing dichotomy has been created by Williams's study. On the one hand, markets converge to the CE. Clearly the *contracts being written* suggest that subjects do have RE in some 'aggregate' sense, i.e. we could properly say that 'this market behaved as if it had an RE that the price would be the CE price'. On the other hand, *individual subject forecasts* do not seem to have this same convergence property.

One feature of DA markets may account for this dichotomy: the intensive learning process that goes on 'continuously' *within* each trading period. Individual's forecasts were made at the beginning of each period before any such learning had taken place. Observed market prices, however, were the result of that learning process. In Bayesian terms, it is as if the initial prior distribution over prices is being compared with the final posterior distribution; to the extent that the observed sample is informative, the prior and posterior could be very different. Since *forecasts* are based on the initial prior, whereas *observed prices* are strongly influenced by the posterior that is evolving during the trading process, we might expect that they would have very different descriptive statistics if the sample were informative.[10]

It is premature to draw any broad conclusions from these experiments as to the validity of the RE hypothesis, given the problems of experimental design noted earlier. None the less, they do illustrate the sort of data on expectations that can be readily collected in an experiment. Moreover, the use of *any* salient reward represents an important methodological contribution over the use of panel survey data typically used to test the RE hypothesis in the field.

Price control experiments

The standard partial equilibrium model of price controls offers an interesting challenge to MRE. Consider the following question. Given a standard Marshallian market (i.e. downward-sloping aggregate demand and upward-sloping aggregate supply) with a unique CE, and given that the market is at the CE, what is the effect of lifting a non-binding price ceiling?

Since the market is in equilibrium, and there are no stochastic shocks, the objective distribution of outcomes assigns all its weight to the unique CE. If the CE is also a MRE equilibrium, then each agent's subjective distribution must also assign all its weight to the CE. Finally, since lifting a non-binding price ceiling does not change the objective distribution of outcomes (i.e. the CE), we should see no effect on agents' subjective distributions.

Isaac and Plott (1981), Smith and Williams (1981) and Coursey and Smith (1983) have examined the effect of price controls in experimental markets. In the first two papers price controls in the DA institution are examined, while in the third paper price controls in the posted offer institution are examined. In these experiments the effect of lifting a non-binding ceiling is to cause a jump (above the CE price) in contract prices which then gradually decline back to the CE price.

In the long run the market returns to the MRE–CE prediction. However, the irrelevant information that the price ceiling is lifted results in a short-run dynamic which cannot be explained by MRE. The MRE assumption that, for the same information set, subjective beliefs will tend to be distributed about the prediction of the theory is essentially a static description of the state of expectations that simply cannot explain the observed short-run behaviour.

Short-lived-asset markets

A series of experiments dealing with 'short-lived assets' has been conducted by Forsythe *et al.* (1982) and Friedman *et al.* (1983, 1984). These experiments provide a basis for evaluating the ability of spot and futures markets to attain the MRE equilibrium under a variety of environments which differ with respect to public and private information sets.

Consider the basic design of Friedman *et al.* (1984) (hereafter FHS) reflected in the numerical parameters in Table 4.1. There are nine agents grouped into three 'types', with a different dividend

Table 4.1 Parameters for an experimental asset market

Agents		*Dividend profile*		
Type	*ID*	*Period A*	*Period B*	*Period C*
I	1, 2, 3	0.45	0.45	0.45
II	4, 5, 6	0.70	0.30	0.10
III	7, 8, 9	0.10	0.30	0.70

profile for each type. Each trading year is divided into three periods, denoted A, B and C. An asset, called a 'certificate', can be purchased or sold by any agent during any period. To purchase a certificate the agent must have cash (each agent receives an interest-free loan of \$20 at the beginning of each year), and to sell a certificate the agent must already own at least one certificate (each agent is endowed with two certificates at the beginning of each year). All trades in this initial design are for spot delivery.

An agent holding a certificate at the *end* of a trading period receives a dividend as shown in Table 4.1. Thus if agent 4, with a type II dividend profile, holds three certificates at the end of period A he receives \$2.10 = \$0.70 + \$0.70 + \$0.70. All assets carry over from period A and period B into the next period, but at the end of period C all assets are 'consumed'. Thus each certificate has a three-period 'life'. These valuations do not vary from year to year, and the foregoing is common information for all agents. However, each agent knows only his own private valuations.

It is straightforward to derive the MRE predictions in this design. Using backward induction, consider the CE price in period C. Assuming that agents, 7, 8 and 9 act non-cooperatively, they would bid the price of a certificate up to \$0.70 rather quickly. Clearly, they will be willing to pay more than \$0.10 for the certificates held by type II agents, and more than \$0.45 for the certificates held by type I agents. Thus the CE price in period C will be greater than \$0.45, since no type I agent will sell for less. Competition between type III agents will further force the price up to \$0.70. We therefore predict that agents 7, 8 or 9 will buy all available certificates in period C at a price of \$0.70. Note that this prediction does not employ any assumption about expectations.

In period B, if agents have an MRE that the period C price will be the CE just derived, what will be their reservation prices? Type I agents will be willing to pay up to \$0.45 + \$0.70 = \$1.15 for each certificate that they buy in period B, since they receive $0.45 in dividends at the end of period B and can sell the certificate for $0.70 in period C. Similarly, the period B reservation prices for type II (III) agents will be $0.40 ($1.00). Therefore we predict that traders 1, 2 or 3 will buy up all the available certificates in period B for a price of $1.15, since the certificates are not worth this much to any other agent. Note that this prediction *does* require some assumption about the period C price that is expected to prevail in period B. As such, it does provide a test of the MRE hypothesis.

What alternative hypothesis might we entertain as to period B behaviour? One simple alternative is that agents do not form a MRE of the period C price, but use only their own private valuation when forming their period B reservation prices. Thus type I agents would have reservation prices of $0.90 = $0.45 + $0.45 in period B, since the period C sale price of $0.70 is replaced in this calculation by the lowly period C dividend of $0.45. Similarly, the reservation prices for type II (III) agents are $0.40 ($1.00). Thus the alternative hypothesis is that type III agents will buy up all the certificates at a price of $1.00. There is a clear separation of predictions here between the MRE hypothesis and a simple alternative.

Finally, in period A, the MRE reservation price is $1.60 = $0.45 + $1.15 for type I agents, since they would receive a period A dividend of $0.45 and be able to 'sell' the asset for $1.15 in period B (in fact they would hold the asset themselves, but the general logic is that the asset is worth $1.15 in the period B market). Type II (III) agents would have period A reservation prices of $1.85 ($1.25) by a similar MRE logic. Thus we would predict that type II agents would buy up all certificates in period A for a price of $1.85.

Under our alternative hypothesis to MRE, the reservation prices in period A would be $1.35, $1.10 and $1.10 for agents of types, I, II and III respectively. Thus we would predict under this hypothesis about 'expectations' that type I agents would buy up all the certificates for only $1.35.

Note that the MRE hypothesis implies sharply different behaviour with respect to market prices in periods A and B, and also with respect to which agent type will hold all the assets in these two periods. Figure 4.2 displays the observed behaviour with experienced subjects in experiment 1 of FHS, who refer to the MRE prediction as the perfect foresight (PF) prediction and to the alternative prediction as the private information (PI) prediction.

Note first the steady convergence of period C price to the CE of $0.70 over several trading years. Clearly, the observed price in period

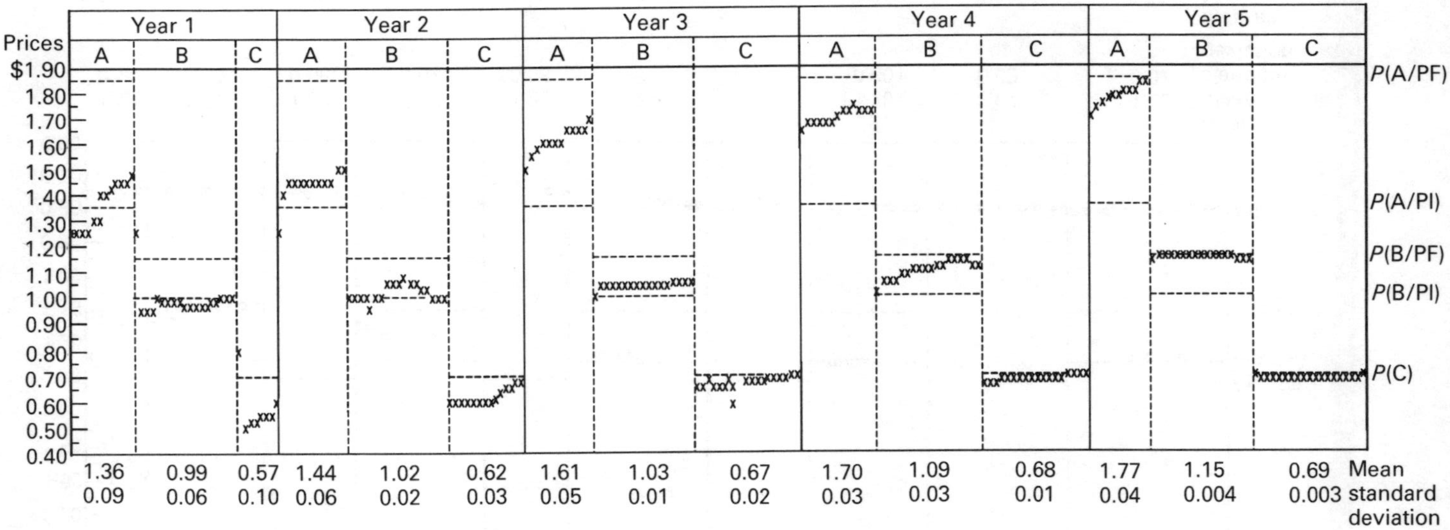

Figure 4.2 Experimental asset market behaviour (spot only)

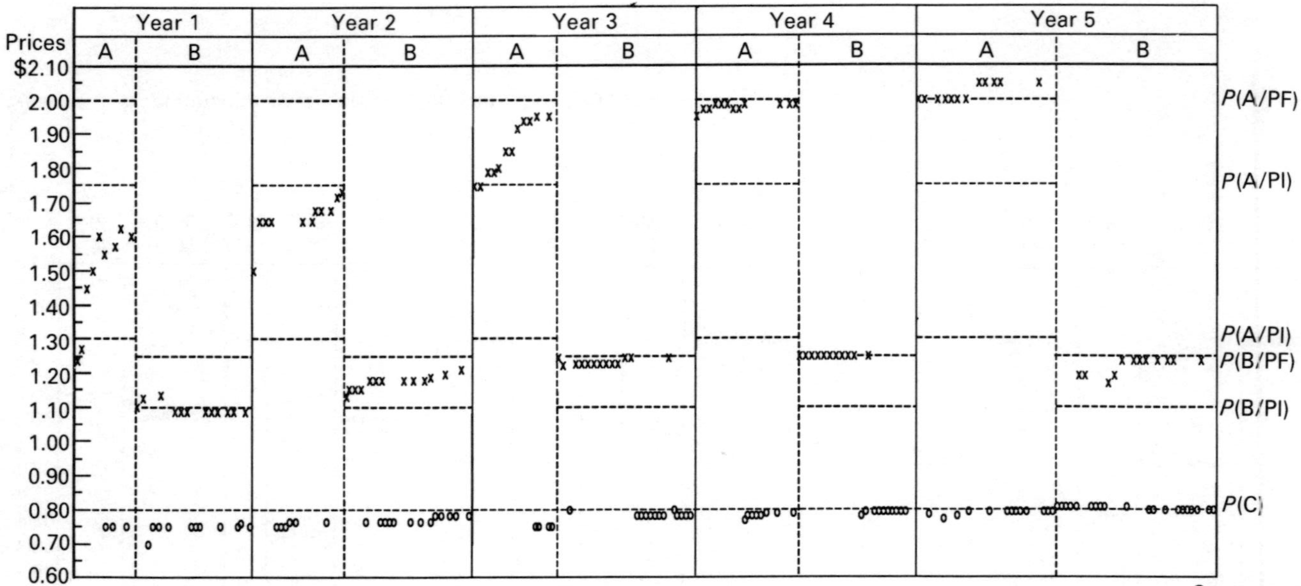

	Year 1 A	Year 1 B	Year 2 A	Year 2 B	Year 3 A	Year 3 B	Year 4 A	Year 4 B	Year 5 A	Year 5 B
Spot										
Mean	1.49	1.07	1.67	1.17	1.85	1.24	1.98	1.25	2.02	1.23
standard deviation	0.14	0.10	0.06	0.02	0.08	0.01	0.01	0.001	0.03	0.02
Futures										
Mean	0.75	0.72	0.76	0.78	0.75	0.79	0.78	0.80	0.80	0.81
standard deviation	0.001	0.09	0.01	0.01	0.001	0.004	0.01	0.003	0.01	0.01

Figure 4.3 Experimental asset market behaviour (spot and futures)

C does not attain the CE until around year 3. However, the average market price of $0.57 in year 1 is significantly greater than the period C valuations of type I and II agents. Thus the period C market in year 1 is sending a correct signal that 'the market' is willing to pay more for each certificate than it is worth to these agents.

In year 1 we observe period A and B prices around the PI (or non-MRE) prediction. Agents have no way of knowing what the market price of a period B or period C certificate will be, and bid solely according to their own private information. In year 2, however, they have observed the period B and C market outcomes of year 1 and have clearly factored these into their period A and B reservation prices. In period A, year 2 prices are significantly greater than the PI prediction, and in the direction of MRE. This process continues monotonically over the remaining years, with closing period A (B) prices in year 5 (4) reaching the MRE. The allocation of certificates between agent types reflects this transition from one prediction to the other.

Now consider the effect of adding a 'period C futures market', which is open during periods A and B and allows agents to contract for the purchase or sale of a period C spot certificate. The PF (or MRE) and PI (or non-MRE) predictions are just as applicable here. Figure 4.3 (based on experiment 2 of FHS) illustrates that we observe dramatically faster convergence to the MRE equilibrium with a futures market present. (This experiment employed valuations different from those in Table 4.1.) Futures contract prices are marked as circles, to distinguish them from spot prices. It is apparent that futures markets improve the performance of the MRE prediction: by allowing agents to form relatively tight expectations about the market price for a period C certificate during period A and period B trading in year 1, it simply speeds up the learning process of experiment 1.

Similar qualitative results are observed in richer informational environments considered by FHS. These environments include the introduction of some 'event uncertainty' in the form of a chance drawing by Nature of dividend profiles for all agents. One event corresponds to a 'high' set of dividends. Agents know the probability of each event, leading to a simple generalization of the distinction between PI and PF when we take the expectation over the events determined by Nature. Again we observe a clear transition process towards the MRE prediction (referred to by FHS as the uninformed rational expectations equilibrium). The introduction of a period C futures market also speeds up this transition process.

The other informational environment considered by FHS is the effect of 'insider' agents with better information than other agents as to which state of Nature prevails in any particular year. Identical qualitative results are observed: steady convergence towards the appropriate MRE equilibrium, and even faster convergence with the orthogonal introduction of a futures market.

These experimental results support two general conclusions. The first is the importance of allowing for a learning process before observing the MRE. In none of these asset market experiments do we observe the market immediately jumping to the MRE prediction; steady convergence over a number of stationary repetitions is the order of things. We could take this as evidence for or against the MRE hypothesis, depending on how rapidly we expect the MRE to be established.

The second conclusion follows from the first: the learning process appears to proceed on Bayesian lines. Agents begin with diffuse priors as to the prices likely to obtain in future trading periods. As they observe more data, and as they observe more informative data (i.e. less noisy data), their expectations are adjusted. The evidence for this conclusion comes from the orthogonal effect of adding a futures market. In these designs the role of a futures market is purely informational. It provides agents with 'better data' earlier than when there are no futures markets. The effect of providing these 'better data' earlier is to generate non-diffuse MRE quicker, and to permit more rapid convergence to the MRE.

Long-lived-asset markets

Early research on experimental asset markets fixed the asset life to one, two or three periods. It is natural to ask whether the trading of assets with longer lives gives different results. Smith *et al.* (1988) present interesting experimental data on this issue. They report twenty-two experiments in which nine to twelve traders with DA experience (and either inexperienced, once experienced or twice experienced in asset markets) traded a number of fifteen- or thirty-period assets with the same common value distribution of dividends.

In these experiments all assets are contracted for in a spot market. Valid contracts specify the selling price of a single asset together with identification of both buyer and seller. The seller must deliver and the buyer must make full payment when the contract is made. Contracts are made in a DA which enforces improvement in the standing bid and ask. Non-improving bids and asks are put in a 'rank queue'; after a contract is made the highest bid and lowest offer in the rank queue become the standing bid and offer respectively. Subjects can enter bids provided that they can pay and can enter offers provided that they have an asset. At any time a subject can accept a standing bid or a standing offer, subject to the same conditions.

If all subjects are risk neutral with identical price expectations, there would be no reason for trade. Diversity in price expectations and/or attitude to risk will generate trade in this market. Heterogeneous price expectations may lead to contract prices above the expected dividend value provided that some subjects believe that there are others who believe that the price will go even higher. This phenomenon is called a price bubble.

The major empirical result is the large number of observed price bubbles: fourteen of the twenty-two experiments provide such an outcome. The mean price path in markets with bubbles invariably starts below the expected dividend value, which is interpreted to mean that initial diversity in attitude to risk leads to a sequence of contract prices resulting in diverse price expectations. Heterogeneous expectations make it possible for subjects to speculate on capital gains. As prices move above the expected dividend value, this speculative behaviour is reinforced as subjects update their beliefs that other subjects have even higher price expectations.

Most of the bubbles ended in a crash, with the price path ending near the MRE price (i.e. the expected dividend value). As trading nears the end, the subjects who are trading on the bubble are essentially playing a game of chicken. In particular, some subjects will be caught holding assets which cost more than the expected value. It is not surprising that collapses in bubbles tend to be preceded by a thinning of bids relative to asks and a drop in trading volume, causing the 'weak of heart' to panic and precipitating a sell-off.

Smith *et al.* (1988) conducted experiments covering a wide range of experimental treatments in order to determine which set of treatments is most likely to result in a bubble. A review of their results reveals some insights. In their notation 'x' denotes experienced subjects, 'xx' denotes highly experienced subjects, 'n' indicates that some inexperienced subjects participated with experienced subjects, 'f' denotes experiments in which subjects were asked for their price forecasts and 'pc' indicates that price controls were binding close to the expected dividend value for several initial periods. A final treatment was the use of a positive 'buyout' price for assets held at the end of the experiment (all experiments except one lasted for fifteen periods).

Consider Smith *et al.*'s experiments 5 and 6x on their Figure 1. In their experiment 5, with inexperienced subjects, there was a significant and high-volume bubble for the first eleven periods. In their experiment 6x, with experienced subjects, there is *no* sign of a bubble, with prices tracking the expected dividend value closely.[11] This pair of experiments suggests that the experience level of subjects could be important for the likelihood of bubbles. Indeed, the observed bubbles in ten experiments could be 'explained' solely on the basis of the inexperience of the subjects (experiments 5, 7, 16, 17, 23, 26, 10, 18, 41f and 90f). It could also be argued that the subjects in two further 'bubble experiments' (30xsf and 39xsf) were not 'fully' experienced in the sense that they had only previously participated in a *short-lived-*asset experiment.[12]

An interesting feature of most of the price bubbles was that the market became thin. In some cases only one or two trades were observed at the 'mean' price (19x and 36xx).

Three experiments with experienced subjects had price bubbles in early periods of trading (up to period 8 or 9), but traded the MRE price thereafter (experiments 48xnf, 49xnf and 28x). One experiment with experienced subjects had a heavy-volume price bubble, but may have been contaminated by subject confusion (25x). This experiment was the first of those with *no* 'terminal buyout'. The subjects that participated in it gained their experience in experiment 23, which *did* have the 'terminal buyout' in effect.

These possible explanations for the observed bubbles are not intended to dismiss them, but rather to offer plausible rationalizations for observed deviations from MRE. There remains one experiment, 124xxf, which had a significant price bubble that does not have such a ready explanation. On the other hand, this outcome should be seen in the context of seven experiments with experienced subjects in which there was no trace of any bubble (6x, 9x, 12xx, 20x, 42xf, 43xnf and 50xxf).

Experience in asset markets tends to lessen the volume of trade and improve the MRE prediction. Note that the bubble is likely to become a game of chicken even earlier given the experience factor. In particular, price bubbles almost disappear (except for small price fluctuations) in markets with twice experienced subjects. This evidence supports the conjecture that experienced traders are less likely to fall victim to a bubble.

In ten of the twenty-two experiments subjects were asked to predict the mean price for the trading period that they were about to enter, using the same incentive scheme as employed by Williams (1987).

Several features of the forecasts tend to reinforce the behavioural interpretation of bubbles given above. First, forecasts tend to be highly adaptive and fail to predict turning points. In particular, there is a tendency for forecasts to underpredict mean price in a boom and overpredict mean price in a crash. Second, within an experiment, subjects who forecast better made more money relative to poorer forecasters. This suggests that subjects were able to act on their price inferences in ways which improved their earnings potential. Third, across experiments, experienced subjects exhibit more homogeneity in their forecasts compared with inexperienced subjects. This reinforces the notion that experienced subjects (who know that each other subject is experienced) tend to start closer to a state of common price priors and tend to converge more quickly to a common price expectation.

CONCLUDING REMARKS

A rational expectation is a conjecture about behaviour that meets certain consistency requirements. Three sets of such requirements have been proposed and have been demonstrated to be of some importance in evaluating evidence from recent laboratory experiments. Such evidence is uniquely valuable in any evaluation of the rationality of expectations since it directly controls for 'fundamentals' *and* the underlying 'true model'.

It is difficult to find any evidence that is in conflict with the weakest notion of RE posed here – RAE. There is *some* evidence, far from overwhelming, against the stronger notion of RE embodied in the game-theoretical concept of NE – REE. On the other hand, there is considerable evidence against the strongest notion of RE proposed here – MRE. To some extent this contrary evidence is attributable to subject inexperience, but these defences are admittedly forced.

The evidence strongly supports simple models of the learning process, albeit models that must be conditioned on the institutional environment in which the process takes place. Subjects behave as if they develop 'common expectations' by an adaptive Bayesian process. The *limit* of this process often, but not always, appears to be consistent with MRE. A diverse range of experimental institutions displays a wide range of speeds of convergence to REE and MRE equilibria.

It is likely that the next generation of experiments will *directly* gather data on subject expectations, but with tighter incentive structures than in previous studies. We may then be in a position to explain the wide range of experimental evidence for and against MRE.

NOTES

I am grateful to Dan Friedman, Kevin McCabe, E.E. Rutström and Arlington Williams for stimulating discussions.

1 Or any correlating device that could allow us to reach a correlated equilibrium in the sense of Autumn (1987). We do not consider correlated equilibria here on the simple grounds that any such device should be included formally in the rules of the game and the normal form for that game studied. In other words, we assume that all aspects of the game are embodied in the description of the game. For a useful comparison of rationalizable equilibria and correlated equilibria see Bernheim (1986).

2 Note that no set of necessary conditions has been proposed, and that the set of sufficient conditions proposed by Smith (1982) has achieved a wide consensus amongst experimentalists. Thus one can view these conditions as 'necessary' if one is to convince a sceptical reader that one has conducted an experiment with 'adequately motivated' subjects. We emphasize that the words in quotation marks involve some degree of professional consensus, and cannot yet be defined independently of such a consensus. Having said that, we do not regard them as particularly controversial notions.

3 One of the experimental studies referred to is by Hoffman and Spitzer (1982), who found in a simple bargaining environment that agents did not use their threat points in an individually rational manner (see Binmore *et al.* 1988: 838) for further references to this 'anomalous' outcome). Harrison and McKee (1985) show that agents do (rationally) use their threat points when the experimental instructions are changed to highlight the nature of the threat point. They argue, therefore, that the observed irrational behaviour was due to the subjects' having an incomplete understanding of the 'rules of the game'. In subsequent bargaining experiments in a complicated environment Harrison *et al.* (1987) similarly find that subjects behave rationally when one employs experimental procedures to ensure that the subjects completely understand the 'rules of the game'. These experiments demonstrate that it is not *necessary* that subjects believe that they have 'earned' the right to demand an individually rational slice of the pie in order that they actually demand such a slice. This is not to deny that such beliefs, when engendered in a controlled fashion, are *sufficient* to generate individually rational behaviour (see Hoffman and Spitzer 1985).

4 Consider the outcome in which player 1 receives sixty tickets and player 2 receives forty tickets. A pair of strategies supporting this outcome in a subgame perfect NE are as follows. Player 1: 'Demand $\alpha = 60$. For every pair of demands $(60, \beta')$ such that $60 + \beta' > 100$, repeat. For every pair of demands $(\alpha', 40)$ such that $\alpha' + 40 > 100$, accept. Otherwise, if the subgame is reached, repeat'. Player 2: 'Demand $\beta = 40$. For every pair of

demands (α', 40) such that $\alpha' + 40 > 100$, repeat. For every pair of demands (60, β') such that $60 + \beta' > 100$, accept. Otherwise, if the subgame is reached, accept'. Clearly the subgame perfection refinement can serve to eliminate many outcomes in different bargaining games (see, for example, Binmore *et al.* 1985).

5 Roth *et al.* (1988). have considered the relevance of complete and incomplete information models of sequential non-cooperative bargaining to these experiments. Their primary objective was to explain their empirical finding that a vast number of agreements occur in the final seconds before a negotiation deadline. They argue (Roth *et al.* 1988: 821) that incomplete information models can account for observed disagreements *if* one posits that at least one of the bargainers has private information as to his own subjective probability distribution over the time remaining for negotiation.

6 To some extent this line of argument has been anticipated by several people. Wilson (1985: 51) notes that an 'alternative view of Roth and Schoumaker's experimental results ... is that the game ordinarily has multiple equilibria and therefore the players face an initial task of focusing on one equilibrium. Experience with one equilibrium could be the basis for a player's expectation that it will be repeated in subsequent encounters. A formal development of this view is given by Rosenthal and Landau (1979).' However, Rosenthal (1985: 64) explicitly notes that his 'approach deviates from the pervasive rationality normally assumed in game-theoretic modeling' by assuming that individual agents neglect the influence of their actions on the (large) population of opponents.

Roth (1985) proposes a non-cooperative co-ordination game in which two bargainers either demand a preferred 'focal point' or accept a less-favourable 'focal point'. Interesting as this model may be, it does not address the issue of the rationality of the focal points assumed. Roth (1985: 265) argues that the experiments of R2 show that 'focal points are not determined by the usual (strategic) data with which existing theories describe a game. Nevertheless, focal points appear to play a significant role in determining the outcome of bargaining. For this reason, it seems sensible to attempt to construct theories of bargaining that treat focal points as an (empirically determined) part of the data used to model a game, and to test the ability of such theories to predict and explain other observable regularities of bargaining behaviour. Let us therefore take the focal points in a bargaining situation as given.' Actually we do not argue at all with this approach. Rather, we simply want to clarify that these focal points are perfectly consistent with subject rationality (and the strategic data of the non-cooperative game they face), even if rationality alone is unable to determine which particular points are 'focal' and which are not.

7 The game in Figure 4.1 has two NE in the off-diagonal cells, with disagreement being one of the diagonal cells. What if each player conjectured that the other player was going to 'play Nash' and to choose his strategy component from these NE by 'the flip of a coin'? In effect, each player is simply guessing as to which of the NE will obtain, and has no reason to suspect that either NE is more likely. In this case we would observe, over enough repetitions, each cell in Figure 4.1 played exactly 25 per cent of

the time for the subgame to be reached. We should emphasize that this particular set of conjectures is only one of many possible, although it is clearly plausible on *a priori* grounds.

8 It might be tempting to conclude that these experiments are indiscriminate vehicles for testing non-cooperative models of bargaining games, since a wide range of outcomes is consistent with popular solution concepts (i.e. there is virtually 'nothing to reject'). On the contrary, we believe that such experiments can provide fertile grounds to test alternative refinement hypotheses in future research.

9 A simple way of avoiding this problem is to ask whether one set of agents could forecast the market prices being set by a completely different set of agents. If the forecasts from this experiment did not differ greatly from those that were observed when the two sets of agents coincide, then it could be concluded that this problem is not serious.

10 This argument suggests that a particularly interesting variant would be to conduct such forecasting exercises with comparable posted offer (PO) markets. In a PO market, unlike a DA market, the sellers must post a 'take it or leave it' price at the outset of each trading period. They may not change their prices during the period. Thus the costliness of intraperiod price search by sellers is significantly higher in PO markets than in DA markets. There is considerable evidence that this lack of intraperiod learning accounts for the relatively slower adaptability of prices in PO markets to changes in fundamentals (see Davis *et al.* 1989).

11 There is one other difference between the two experiments: the first had twelve subjects and the second had only nine subjects. There is no reason to imagine that this could make much difference in market behaviour.

12 In these training experiments asset endowments were re-initialized after each period of trading, in sharp contrast with the situation that the subjects faced in the experiments of Smith *et al.* (1988).

REFERENCES

Aumann, R.J. (1987) 'Correlated equilibrium as an expression of Bayesian rationality', *Econometrica* 55: 1–18.

Bernheim, B.D. (1984) 'Rationalizable strategic behaviour', *Econometrica* 52: 1007–28.

—— (1986) 'Axiomatic characterizations of rational choice in strategic environments', *Scandinavian Journal of Econometrics* 88: 473–88.

Binmore, K., Shaked, A. and Sutton J. (1985) 'Testing noncooperative bargaining theory: a preliminary study', *American Economic Review* 75: 1178–80.

—— (1988) 'A further test of noncooperative bargaining theory: reply', *American Economic Review* 78: 837–9.

Chatterjee, K. (1985) 'Disagreement in bargaining: models with incomplete information', in A.E. Roth (ed.) *Game-Theoretic Models of Bargaining*, Cambridge: Cambridge University Press.

Coursey, D.L. and Smith, V.L. (1983) 'Price controls in a posted offer market', *American Economic Review* 73: 218–21.

Davis, D.D., Harrison, G.W. and Williams, A.W. (1989) 'Convergence to nonstationary competitive equilibria: an experimental analysis', *unpublished manuscript*, Department of Economics, Virginia Commonwealth University.

Forsythe, R., Palfrey, T.R. and Plott, C.R. (1982) 'Asset valuation in an experimental market', *Econometrica* 50: 537–67.

Friedman, D., Harrison, G.W. and Salmon, J.W. (1983) 'The informational role of futures markets: some experimental evidence', in M.E. Streit (ed.) *Futures Markets: Modelling, Managing and Monitoring Futures Trading*, Oxford: Basil Blackwell.

—— (1984) 'The informational efficiency of experimental asset markets', *Journal of Political Economy* 92: 349–408.

Grether, D.M. and Plott, C.R. (1979) 'Economic theory of choice and the preference reversal phenomenon', *American Economic Review* 69: 623–38.

Harrison, G.W. (1989) 'Theory and misbehavior of first-price auctions', *American Economic Review* 79: 749–62.

—— (1990a) 'The payoff dominance critique of experimental economics', *unpublished manuscript*, Department of Economics, University of South Carolina.

—— (1990b) 'Expected utility theory and the experimentalists', *unpublished manuscript*, Department of Economics, University of South Carolina.

Harrison, G.W. and McKee, M. (1985) 'Experimental evaluation of the Coase theorem', *Journal of Law and Economics* 28: 653–70.

Harrison, G.W., Hoffman, E., Rutström, E.E. and Spitzer, M.L. (1987) 'Coasian solutions to the externality problem in experimental markets', *Economic Journal* 97: 388–402.

Hoffman, E. and Spitzer, M.L. (1982) 'The Coase theorem: some experimental results', *Journal of Law and Economics* 25: 73–98.

—— (1985) 'Entitlements, rights and fairness: an experimental examination of subjects' concepts of distributive justice', *Journal of Legal Studies* 14: 259–97.

Isaac, R.M. and Plott, C.R. (1981) 'Price controls and the behaviour of auction markets: an experimental examination', *American Economic Review* 71: 449–59.

Kahneman, D. and Tversky, A. (1979) 'Prospect theory: an analysis of decision under risk', *Econometrica* 47: 263–91.

Kahneman, D., Knetsch, J.L. and Thaler, R. (1986) 'Fairness as a constraint on profit seeking: entitlements in the market', *American Economic Review* 76: 728–41.

Machina, M.J. (1987) 'Choice under uncertainty: problems solved and unsolved', *Journal of Economic Perspectives* 1: 121–54.

Muth, J.F. (1961) 'Rational expectations and the theory of price movements', *Econometrica* 29: 315–35.

Nash, J.F. (1950) 'The bargaining problem', *Econometrica* 28: 155–62.

—— (1951) 'Non-cooperative games', *Annals of Mathematics* 54: 286–95.

—— (1953) 'Two person cooperative games', *Econometrica* 21: 128–40.

Pearce, D.G. (1984) 'Rationalizable strategic behavior and the problem of perfection', *Econometrica* 52: 1029–50.

Plott, C.R. (1982) 'Industrial organization and experimental economics',

Journal of Economic Literature 20: 1485–527.
Rosenthal, R.W. (1985) 'An approach to some noncooperative game situations with special attention to bargaining', in A.E. Roth (ed.) *Game-Theoretic Models of Bargaining*, Cambridge: Cambridge University Press.
Rosenthal, R.W. and Landau, H. (1979) 'A game-theoretic analysis of bargaining with reputations', *Journal of Mathematical Psychology* 20: 233–55.
Roth, A.E. (1979) *Axiomatic Models of Bargaining*, Berlin: Springer-Verlag.
—— (1985) 'Toward a focal-point theory of bargaining', in A.E. Roth (ed.), *Game-Theoretic Models of Bargaining*, Cambridge: Cambridge University Press.
Roth, A.E. and Malouf, M.W.K. (1979) 'Game-theoretic models and the role of information in bargaining', *Psychological Review* 86: 574–94.
Roth, A.E. and Murnighan, J.K. (1982) 'The role of information in bargaining: an experimental study', *Econometrica* 50: 1123–42.
Roth, A.E., Malouf M.W.K. and Murnighan, J.K. (1981) 'Sociological versus strategic factors in bargaining', *Journal of Economic Behavior and Organization* 2: 153–77.
Roth, A.E. and Schoumaker, F. (1983a) 'Expectations and reputations in bargaining: an experimental study', *American Economic Review* 73: 362–72.
—— (1983b) 'Subjective probability and the theory of games: some further comments', *Management Science* 29: 1337–40.
Roth, A.E., Murnighan, J.K. and Schoumaker, F. (1988) 'The deadline effect in bargaining: some experimental evidence', *American Economic Review* 78: 806–23.
Rubinstein, A. (1982) 'Perfect equilibrium in a bargaining model', *Econometrica* 50: 97–109.
Smith, V. L. (1982) 'Microeconomic systems as an experimental science', *American Economic Review* 72: 923–55.
Smith, V.L. and Williams, A.W. (1981) 'On non-binding price controls in a competitive market', *American Economic Review* 71: 467–74.
Smith, V.L., Suchanek, G.L. and Williams, A.W. (1988) 'Bubbles, crashes, and endogenous expectations in experimental spot asset markets', *Econometrica* 56: 1119–52.
Tversky, A. and Kahneman, D. (1986) 'Rational choice and the framing of decisions', in R.M. Hogarth and M.W. Reder (eds) *Rational Choice*, Chicago, Il: University of Chicago Press.
Williams, A.W. (1987) 'The formation of price forecasts in experimental markets', *Journal of Money, Credit and Banking* 19: 1–18.
Wilson, R. (1985) 'Reputations in games and markets', in A.E. Roth (ed.) *Game-Theoretic Models of Bargaining*, Cambridge: Cambridge University Press.
Zeckhauser, R. (1986) 'Comments: Behavioral versus rational economics: what you see is what you conquer', in R.M. Hogarth and M.W. Reder (eds) *Rational Choice*, Chicago, Il: University of Chicago Press.

5 Efficiency of the yen futures market at the Chicago Mercantile Exchange

Stephen J. Taylor

INTRODUCTION

A financial market can be said to make efficient use of information if prices adjust fully and instantaneously when new information becomes available (Fama 1976). This demanding requirement for an efficient market is often relaxed to a statement that trading systems cannot use information to outperform passive investment strategies when transaction costs and risk are considered (Jensen 1978). It is claimed in this chapter that currency futures markets are not efficient according to Fama's definition and that there is strong evidence that they also fail to be efficient with respect to Jensen's definition. Detailed results are given for yen–dollar futures traded at the International Monetary Market (IMM) of the Chicago Mercantile Exchange from 1979 to 1987, complementing studies of European currency futures traded at the same market (Taylor 1986; Taylor and Tari 1989). It is shown that yen trading would have been profitable, and more so than trading other currencies.

One of the major features of the chapter is the application of a satisfactory method for adapting Jensen's definition from stock markets to futures markets. This is non-trivial because futures contracts are more like bets than securities: capital is not invested in futures and the market aggregate position in futures is always zero (Black 1976).

Results for trading rules applied to futures prices have often cast doubt on the weak form efficiency of futures markets. It is well known that the early studies of Stevenson and Bear (1970) and Leuthold (1972) for US agricultural futures have methodological weaknesses (Praetz 1976a, b). Recent studies by Bird (1985), Taylor (1986) and Lukac *et al.* (1988) are more rigorous, and claim trading profits for currencies, metals and crops at various US and UK forward and futures markets. Similar research by Sweeney (1986) for spot foreign exchange provides additional evidence against market efficiency.

In this chapter we present results for the trading rule of Taylor (1983). Unlike the filter rule of Alexander (1961), the Taylor rule is based upon optimal time series forecasts. In the next section we describe time series models for futures prices. Accurate models have to take account of the stochastic volatility of prices, and this is the subject of much interesting contemporary research (for example, Engle and Bollerslev 1986). Plausible models for price trends are also mentioned in this section. Adding an AR(1) trend component to residual white noise gives an ARMA(1, 1) model for returns (the first differences of price logarithms) which is well supported by empirical evidence. It is shown in the third section, by using a test statistic that has a high power to detect price trend behaviour, that yen futures prices are not random walks. The test statistic exploits the prediction that trends will cause positive autocorrelation at several lags. The detected autocorrelation is asserted to be too large to be merely the result of time-dependent risk premiums, and so the yen market is not 'Fama efficient'.

The time series results show that there is sufficient autocorrelation to warrant evaluating trend-following trading rules and hence Jensen's definition of efficiency. A performance measure for trading rules in a portfolio context is proposed in the fourth section. The trader invests in bills and stocks and can also invest in a futures strategy. Trading profits in excess of transaction costs are evidence against an efficient market as bills are adequate for margin purposes and futures (and likewise futures rules) have negligible betas. This proposition is made rigorous by inventing a hypothetical security called a risky bill.

In the fifth section we describe a trading rule which is based upon optimal forecasts for an ARMA(1, 1) model. This rule has four parameters. Two of these specify the autocorrelations of the time series model, and two control the beginnings and ends of trades. In the sixth section we give the trading results when the parameter values are as selected in Taylor (1983) for European currency futures using prices prior to 1979. The rule makes net profits from 1979 to 1987 for every currency considered: the yen, sterling, the Deutschmark and the Swiss franc. The yen profits are higher and more consistent than those for the European currencies. Average returns on a bill used as collateral for the yen trades are 6.5 per cent per annum above the average risk-free rate of interest, so that if US investors averaged 10 per cent from risk-free bills, they could have averaged 16.5 per cent on capital assigned to yen futures trading. The average excess return over all four currencies is an appealing 5.2 per cent per annum. Straightforward tests show that the net profits are statistically significant. In the final section, we present the conclusion that these trading results show that currency futures markets have been inefficient.

STOCHASTIC PROCESSES FOR CURRENCY FUTURES PRICES

Research into the behaviour of currency prices has sought models for the time-varying means and variances of day-to-day changes in the logarithms of prices. Risk premiums or trends in prices can explain time-varying means. Changes in variance, also referred to as conditional heteroscedasticity or stochastic volatility, can be attributed to variations in the amount and importance of relevant price information. An understanding of realistic price models is helpful for motivating random walk tests and trading rules.

Let Z_t be the closing price on day t for some price model and let

$$X_t = \log Z_t - \log Z_{t-1}$$

be the so-called return on day t. Let $\{X_t\} = \{X_1, X_2, \ldots\}$ be a set of random variables. Then, if a model is to be of value, the observed market returns $\{x_t\} = \{x_1, x_2, \ldots\}$ must be reasonably consistent with the generating process $\{X_t\}$. There is no need to interpret x_t as a return on an investment, which is a problematic concept for futures. Rather, x_t is a conventional measure of the change in price from day $t-1$ to day t.

First, suppose that prices follow random walks so that our only concern is to model stochastic volatility. A general approach supposes that

$$X_t = \mu + e_t \tag{5.1}$$

$$e_t = V_t \varepsilon_t \tag{5.2}$$

where μ is a constant expected return (zero is theoretically plausible (see Black 1976)), V_t represents volatility and the ε_t are independent and identically distributed with zero mean and unit variance. Past returns cause present volatility in the autoregressive conditional heteroscedasticity (ARCH) models discussed by Engle and Bollerslev (1986), Bollerslev (1987) and Baillie and Bollerslev (1989). A suitable ARCH model is

$$V_t^2 = \omega + \alpha X_{t-1}^2 + \beta V_{t-1}^2 \quad (5.3)$$

with $\omega \geq 0$, $\alpha, \beta > 0$, $\alpha + \beta$ near or equal to 1 and ε_t having a Student's t distribution. Past returns have a less direct influence on present volatility in models discussed by Taylor (1986), Scott (1987), Wiggins (1987), Hull and White (1987) and Johnson and Shanno (1987). An example is the model

$$\log V_t = \delta + \phi \log V_{t-1} + \eta_t \quad (5.4)$$

with ϕ near or equal to 1 and η_t a zero-mean normal variable perhaps correlated with ε_t. ARCH models have the advantage that their parameters can be estimated using maximum likelihood. Research is needed to discover which of (5.3) or (5.4) better explains observed returns.

Second, suppose that there are risk premiums or trends in prices but volatility is non-stochastic. The simplest plausible stationary model is given by

$$X_t = \mu_t + e_t \quad (5.5)$$

$$\mu_t - \mu = p(\mu_{t-1} - \mu) + \omega_t \quad (5.6)$$

where $\{e_t\}$ and $\{\omega_t\}$ are stochastically independent zero-mean noise processes. Let μ and σ^2 be the mean and variance of X_t. Also, let var $\mu_t = A\sigma^2$ and var $e_t = (1 - A)\sigma^2$. Note that $\{\mu_t\}$ is AR(1), $\{X_t\}$ is ARMA(1, 1) and the X_t have autocorrelations

$$\rho_{\tau,X} = \text{cor}(X_t, X_{t+\tau}) = Ap^\tau \qquad \tau \geq 1 \quad (5.7)$$

Empirical evidence favours $0 < A < 0.05$ and p close to 1 for currency futures.

Finally, it is observed that mixing of trend and volatility effects is necessary, but it is not obvious how this should be done. Two plausible possibilities are described by Taylor (1986). They retain equation (5.5) and suppose that $\text{cov}(\mu_t, \mu_{t+\tau}) > 0$ and $\text{cov}(\mu_s, e_t) = \text{cov}(e_t, e_{t+\tau}) = 0$ for all s, t and all positive τ. In one method it is assumed that stochastic volatility effects are confined to the residual term e_t, while in the other it is assumed that $\mu_t - \mu$ and e_t are multiples of a common volatility term V_t. Either way, if all processes are stationary, then the autocorrelations of X_t are exactly the same as or similar to Ap^τ, as in equation (5.7) with $A = \text{var } \mu_t/\text{var } X_t$ and p a measure of how slowly some information is reflected by prices. The autocorrelation function Ap^τ is identical with that of an ARMA(1, 1) process which motivates the subsequent tests, forecasts and trading rule.

AUTOCORRELATION ANALYSIS FOR YEN–DOLLAR FUTURES

Prices studied

The data are daily closing prices from the Chicago Mercantile Exchange IMM *Yearbook* 1979–87. Results are presented for all IMM June and December yen–dollar contracts available to the author when this chapter was written. Closing prices are considered for seventeen contracts beginning with the December 1979 contract and ending with the December 1987 contract. December contracts are used to provide daily prices from June to November inclusive. June contracts provide prices from the preceding December to May inclusive. Each of the seventeen contracts provides about 126 prices for the calculation of autocorrelations and the evaluation of a trading rule. Returns are always calculated using consecutive closing prices for the same contract. A total of $n = 2{,}147$ returns are used for calculations.

Autocorrelations

The sample autocorrelation at lag τ for the series of returns $\{x_t\}$ is defined using returns for all seventeen contracts by

$$r_{\tau,x} = \sum_{T_\tau} (x_t - \bar{x})(x_{t+\tau} - \bar{x}) \Big/ \sum_{t=1}^{n} (x_t - \bar{x})^2 \qquad (5.8)$$

where T_τ is the set of times for which t and $t + \tau$ refer to the same futures contract. As usual $\bar{x}$ is the sample mean $(x_1 + \ldots + x_n)/n$. The autocorrelations of the time series $\{|x_t|\}$ and $\{x_t^2\}$ have been calculated in the same manner. Following Taylor (1986: Ch. 5) and for a reason described below, autocorrelations have also been calculated for so-called rescaled returns defined by

$$y_t = \frac{x_t - \bar{x}}{\hat{v}_t} \qquad (5.9)$$

with the estimate $\hat{v}_t$ of the realized volatility v_t on day t given by the recursive equation

$$\hat{v}_t = 0.9\,\hat{v}_{t-1} + 0.1253|x_{t-1}| \qquad (5.10)$$

The initial $\hat{v}_t$ for a contract was calculated from the twenty returns for that contract from times $t - 20$ to $t - 1$ (here t refers to the first return in some June or December).

Table 5.1 presents the autocorrelations of x_t, y_t, $|x_t|$ and x_t^2 for lags τ ranging from 1 to 30 trading days. Notice first that the autocorrelations of the absolute and squared returns are greater than the autocorrelations of the returns. This is an immediate and now well-documented consequence of conditional heteroscedasticity (Engle and Bollerslev 1986; Taylor 1986: Chs 2, 3; Baillie and Bollerslev 1989). Considering the absolute returns, all thirty coefficients are positive and the first six exceed $1.96/n^{1/2}$. Thus it is clear that the

Table 5.1 Autocorrelations for yen futures, daily data 1979–1987

Lag in days τ	*Returns* $r_{\tau,x}$	*Rescaled returns* $r_{\tau,y}$	*Absolute returns* $r_{\tau,\|x\|}$	*Squared returns* r_{τ,x^2}
1	−0.0289	0.0227	0.1268	0.0824
2	−0.0033	0.0168	0.0715	0.0576
3	0.0595	0.0562	0.1582	0.1574
4	0.0259	0.0350	0.0715	0.0478
5	0.0171	0.0386	0.1125	0.0599
6	0.0318	0.0431	0.0859	0.0530
7	−0.0106	−0.0088	0.0330	0.0012
8	0.0291	0.0140	0.0484	0.0175
9	0.0489	0.0327	0.0506	0.0224
10	0.0210	0.0139	0.0734	0.0512
11	0.0257	0.0329	0.0487	0.0217
12	−0.0042	0.0079	0.0350	0.0114
13	0.0370	0.0253	0.0134	−0.0103
14	0.0303	0.0147	0.0582	0.0231
15	−0.0071	−0.0061	0.0843	0.0529
16	−0.0130	−0.0086	0.0207	−0.0017
17	−0.0088	−0.0124	0.0124	−0.0013
18	0.0134	0.0120	0.0469	0.0224
19	0.0064	0.0068	0.0434	0.0208
20	0.0084	0.0132	0.0401	0.0208
21	0.0047	0.0129	0.0177	0.0071
22	0.0218	0.0203	0.0340	0.0152
23	−0.0028	−0.0035	0.0477	0.0244
24	0.0300	0.0289	0.0651	0.0349
25	−0.0449	−0.0308	0.0488	0.0100
26	0.0054	−0.0044	0.0205	0.0145
27	−0.0084	−0.0107	0.0392	0.0234
28	−0.0027	0.0138	0.0124	−0.0052
29	−0.0093	−0.0156	0.0801	0.0609
30	0.0041	0.0028	0.0458	0.0129

Note: The coefficients are calculated from 2,147 observations and seventeen futures contracts.

returns are not generated by a set of independent and identically distributed random variables. This does not tell us anything about the validity of the random walk hypothesis, but it does imply that extra care is needed when testing the hypothesis.

Random walk tests

The random walk hypothesis (RWH) is defined here in terms of the returns-generating process $\{X_t\}$ by

$$\mathrm{E}[X_t] = \mathrm{E}[X_{t+\tau}] \qquad \mathrm{cov}(X_t, X_{t+\tau}) = 0 \tag{5.11}$$

for all t and all $\tau > 0$. If the RWH holds, the presence of conditional heteroscedasticy will increase the standard error of

$$R_{\tau,X} = \frac{\Sigma(X_t - \bar{X})(X_{t+\tau} - \bar{X})}{\Sigma(X_t - \bar{X})^2} \tag{5.12}$$

to a number above the conventional figure of $1/n^{1/2}$. By their construction, however, the autocorrelations $r_{\tau,y}$ of rescaled returns will be observations from distributions whose standard errors are close to $1/n^{1/2}$ (Taylor 1986: ch. 5). Thus the autocorrelations $r_{\tau,y}$ are preferred for tests.

Routine test statistics such as the sum of squared autocorrelations have low power to detect price trends. Test statistics which have high power when the population autocorrelations are Ap^{τ} with $A > 0$ and p near 1 (as for the price trend models of the previous section) are preferred. Following Taylor (1982, 1986: Ch. 6) such a test statistic is given by

$$T^* = 0.4274n^{1/2} \sum_{\tau=1}^{30} 0.92^{\tau} r_{\tau,y} \tag{5.13}$$

When the RWH applies $T^* \sim \mathrm{N}(0, 1)$ and when a trend model is relevant T^* is expected to be positive. Thus the RWH is rejected at the 5 per cent significance level whenever $T^* > 1.65$. The yen–dollar series for rescaled returns, as defined in (5.9), gives a test value of 4.12 (using the $r_{\tau,x}$ instead gives 2.72). Clearly, a price trend model describes the observed prices better than does a random walk. This is consistent with the large number of observed positive coefficients: seven of the first ten for returns and nine of the first ten for rescaled returns. The spectral density for rescaled returns has a significant peak at zero frequency, lending further support to the presence of trends in the prices.

Comparing $T^* = 4.12$ for yen–dollar futures with test values for other IMM currency futures for the same period shows that yen-dollar prices were relatively easy to predict: T^* is higher at 4.36 for the Deutschmark but lower at 2.02 for sterling and at 1.75 for the Swiss franc.

Magnitude and duration of trends

Following Taylor (1986: Ch. 7) simple estimates of the trend model parameters A and p are given by minimizing

$$\sum_{\tau=1}^{30} (r'_{\tau,y} - Ap^{\tau})^2 \tag{5.14}$$

where $r'_{\tau,y}$ is $r_{\tau,y}$ multiplied by n and divided by the number of terms in the numerator set T_τ of equation (5.8). This gives the estimates $A = 0.0429$ and $p = 0.9091$, which are measures of trend magnitude and trend duration respectively. Here, A is the proportion of the variance of rescaled returns attributable to trends. The estimates are known to be inaccurate. Alternative estimates are probably no more accurate when p is near 1. Unpublished simulation results for least squares estimates show that they are more biased and less accurate than estimates given by minimizing the function in equation (5.14).

The standard deviation of the returns is $s = 0.0071$. A plausible estimate of the proportion of the variance of returns due to trends is given by replacing y by x in equation (5.14) and p by 0.9091. This gives the estimate $A_1 = 0.028$. Thus an estimate of the standard deviation of the trend component μ_t is $sA_1^{1/2} = 0.0012$. Therefore, if the trend on any day is as large as its long-run standard deviation, the expected return over one trading day measured in annual terms is about $252sA_1^{1/2} = 30$ per cent. The expected long-run change in price when $\mu_t = 0.0012$ is $sA^{1/2}/(1 - p) = 1.3$ per cent. These rough calculations suggest that trading profits are possible if the trend component can be forecast with sufficient accuracy.

The case against the risk premium explanation

The trend term μ_t which is the non-random component of the daily return X_t could be called a time-varying risk premium if its magnitude were consistent with observed premium estimates. It is claimed, however, that the variance of μ_t for yen futures is far higher than the variance of observed premium estimates. For, suppose that μ_t is merely a time-varying risk premium. From Wolff (1987), whose figures appear typical, we can assume that the absolute premium for one year is less than 5 per cent, so that $|\mu_t| < 0.05/250 = 0.0002$. Assuming that μ_t has a uniform distribution over the range -0.0002 to 0.0002 gives var $\mu_t = (0.0004)^2/12$ (a generously high estimate). The variance of the yen returns is about 0.00005. Thus, the proportion of returns variance attributable to time-varying risk premiums is less than

$$\frac{(0.0004)^2}{12 \times 0.00005} \approx 0.0003$$

This proportion is very small compared with the proportion of returns variance attributed here to trends and denoted by A_1. The estimate of A_1 for the yen exceeds 0.02. To explain such a value of A_1 using time-varying risk premiums would require the premium in annual terms to have a standard deviation greater than 25 per cent.

DEFINING EFFICIENCY FOR FUTURES MARKETS

A definition

The results of the previous section cannot, it is argued, be reconciled with the view that yen futures prices adjust fully and instantaneously when new information becomes available. Thus the market is not efficient in the manner defined by Fama (1976: 140). It is arguable that Fama's definition is only of theoretical interest – for practical purposes it is more helpful to use a definition of efficiency based upon the impossibility of exploiting available information. Therefore a definition of efficiency in line with that of Jensen (1978) is adopted.

The efficient market hypothesis will be said to be true if the risk-adjusted return, net of all costs, from the best trading rule is not more than the comparable figure when assets are traded infrequently. It is assumed that trading rules buy and sell the same goods, here yen futures, fairly often, typically more than once per futures contract. In comparison, goods should be traded at efficient markets as little as possible to minimize costs. Of course, investors and institutions may never want to trade futures when they believe that such markets are efficient.

The above definition of an efficient market has the advantage of being practical at the cost of being person dependent. Resources, costs, opportunities to diversify and attitudes to risk vary between people.

To obtain useful results with the Jensen definition it is necessary to consider costs and the meaning of risk-adjusted return in the context of futures (see the following two subsections). Ball (1989) has recently surveyed definitions of cfficiency in great detail for security markets. He prefers Fama's definition to that of Jensen, but a practical definition is preferred here.

Costs

Trading rules generate more business for brokers than efficient market policies and therefore have higher transaction costs. Further costs for traders arise from differing bid and ask prices, and the acquisition and interpretation of information. Daily closing prices, which cost little to acquire, are used in this study. The rule to be described in the next section produces decisions using negligible time and computer resources. Developing useful trading systems requires specialist skills. The associated costs cannot be measured with any accuracy. Only the inventor or purchaser of a system can compare development or acquisition costs with net returns, and of necessity such costs are ignored here.

Returns and risk

The margin system prevents a precise description of the capital invested in a futures position. As treasury bills are acceptable margin for some traders, it can be argued that no capital is required to finance a position. Thus, the definition of a return on futures positions is not clear. Adjustments for the risks incurred by trading futures are also problematic. Asset-pricing models can imply that risk adjustments are not required because (a) futures risks can be diversified away (Black 1976) and (b) futures betas are often empirically close to zero (see Dusak 1973; Bodie and Rosansky 1980; Elton *et al.* 1987), although Lukac *et al.* (1988) claim significant negative betas for technical rules applied to futures.

To cope with the problems of defining returns and adjusting for risk, the approach of Taylor and Tari (1989) is followed in assuming that the individual agent is interested in constructing an optimal mean–variance portfolio. It will be supposed that the trader has no capital constraints (i.e. has substantial assets). These assets form a portfolio which is assumed to be well diversified and to include cash on deposit, short-term bills and stocks. It is reasonable to concentrate on results for traders commanding substantial resources.

The trader is assumed not to be a floor trader. When a futures position is opened, the trader sends a bill to a broker as deposit margin. The bill will be a zero-coupon risk-free government security and is chosen to have a maturity date after the futures contract expires. Furthermore, the price paid for the bill is equated with the value of the futures contract when the position is opened (see Taylor and Tari (1989) for a numerical example).

The agent organizes its affairs so that for a given futures contract the same bill is always used as collateral. If we consider all the cash flows associated with the risk-free bill (commission, trading gains and losses, interest on the bill) we can construct a new security which we call a risky bill. At maturity the value of the risky bill is taken to be the value of the risk-free bill plus trading profit less transaction costs. Define the excess return on the risky bill at maturity to be its maturity value less the maturity value of the risk-free bill divided by the price paid for the risk-free bill. Likewise, define the excess return for any subperiod of the life of the bill as gross trading profits less transaction costs for the same time interval divided by the price paid for the risk-free bill.

We have available a conceptual security (the risky bill) for futures trades that has a well-defined return and well-defined excess return compared with a risk-free bill. This security could be part of the trader's portfolio. To make risk adjustments for the risky bill it is assumed that its beta (systematic risk) with respect to a market portfolio of stocks is zero or negative. This is consistent with the studies previously cited and is shown to be valid for yen futures trades on p. 125.

In conclusion, the futures market will be called inefficient if expected excess returns on risky bills are positive and the beta assumption applies, because the trader can then arrange a portfolio including risky bills that is superior to a benchmark portfolio that does not include risky bills. By 'superior' we mean a lower variance without any decrease in the expected return of the portfolio (Taylor and Tari (1989) give a numerical example). Thus it will suffice to consider expected excess returns on risky bills, or equivalently to consider expected net trading profits (gross trading profits less transaction costs) divided by the futures price of goods traded (see also equation (5.23) on p. 12.

The possibility of taking geared positions in the futures market is ignored because gearing is irrelevant when assessing efficiency. Gearing has no effect on the least variance portfolio obtainable for a specified expected return. Cash flows for daily marking to market are also ignored because they have a negligible impact upon excess returns.

A TRADING RULE

The trading rule defined in this section is based upon return and volatility forecasts. The forecasts are derived from the price trend model given earlier with modifications for stochastic volatility.

Forecasts

The rule makes use of standardized forecasts k. As in Taylor (1986: Ch. 8), at time t the latest return x_t (calculated from closing prices z_{t-1} and z_t) is used to forecast the next day's volatility and return using simple updating equations. The volatility forecast $\hat{v}_{t+1}$ made at time t is a function of the return x_t and the forecast $\hat{v}_t$ made at time $t-1$:

$$\hat{v}_{t+1} = 0.9\hat{v}_t + 0.1(1.253|x_t|) \tag{5.15}$$

Likewise, the return forecast $f_{t,1}$ made at time t is a function of x_t and the forecast $f_{t-1,1}$ made at time $t-1$:

$$f_{t,1} = \frac{\hat{v}_{t+1}}{\hat{v}_t}[(p-q)x_t + qf_{t-1,1}] \tag{5.16}$$

In equation (5.16), q is the moving-average parameter when an ARMA(1, 1) process has autocorrelations Ap^{τ}. It is the solution to

$$q^2 - \frac{q[1+(1-2A)p^2]}{(1-A)p} + 1 = 0 \qquad q < 1 \tag{5.17}$$

An estimate of the standard deviation of the variable $F_{t,1}$ that generates $f_{t,1}$, conditional upon the observed volatility forecast, is

$$\hat{\sigma}_F = \hat{v}_{t+1}\left[\frac{Ap(p-q)}{(1-pq)}\right]^{1/2} \tag{5.18}$$

Dividing the forecast $f_{t,1}$ by its estimated standard deviation gives the standardized forecast

$$k = f_{t,1}/\hat{\sigma}_F \tag{5.19}$$

The variable k is intended to have zero mean and unit variance.

The definition of k and the trading rule first appeared in Taylor (1983), except that the number 1.253 is used in equation (5.15) instead of 1.333. Initial values are needed for the various forecasts and the previous methods have been followed.

The rule

The rule, or strategy, has two parameters: the first, k_1, controls opening market positions and the second, k_2 controls their closure. The trader will have one of three possible market commitments when the market opens on day t: long, short or none. Later, the market will close at z_t giving a return x_t and hence k, and the trader can buy or sell at the closing price. This is realistic for yen prices.

This rule (strategy 2 of Taylor (1986)) aims to profit from substantial trends in either direction. Initially, the position is none and decisions are then as given in Table 5.2. Positions are not opened during the final fifteen days considered for a contract. Also, if necessary, positions are closed on the final day of the month preceding the delivery month of the contract.

Table 5.2 Decision rules for yen futures trading

Position at start of day t	*Forecast range*	*Decision*	*Position after decision*
None	$k > k_1$	Buy	Long
None	$k_1 \geq k \geq -k_1$	Do nothing	None
None	$k < -k_1$	Sell	Short
Long	$k \geq k_2$	Do nothing	Long
Long	$k < k_2$	Sell	None
Short	$k \leq -k_2$	Do nothing	Short
Short	$k > k_2$	Buy	None

A note on simulations

The rule aims to take advantage of trends associated with very small return autocorrelations. However, the total of the autocorrelations $\rho_{\tau,X}$ (over $\tau > 0$) is reasonably high for observed trend model parameter estimates. This suggests that the rule may be able to deliver excess returns. Results for simulated prices given by Taylor and Tari (1989) confirm this. Using $A = 0.021$, $p = 0.95$, $k_1 = 0.8$, $k_2 = -0.3$ and other appropriate parameters, they reported an average excess return of 6.3 per cent per annum (standard error 0.35 per cent).

TRADING RESULTS FOR YEN FUTURES

Parameter values

It is necessary to choose values for k_1, k_2 (rule parameters) and A, p (trend model parameters) to obtain trading decisions. In order to provide results for all seventeen yen contracts from December 1979 to December 1987, use is made of parameter values obtained for sterling, Deutschmark and Swiss franc futures prices from 1974 to 1978. These prices were used by Taylor (1983) to select

$$A = 0.028 \qquad p = 0.95 \tag{5.20}$$

Simulation of 400 hypothetical contracts with these A and p gave

$$k_1 = 0.8 \qquad k_2 = -0.3$$

These k_1 and k_2 values maximized an objective function similar to the average excess return. It is preferable to choose k_1 and k_2 by simulating the price trend model many times rather than by evaluating a small number of actual contracts. The results given by Taylor (1983) for trades in 1979 and 1980 are not impressive. Better results are obtained for 1981 and were first published by Taylor (1986). Subsequent results for the three European currencies from 1982 to 1987 are given by Taylor and Tari (1989) and are repeated here.

A second set of parameters is given by replacing A and p by the estimates given on p. 116, namely $A = 0.0429$ and $p = 0.9091$. Of course, these could not have been available to any trader and so the results are less realistic.

It is quite possible that the A, p, k_1 and k_2 of the 1983 study could be improved upon, although this is not attempted here.

Excess returns

It is assumed for convenience that the costs for a round trip (one buy and one sell order) are proportional to the value of the goods traded when the trade commences. Costs are assumed to be $c = 0.2$ per cent of the value of goods. For example, with a futures price of \$0.007 for 1 yen (i.e. 143 yen per dollar) and trading one IMM contract of 12,500,000 yen, the costs are \$0.002 × 0.007 × 12,500,000 = \$175. This is a conservative figure; many non-floor traders would pay less.

Suppose that the trader uses a bill that cost F as margin for a particular contract and makes N trades, commencing trade i at a price P_i and concluding it at a price Q_i. Also, let π_i be either 1 for a long trade or −1 for a short trade. Then the trader takes a position in $F/12{,}500{,}000P_i$ contracts for trade *i* and pays costs totalling *cF*. The net profit for trade *i* is

$$\frac{\pi_i(Q_i - P_i)F}{P_i} - cF \tag{5.22}$$

The excess return on the risky bill security described on p. 119 is the sum of the net profits divided by the price paid for the bill, i.e.

$$\sum_{i=1}^{N} [\pi_i(Q_i - P_i)/P_i - c] \tag{5.23}$$

Positive excess returns will be interpreted as evidence against an efficient futures market.

Results

Table 5.3 presents excess returns over six-month periods obtained using (5.20), (5.21) and (5.23). Trades are evaluated from June to November for December contracts and from December to May for June contracts. The IMM had limit rules for some of the contracts and it has been necessary to adjust one yen figure because of these rules (a trade had to be postponed for one day, thus reducing the June 1984 excess return by 2.05 per cent). Table 5.3 also presents comparable figures for the three European currencies and averages across all four currencies.

It is apparent that the trading rule was a success for yen trades, particularly from 1985 to 1987 inclusive. The average excess return in annual terms over 8.5 years is 6.49 per cent, and so if risk-free bills average 10 per cent per annum, then risky bills average 16.49 per cent per annum.

The yen results are better than those for any other currency, having both the highest mean and the least standard deviation. However, a standard two-way analysis of variance on the figures in Table 5.3 shows no evidence of a significant currency effect. Standard *t* ratios for testing a null hypothesis of zero or negative expected excess return are also given in Table 5.3. These are significant at the 5 per cent level for both the yen and the currency average.

Taylor (1983, 1986) employed price data up to December 1981. For the subsequent six years (1982–7) all currencies have positive average excess returns and the yen average is highly significant. The trading rule only became publicly available in 1983. Therefore it could be argued that traders could only have tried to use it for the

Table 5.3 Excess returns for currency futures trades over six-month periods

Contract	*Yen*	*Sterling*	*Deutschmark*	*Swiss franc*	*Average*
Dec 1979	7.02	4.55	−0.71	−1.87	2.25
June 1980	−1.10	4.84	1.96	3.16	2.22
Dec 1980	−0.63	−1.84	5.65	2.59	1.44
June 1981	5.73	6.78	16.34	15.15	11.00
Dec 1981	−3.30	0.55	1.62	12.16	2.76
June 1982	4.18	−7.25	3.15	−8.61	−2.13
Dec 1982	5.24	−5.66	−9.34	−13.61	−5.84
June 1983	0.59	11.93	−5.59	−0.73	1.55
Dec 1983	−0.53	−11.19	6.34	−3.91	−2.32
June 1984	−2.63	1.02	4.80	2.62	1.45
Dec 1984	3.28	6.31	8.33	10.63	7.14
June 1985	2.39	11.39	−1.67	1.49	3.40
Dec 1985	10.05	−8.22	7.59	10.69	5.03
June 1986	9.01	−2.90	2.33	3.28	2.93
Dec 1986	2.92	−1.54	−3.07	−3.19	−1.22
June 1987	7.62	14.96	1.33	2.97	6.72
Dec 1987	5.34	8.75	8.94	8.42	7.86
1979–87					
Average	3.25	1.91	2.82	2.43	2.60
St. deviation	4.05	7.64	6.06	7.54	4.18
t ratio	3.31*	1.03	1.92*	1.33	2.57*
1982–7					
Average	3.95	1.47	1.93	0.84	2.05
t ratio	3.61*	0.57	1.15	0.39	1.65
1984–7					
Average	4.75	3.72	3.57	4.61	4.16
t ratio	3.24*	1.33	2.20*	2.67*	3.77*

Notes: *Significant at the 5% level (one-tail test).

All forecasts are obtained using $A = 0.028$ and $p = 0.95$.

four years from 1984 to 1987. For this shorter period the *t* ratios are significant for the yen, the Deutschmark, the Swiss franc and the average. The final year (1987) which follows further publication of the rule by Taylor (1986) has the best results for the currency average with an excess return of 14.6 per cent!

Table 5.4 compares the results for the published values of A and p with those for the yen estimates of A and p. Also included are the results for the strategy of buying and holding yen futures, i.e. always long. The average excess returns are similar for the two (A, p) combinations. Buy and hold has a positive but smaller mean, a far

Table 5.4 Excess returns and betas for yen futures trades over six-month periods

Contract	*(1) A, p from European prices 1974–8*	*(2) A, p from yen prices 1979–87*	*(3) Buy and hold*	*Betas for trades from (1)*	*(3)*
Dec 1979	7.02	8.20	−13.33	−0.002	−0.062
June 1980	−1.10	8.03	8.00	−0.121	0.069
Dec 1980	−0.63	−5.19	3.53	0.012	−0.039
June 1981	5.73	2.17	−5.35	0.074	−0.062
Dec 1981	−3.30	−5.20	−0.29	−0.004	0.002
June 1982	4.18	1.10	−13.86	0.010	0.103
Dec 1982	5.24	−4.41	−5.55	−0.135	0.160
June 1983	0.59	2.09	2.30	0.059	0.172
Dec 1983	−0.53	−1.05	1.55	−0.060	0.101
June 1984	−2.63	−5.26	−1.39	−0.041	−0.017
Dec 1984	3.28	2.39	−10.12	−0.060	0.051
June 1985	2.39	0.76	−3.05	−0.085	0.159
Dec 1985	10.05	14.13	21.28	−0.010	0.203
June 1986	9.01	9.62	16.00	0.126	0.223
Dec 1986	2.92	−2.44	6.39	−0.030	−0.046
June 1987	7.62	10.29	11.75	−0.067	−0.066
Dec 1987	5.34	7.98	8.01	−0.026	−0.048
Average	3.25	2.57	1.52	−0.021	0.053
St. deviation	4.05	6.12	9.81	0.067	0.103
t ratio	3.31	1.73	0.64	−1.29	2.12

Note: The critical values for the t ratios using a 5% significance level are 1.75 for excess returns (one-tail test) and 2.12 and −2.12 for betas (two-tail test).

higher standard deviation and a t ratio which is insignificant.

Estimates of beta are also given in Table 5.4. These have been calculated by regressing trading returns on the return from Standard & Poor's 500 Index. Trading returns are simply the futures return x_t multiplied by 1 if the trader is long from close $t-1$ to close t, by −1 if short and by zero if neither long nor short. It is clear that the contract betas are all small. The trading rule has an average beta of −0.02 (statistically insignificant), whilst buy and hold has an average of 0.05 (just significant at the 5 per cent level). The trading betas support the assumption that a risky bill security has no systematic risk and hence support the claim that the yen futures market is inefficient.

Table 5.5 provides information on the number of trades and days long and short by contract. On average there are three trades per

Table 5.5 Information about yen trades

Contract	Trades	*Days* Long	Short	Neutral
Dec 1979	3	24	63	40
June 1980	4	45	51	27
Dec 1980	4	61	17	47
June 1981	3	34	75	14
Dec 1981	3	0	72	55
June 1982	3	34	70	20
Dec 1982	3	0	96	31
June 1983	3	49	37	39
Dec 1983	3	30	69	27
June 1984	3	46	17	62
Dec 1984	3	12	83	32
June 1985	2	30	73	21
Dec 1985	3	110	14	2
June 1986	2	95	0	29
Dec 1986	3	40	30	56
June 1987	2	103	6	15
Dec 1987	5	58	60	9

Note: Forecasts obtained using $A = 0.028$ and $p = 0.95$.

contract, so that costs average 1.2 per cent per annum. Over the entire 8.5 year period the rule was long 36 per cent of the time, short 39 per cent of the time and neutral on the other days.

CONCLUSIONS

Yen futures could have been traded profitably in recent years by using a trend-following strategy based upon time series models. Furthermore, yen profits are higher and more consistent than those for European currency futures at the same market in Chicago. These two conclusions are further evidence against the efficiency of currency futures markets.

This empirical evidence for currency futures is interpreted to mean that these markets are inefficient: traders can make profits net of transaction costs. Futures prices are not random walks. The detected autocorrelation is theoretically enough to permit profitable trading rules. These results do not prove inefficiencies but they show that the efficiency of the markets is an open issue. Average excess returns over several years are significantly different from zero and their magnitude is non-trivial. Taking averages over four currencies, from Table 5.3 we have the following annual returns in excess of the risk-free rate: 3.7 per cent in 1980, 13.8 per cent in 1981, −8.0 per cent in 1982, −0.8 per cent in 1983, 8.6 per cent in 1984, 8.4 per cent in 1985, 1.7 per cent in 1986 and finally 14.6 per cent in 1987. The average over all eight years is 5.2 per cent per annum.

Prior beliefs naturally influence our interpretation of evidence. The author's prior was tolerant of inefficiencies. Readers with a prior heavily committed to the efficiency of markets may be tempted to evade the message of the evidence presented here by asserting a small sample or time-dependent risk premium. However, they should note that throughout empirical studies in finance disturbing anomalies are continually being unearthed: for example, the Monday, January, earnings and size effects. Two recent collections of papers on anomalous behaviour are Dimson (1988) and Guimaraes *et al.* (1989). The finance journals contain many more. We should be prepared to entertain the possibility that markets are reasonably but not exactly efficient. The yen futures market in particular does not seem to be efficient.

NOTE

I am grateful to Chris Chow for calculating the betas presented in Table 5.4.

REFERENCES

Alexander, S. S. (1961) 'Price movements in speculative markets: trends or random walks?', *Industrial Management Review* 2: 7–26.

Baillie, R. T. and Bollerslev, T. (1989) 'The message in daily exchange rates: a conditional variance tale', *Journal of Business and Economic Statistics* 7: 297–305.

Ball, R. (1989) 'What do we know about stock market "efficiency"', in R. M. C. Guimaraes, B. G. Kingsman and S. J. Taylor (eds) *A Reappraisal of the Efficiency of Financial Markets*, pp. 25–55, Heidelberg: Springer-Verlag.

Bird, P. J. W. N. (1985) 'The weak form efficiency of the London Metal Exchange', *Applied Economics* 17: 571–87.

Black, F. (1976) 'The pricing of commodity contracts', *Journal of Financial Economics* 3: 167–79.

Bodie, Z. and Rosansky, V. I. (1980) 'Risk and return in commodity futures', *Financial Analysts Journal* May–June: 27–39.

Bollerslev, T. (1987) 'A conditionally heteroskedastic time series model for security prices and rates of return data', *Review of Economics and Statistics* 59: 542–7.

Dimson, E. (ed.) (1988) *Stock Market Anomalies*, Cambridge: Cambridge University Press.

Dusak, K. (1973) 'Futures trading and investors returns: an investigation of commodity market risk premiums', *Journal of Political Economy* 81: 1387–406.

Elton, E.J., Gruber, M.J. and Rentzler, J.C. (1987) 'Professionally managed, publicly traded commodity funds', *Journal of Business* 60: 175–99.

Engle, R. F. and Bollerslev, T. (1986) 'Modelling the persistence of conditional variances', *Econometric Reviews* 5: 1–50.

Fama, E. F. (1976) *Foundations of Finance*, Oxford: Basil Blackwell.

Guimaraes, R. M. C., Kingsman, B. G. and Taylor, S. J. (eds) (1989) *A Reappraisal of the Efficiency of Financial Markets*, Heidelberg: Springer-Verlag.

Hull, J. and White, A. (1987) 'The pricing of options on assets with stochastic volatilities', *Journal of Finance* 42: 281–300.

Jensen, M. C. (1978) 'Some anomalous evidence regarding market efficiency', *Journal of Financial Economics* 6: 95–101.

Johnson, H. and Shanno, D. (1987) 'Option pricing when the variance is changing', *Journal of Financial and Quantitative Analysis* 22: 143–51.

Leuthold, R. M. (1972) 'Random walks and price trends: the live cattle futures market', *Journal of Finance* 27: 879–89.

Lukac, L. P., Brorsen, B. W. and Irwin, S. H. (1988) 'A test of futures market disequilibrium using twelve different trading systems', *Applied Economics* 20: 623–39.

Praetz, P. D. (1976a) 'Rates of return on filter tests', *Journal of Finance* 31: 71–5.

—— (1976b) 'On the methodology of testing for independence in futures prices', *Journal of Finance* 31: 977–9.

Scott, L. O. (1987) 'Option pricing when the variance changes randomly: theory, estimation and an application', *Journal of Financial and Quantitative Analysis* 22: 419–38.

Stevenson, R. A. and Bear, R. M. (1970) 'Commodity futures: trends or random walks?' *Journal of Finance* 25: 65–81.

Sweeney, R. J. (1986) 'Beating the foreign exchange market', *Journal of Finance* 41: 163–82.

Taylor, S. J. (1982) 'Tests of the random walk hypothesis against a price-trend hypothesis', *Journal of Financial and Quantitative Analysis* 17: 37–61.

—— (1983) 'Trading rules for investors in apparently inefficient markets', in M. E. Streit (ed.) *Futures Markets – Modelling, Managing and Monitoring Futures Trading*, pp. 165–98, Oxford: Basil Blackwell.

—— (1986) *Modelling Financial Time Series*, Chichester: Wiley.

Taylor, S. J. and Tari, A. (1989) 'Further evidence against the efficiency of futures markets' in R. M. C. Guimaraes, B. G. Kingsman and S. J. Taylor (eds) *A Reappraisal of the Efficiency of Financial Markets*, pp. 577–601, Heidelberg: Springer–Verlag.

Wiggins, J. B. (1987) 'Option values under stochastic volatility: theory and empirical evidence', *Journal of Financial Economics* 19: 351–72.

Wolff, C. C. P. (1987) 'Forward foreign exchange rates, expected spot rates and premia: a signal-extraction approach', *Journal of Finance* 42: 395–406.

6 Simultaneity, forecasting and efficiency in the US oats market

Barry A. Goss, Siang-Choo Chan and S. Gulay Avsar

INTRODUCTION

Oats are the fourth most important crop in the United States, after corn, wheat and soybeans, according to area planted. The United States is an important world producer of oats, ranking second only to the USSR, although Germany, Poland and Canada are also major producers. In 1975–6 US production of oats was 639 million bushels (458 million bushels in 1980–1), while production of corn in 1975–6 was 9 times that of oats (14.5 times in 1980–1) and production of soybeans in 1975–6 was 2.4 times that of oats (3.9 times in 1980–1). Yet, in terms of the volume of futures contracts traded on the Chicago Board of Trade, corn and soybeans are proportionately far more important. In 1975 oats futures contracts representing 772 billion bushels were traded (1,604 billion bushels in 1980), while the volume of corn futures contracts was 31 times that of oats in 1975 (37 times in 1980), and the volume of soybeans futures contracts traded was 25 times that of oats in 1975 (36 times in 1980). This minor status of the oats market is reflected in research on US grains, with most studies concentrating on wheat, corn and soybeans.

The comparative neglect of the oats market may have arisen, in part, because a large proportion of the oats crop is consumed on the farm (38.2 per cent in 1975–6 and 34.9 per cent in 1980–1), and this in turn may be due to the high bulk-to-weight ratio and the relative lack of profitability of oats compared with corn, for example. Another factor contributing to the lack of interest in the oats market may be the low speculative ratio which the oats crop has attracted (see Appendix 1), probably largely because of its relatively smaller price fluctuations compared with soybeans and corn (Inkeles 1972: 129–30).

Oats are an important feed component for horses, dairy cattle, poultry and hogs, being high in protein and fibre content compared with other grains on a weight basis. They also play an important role in crop rotation programmes. In the United States in 1975–6, 86 per cent of the oats crop was fed to livestock (94 per cent in 1980–1), while food uses comprised typically 7–9 per cent, seed comprised about 6–7 per cent and exports accounted for around 2–3 per cent of the crop. In the milling of oats for feed, white oats are preferred. The major oats-producing states in the United States are Minnesota, South Dakota, Iowa, Wisconsin and North Dakota. These states produce essentially white oats, which are grown on a spring planting cycle and are harvested in the summer, some 100–120 days later.

In the preparation of animal feeds, the degree of substitutability between oats and corn is higher than that between oats and any other grain. In practice, the price of corn has a strong influence on the price of oats, and given that the weight of a bushel of oats is only 57.14 per cent of that of a bushel of corn, and that corn has a higher feed value on a volume basis, the price of corn is usually significantly higher than that of oats. Indeed, in the period from 1972–3 to 1980–1 the average ratio of the annual average cash price of oats to the annual average cash price of corn was 58.0 per cent.

The main trading location for oats futures contracts is the Chicago Board of Trade (CBOT), although such contracts are also traded on the Winnipeg Commodity Exchange in Canada and on the Mid-America Commodity Exchange in Chicago. Oats have traded on the CBOT since 1877, where the contract calls for delivery of 5,000 bushels in March, May, July, September and December.

The issue of informational efficiency in futures markets is discussed in the Introduction to this volume. In this chapter it is proposed simply to summarize the results according to the main methodologies employed to explore this question in the area of futures markets. The issue of weak form efficiency has been studied by many writers, including Larson (1960), Stevenson and Bear (1970), Leuthold (1972), Cargill and Rausser (1975) and Praetz (1975), using research methodologies essentially the same as those employed in the equities area (see Fama 1970). While some departures from the strict random walk model have been found, it is not clear that these could have been used to generate returns in excess of transaction costs.

The question of semi-strong form efficiency in futures markets, i.e. efficiency with respect to publicly available information, has been studied using three different approaches. Hansen and Hodrick (1980) investigated whether a relationship existed between the current forecast error for a particular currency and immediately prior forecast errors for related currencies. This approach, which exploits the 'predictive' quality of futures prices, is based upon the idea that the information contained in forecast errors will be immediately exploited in an efficient market, so that there will be no systematic relationship between the current forecast error for a futures contract and the elements assumed to comprise the information set. This method has been applied to a group of non-ferrous metals (Goss 1986: 168–71) and to the Australian wool market (Goss 1987).

Another method used to investigate this question, which also exploits the predictive qualities of futures prices, requires the employment of a quantitative model of the market to forecast the cash price at future dates. If the futures price does not predict at least as well as the model, this suggests that the model contains information not reflected in the futures price. This method has been used by Leuthold and Hartmann (1979) and Leuthold and Garcia (see Chapter 3 of this volume) for US livestock, Rausser and Carter (1983) for the US soybeans complex and Brasse (1986) for the London tin market, all of whom discovered some inefficiencies in the markets studied.

Failure to reject the hypothesis of semi-strong form efficiency, under either of these approaches, is not proof that the market is efficient. There remains the possibility that an alternative model may lead to rejection. More recently Chance (1985a, b) has studied the response of the US Treasury Bond and Government National Mortgage Association futures markets to 'news' (in this case the unanticipated component of inflation rate announcements). The results are generally consistent with the hypothesis of semi-strong form efficiency. In this chapter the second method is employed to examine whether US oats futures prices reflect publicly available information as fully as possible. In the following sections a simultaneous model of the US oats market is developed, and the data are discussed and tests of the hypothesis of a single unit root in oats futures prices are reported. Estimates of the parameters of the simultaneous model are reported and evaluated, and post-sample forecasts of the cash price and tests of the efficient markets hypothesis (EMH) are discussed. Some conclusions are presented in the final section.

The model presented in this chapter draws on the approach of Peston and Yamey (1960) and Giles *et al.* (1985), and extends the work of Goss and Giles (1986a, b) in the analysis of intertemporal price relationships in commodity markets with futures trading. The model presented here comprises separate functional relationships for long and short hedgers, long and short speculators in futures, consumers and holders of unhedged inventories.

It is assumed that there are three submarkets for oats: a storage submarket, a futures submarket and a submarket for present consumption. Within each submarket, appropriate demand and supply relationships can be distinguished. In the storage submarket, the supply of hedged storage is provided by short hedgers, who hold inventories and sell futures contracts as a hedge against the risk of a fall in the cash price. The demand for hedged storage comes from long hedgers, who require the commodity at a later date for processing or to fulfil a forward commitment, and who hedge the risk that the price of the commodity will rise by buying futures contracts.[1]

Storage is held unhedged by agents who anticipate a rise in the cash price. Their price expectations are assumed to involve them in a reciprocal demand for and supply of unhedged storage, so that the quantity of unhedged inventories held by these agents is added equally to the hedged components of demand and supply in the storage submarket to obtain total demand for and supply of storage.

The futures submarket partially overlaps the storage submarket, but the two are not synonymous. In the submarket for futures contracts, supply is provided by short hedgers and short speculators. Short speculators expect the price to fall and sell futures contracts in pursuit of an uncertain gain. Demand for futures is provided by long hedgers and long speculators. Long speculators buy futures because they expect the price to rise and employ risk capital in support of their expectations.

In periods when hedgers are net short, the demand for hedged storage is assumed to be provided by long hedgers and sufficient long speculative positions in futures to balance the hedged storage submarket. Similarly, in periods when hedgers are net long, the supply of hedged storage is assumed to be provided by short hedgers and sufficient short speculative positions in futures to balance the hedged storage submarket.

In the submarket for present consumption, demand is provided by consumers or processors of oats, whose demand is a derived demand. It is further assumed that in each period there is a given amount of the commodity for allocation between current consumption and storage. This amount is the available supply. The supply in the consumption submarket is that part of the available supply which is not allocated to storage. Note that the submarket for present consumption is not the same as the spot market for the commodity because a spot purchase may be made for either consumption or storage purposes.

SPECIFICATION OF THE EQUATIONS

Supply of hedged storage

Hedgers are assumed not only to pursue risk reduction but also to seek gains from their hedging activities. If the forward premium declines, gains will be realized for short hedgers. Hence the volume of hedged storage that is supplied by short hedgers is assumed to be an increasing function of the forward premium and of the volume of inventories eligible for hedging. The supply of hedged storage also varies inversely with the marginal net cost of storage, represented here by the marginal interest cost m_t (the dominant component of storage cost) because warehousing costs of oats are not available to us.

Since hedging is usually done in the expectation of a favourable change in the price spread (Working 1953: 325) we expect the supply of hedged storage to be inversely related to the expected price spread. The specification of the short-hedging equation is therefore

$$\mathrm{SH}_t = \alpha_0 + \alpha_1(P_t - A_t) + \alpha_2\mathrm{CK}_t + \alpha_3(P_{t+1} - A_{t+1})^* + \alpha_4 m_t + e_{1t} \tag{6.1}$$

where α_1, $\alpha_2 > 0$ and α_3, $\alpha_4 < 0$. SH_t is the supply of storage (and futures) by short hedgers, P_t is the current futures price of oats, A_t is the current cash price of oats, CK_t is the indicator of the quantity of oats eligible for hedging and $(P_{t+1} - A_{t+1})^*$ is the expected price spread for period $t + 1$.

The oats market has a lower speculation ratio than the soybeans market (see Appendix 1), so that expectations in the oats market are likely to respond less rapidly to new information; hence price expectations are assumed here to be represented by the adaptive expectations hypothesis (Nerlove 1958). This hypothesis assumes that the current revision of expectations is a proportion of the immediately prior expectational error:

$$(P_{t+1} - A_{t+1})^* - (P_t - A_t)^* = \alpha[(P_t - A_t) - (P_t - A_t)^*]$$

where $0 < \alpha < 1$. Hence

$$(P_{t+1} - A_{t+1})^* = \frac{(1 - \beta)(P_t - A_t)}{1 - \beta L} \tag{6.2}$$

where $\beta = 1 - \alpha$ and L is the lag operator. This hypothesis implies that the current expectation is a geometrically weighted average of past actual values, with backwardly declining weights, and will underpredict on a rising market and overpredict on a falling market. Substitution from (6.2) into (6.1) yields the following:

$$\mathrm{SH}_t = \phi_1 + \phi_2(P_t - A_t) + \phi_3(P_{t-1} - A_{t-1}) + \phi_4\mathrm{CK}_t + \phi_5\mathrm{CK}_{t-1} + \phi_6 m_t + \phi_7 m_{t-1} + \phi_8\mathrm{SH}_{t-1} + u_{1t} \qquad (6.3)$$

While inclusion of the price spread yields parameter estimates of the expected signs, the significance of these estimates improves, as does simulation by the model generally, when cash and futures prices are included, in both current and lagged form, as separate variables, thus supporting an alternative hypothesis. The marginal net cost of storage was deleted from the equation for the same reason.[2] The final specification is therefore based on the hypothesis that short hedging varies directly with the current futures price and the volume of inventories eligible for hedging, and inversely with the expected futures price and the current cash price:

$$\mathrm{SH}_t = \alpha_0 + \alpha_1 P_t + \alpha_2 P^*_{t+1} + \alpha_3 A_t + \alpha_4\mathrm{CK}_t + e_{1t} \qquad (6.4)$$

where $\alpha_1, \alpha_4 > 0$ and $\alpha_2, \alpha_3 < 0$, and

$$P^*_{t+1} = \frac{(1-\beta)P_t}{1-\beta L} \qquad (6.5)$$

Substitution from (6.5) into (6.4) yields the final specification:

$$\mathrm{SH}_t = \phi_1 + \phi_2 P_t + \phi_3 A_t + \phi_4 P_{t-1} + \phi_5 A_{t-1} + \phi_6\mathrm{CK}_t + \phi_7\mathrm{CK}_{t-1} + \phi_8\mathrm{SH}_{t-1} + u_{1t} \qquad (6.6)$$

where $\phi_2 > 0$ if $\alpha_1 > |\alpha_2(1-\beta)|$, otherwise $\phi_2 < 0$; $\phi_3, \phi_4, \phi_7 < 0, \phi_5, \phi_6 > 0$ and $0 < \phi_8 < 1$. If e_{1t} is independently and identically distributed then u_{1t} follows a first-order moving-average (MA1) process.

Demand for hedged storage

Long hedgers will suffer a loss if the price spread narrows; i.e. if the forward premium at the time that a hedge is lifted is less than the difference between the futures price and the forward actuals price at the time that the hedge is opened, the long hedger will incur a loss. The cash price has been used as a proxy for the forward actuals price, which is generally unobservable. Therefore it is expected that the demand LH for hedged storage by long hedgers will be inversely related to the current price spread and directly related to the expected price spread. Forward actuals commitments of long hedgers are measured by planned exports X_{t+1} and planned consumption C_{t+1} in period $t+1$, where the plans are assumed to be realized. Hence the long-hedging equation is

$$\mathrm{LH}_t = \alpha_5 + \alpha_6(P_t - A_t) + \alpha_7(P_{t+1} - A_{t+1})^{**} + \alpha_8 C_{t+1} + \alpha_9 X_{t+1} + e_{2t} \quad (6.7)$$

where $\alpha_6 < 0$ and $\alpha_7, \alpha_8, \alpha_9 > 0$. Adaptive expectations implies that

$$(P_{t+1} - A_{t+1})^{**} = \frac{(1-\lambda)(P_t - A_t)}{1 - \lambda L} \qquad 0 < \lambda < 1$$

Substitution of this expected price spread expression into (6.7) gives

$$\mathrm{LH}_t = \phi_9 + \phi_{10}(P_t - A_t) + \phi_{11}(P_{t-1} - A_{t-1}) + \phi_{12} C_{t+1} + \phi_{13} C_t + \phi_{14} X_{t+1} + \phi_{15} X_t + \phi_{16}\mathrm{LH}_{t-1} + u_{2t} \quad (6.8)$$

Again, inclusion of the price spread led to deterioration of the parameter estimates and model simulation, so that it was replaced by the ratio P_t/A_t of the futures price to the cash price. The variables representing planned exports and planned consumption were deleted from the relationship for the same reason. The long-hedging equation is therefore

$$\mathrm{LH}_t = \alpha_5 + \alpha_6\left(\frac{P_t}{A_t}\right) + \alpha_7\left(\frac{P_{t+1}}{A_{t+1}}\right)^* + e_{2t} \quad (6.9)$$

where $\alpha_6 < 0$, $\alpha_7 > 0$ and

$$\left(\frac{P_{t+1}}{A_{t+1}}\right)^* = \frac{(1-\lambda)(P_t/A_t)}{1 - \lambda L}$$

Substitution for $(P_{t+1}/A_{t+1})^*$ in (6.9) gives

$$\mathrm{LH}_t + \phi_9 + \phi_{10}\left(\frac{P_t}{A_t}\right) + \phi_{11}\left(\frac{P_{t-1}}{A_{t-1}}\right) + \phi_{12}\mathrm{LH}_{t-1} + u_{2t} \quad (6.10)$$

where $\phi_{10} < 0$ if $|\alpha_6| > \alpha_7(1-\lambda)$, otherwise $\phi_{10} > 0$; $\phi_{11} < 0$ and $0 < \phi_{12} < 1$.

Unhedged storage

Unhedged storage is held by agents who purchase stocks spot in the expectation of a rise in the spot price. Following Brennan (1958) and Telser (1958), the demand U_t for unhedged storage is related directly to the expected spot price A^*_{t+1}, and inversely to the current spot price A_t, the marginal risk premium r_t and the marginal net cost of storage m_t. The specification of this equation is

$$U_t = \alpha_{10} + \alpha_{11}A_t + \alpha_{12}A^*_{t+1} + \alpha_{13}m_t + \alpha_{14}r_t + e_{3t} \qquad (6.11)$$

where α_{11}, α_{13}, $\alpha_{14} < 0$, $\alpha_{12} > 0$ and

$$A^*_{t+1} = \frac{(1-\gamma)A_t}{1-\gamma L}$$

with $0 < \gamma < 1$. Inclusion of the marginal net cost of storage had a detrimental impact on the significance of the estimated coefficients and on the model simulation, and so m_t was deleted, although this is not a cause for concern (see note 2).

Substituting for A^*_{t+1} in (6.11) gives

$$U_t = \phi_{13} + \phi_{14}A_t + \phi_{15}A_{t-1} + \phi_{16}r_t + \phi_{17}r_{t-1} + \phi_{18}U_{t-1} + u_{3t} \qquad (6.12)$$

where ϕ_{15}, $\phi_{17} > 0$, $\phi_{16} < 0$, $0 < \phi_{18} < 1$, and $\phi_{14} < 0$ if $|\alpha_{11}| > \alpha_{12}(1-\gamma)$, otherwise $\phi_{14} > 0$.

Demand for futures by long speculators

Long speculators purchase futures contracts expecting the futures price to rise. Their demand LS for futures is assumed to vary inversely with the current futures price and marginal risk premium, and directly with their expected futures price. Such speculators, however, are likely to take into account the relative profitability of speculating in oats and other grain futures such as corn. Account was taken of this substitution through the spread between the oats futures price P_t and the corn futures price P^c_t; this spread performed better in preliminary estimation than a ratio of these prices, in that the latter had a detrimental effect on signs and significance in the model generally. Hence the specification of this relationship is

$$LS_t = \alpha_{15} + \alpha_{16}(P_t - P^c_t) + \alpha_{17}(P_{t+1} - P^c_{t+1})^* + \alpha_{18}r_t + e_{4t} \qquad (6.13)$$

where α_{16}, $\alpha_{18} < 0$, $\alpha_{17} > 0$ and $(P_{t+1} - P^c_{t+1})^*$ is the expected spread between oats and corn futures prices for next period formed in the current period.

Adaptive expectations implies that

$$(P_{t+1} - P^c_{t+1})^* = \frac{(1-\delta)(P_t - P^c_t)}{1-\delta L} \qquad 0 < \delta < 1 \qquad (6.14)$$

Inclusion of the marginal risk premium, however, adversely affects the signs of the parameter estimates of the model, and this variable was deleted, although again this is not a cause for concern (see note 2).

Substituting from (6.14) into (6.13) for $(P_{t+1} - P^c_{t+1})^*$ yields

$$\mathrm{LS}_t = \phi_{19} + \phi_{20}(P_t - P^c_t) + \phi_{21}(P_{t-1} - P^c_{t-1}) + \phi_{22}\mathrm{LS}_{t-1} + u_{4t} \qquad (6.15)$$

where $\phi_{21} > 0$, $0 < \phi_{22} < 1$, and $\phi_{20} < 0$ if $|\alpha_{16}| > \alpha_{17}(1-\delta)$, otherwise $\phi_{20} > 0$.

Supply of futures by short speculators

Futures contracts are also supplied by speculators, i.e. economic agents without actuals commitments who expect the futures price to fall. Again, to take account of the relative profitability of speculating in oats futures and corn futures, the spread between these two futures prices is included in the relationship. These agents can be seen as extending their holdings of short positions to the point where the current oats–corn futures price spread does not exceed their expected oats–corn futures price spread plus a marginal risk premium, i.e. until $P_t - P^c_t = (P_{t+1} - P^c_{t+1})^{**} + r_t$, where $(P_{t+1} - P^c_{t+1})^{**}$ is the expected oats–corn futures price spread of short speculators.

The supply of futures SS is assumed to vary directly with the current oats–corn futures price spread and inversely with their expected futures price spread and marginal risk premium, so that

$$\mathrm{SS}_t = \alpha_{19} + \alpha_{20}(P_t - P^c_t) + \alpha_{21}(P_{t+1} - P^c_{t+1})^{**} + \alpha_{22}r_t + e_{5t} \qquad (6.16)$$

where $\alpha_{20} > 0$, α_{21}, $\alpha_{22} < 0$ and

$$(P_{t+1} - P^c_{t+1})^{**} = \frac{(1-\tau)(P_t - P^c_t)}{1-\tau L} \qquad 0 < \tau < 1 \qquad (6.17)$$

Again, inclusion of the marginal risk premium has an adverse effect on the signs of parameter estimates, and this variable was deleted, although this is not disadvantageous.

Substituting from (6.17) into (6.16) for $(P_{t+1} - P^c_{t+1})^{**}$ yields

$$SS_t = \phi_{23} + \phi_{24}(P_t - P_t^c) + \phi_{25}(P_{t-1} - P_{t-1}^c) + \phi_{26}SS_{t-1} + u_{5t} \qquad (6.18)$$

where $\phi_{25} < 0$, $0 < \phi_{26} < 1$, and $\phi_{24} > 0$ if $\alpha_{20} > |\alpha_{21}(1 - \tau)|$, otherwise $\phi_{24} < 0$.

Consumption submarket

The demand C for the consumption of oats by processors is derived from the use of this crop as a feed for dairy cattle, livestock and horses. Hence, the consumption demand for oats is assumed to be dependent upon the parameters of demand for the end-products, the parameters of the supply of other factors employed in making these final products and the cash price of oats. Dairy cattle consume about 34 per cent of oats used for animal feed, and oats make up 35 per cent of all grains fed to dairy cattle (Inkeles 1972: 31). The profitability of feeding oats to dairy cattle can be represented by the oats-to-milk cash price ratio. Inclusion of the cash price of milk, however, detrimentally affected the signs and significance of the parameter estimates of the model, and so this variable was omitted from the relationship.

Corn is also used with oats in preparing livestock feed, and the cash price (A^c) of corn is included as a parameter of the supply of other inputs. Whether corn is a complement to or a substitute for oats will be inferred from the sign of its coefficient (a negative coefficient implies complementarity while a positive coefficient indicates that the grain is a substitute for oats). US real personal income is assumed to be a parameter of end-product demand.

In order to place the anticipations of all agents on the same theoretical footing, the adaptive hypothesis has been extended to income in the consumption equation, so that the relationship is

$$C_t = \alpha_{23} + \alpha_{24}A_t + \alpha_{25}A_t^c + \alpha_{26}Y_{t+1}^* + e_{6t} \qquad (6.19)$$

where $\alpha_{24} < 0$, $\alpha_{25} \gtrless 0$, $\alpha_{26} > 0$ and Y_{t+1}^* is the anticipated US real personal income for period $t + 1$:

$$Y_{t+1}^* = \left(\frac{1 - \omega}{1 - \omega L}\right) Y_t \qquad 0 < \omega < 1$$

Substituting for Y_{t+1}^* in (6.19) gives

$$C_t = \phi_{27} + \phi_{28}A_t + \phi_{29}A_t^c + \phi_{30}A_{t-1} + \phi_{31}A_{t-1}^c$$

$$+ \phi_{32} Y_t + \phi_{33} C_{t-1} + u_{6t} \tag{6.20}$$

where $\phi_{28} < 0$, ϕ_{29}, $\phi_{31} \gtrless 0$, ϕ_{30}, $\phi_{32} > 0$ and $0 < \phi_{33} < 1$.

Identities

The model is completed with the following identities:

$$K_t \equiv U_t + \mathrm{HH}_t \tag{6.21}$$

where $\mathrm{HH}_t = \max(\mathrm{SH}_t, \mathrm{LH}_t)$ and K_t is the total inventory of oats and is exogenous; and

$$\mathrm{SH}_t + \mathrm{SS}_t \equiv \mathrm{LH}_t + \mathrm{LS}_t \tag{6.22}$$

The first identity states that the total quantity of stocks equals the demand for unhedged storage plus the demand for hedged storage. It is written in this form because this identity is employed to generate observations on the variable U_t (see the next section). The second identity states that total supply of futures contracts equals the total demand for futures contracts. These are identities of observed values and it is assumed that the storage and futures markets clear every trading period so that only equilibrium values are observed in monthly data. There are eight endogenous variables (SH, LH, U, SS, LS, C, P, A) together with six behavioural relationships and two identities in this model.

DATA

In this section we provide details of the collection and generation of data employed in the estimation of the model. The sample period dates from October 1972 to September 1978; after allowing for lags of up to four periods in the selection of instruments for estimation purposes (see below), this results in seventy-two observations.

Endogenous variables

Oats futures prices P_t are the closing prices in US dollars per bushel for a six-month future[3] on the median trading day of each month. These prices are quotations from the CBOT *Statistical Annual*, 1972–81.

Spot price data A_t are daily cash prices for oats on the median trading day of each month in US dollars per bushel (No.2 Extra

Heavy White) at Minneapolis, as published in the CBOT *Statistical Annual*, 1972–81.

The demand for and supply of hedged storage of oats (LH_t and SH_t respectively) are assumed to be measured by the end-of-month open interest of hedgers at the CBOT. These open-interest data (in thousands of bushels) are reported in the *Commitments of Traders*, 1972–81, published by the US Commodity Futures Trading Commission (CFTC). The reporting level for oats was 200,000 bushels for the sample and forecast periods. The CFTC reports open-position data, both long and short, for large (reporting) hedgers, large (reporting) speculators and non-reporting traders, i.e. the distribution of the positions of these non-reporting traders between hedging and speculation is unknown. How the positions of small traders should be distributed has been the subject of analysis by Peck (1982) who argued that 'virtually all' the 'small traders' in corn, and possibly soybeans, were speculators for most of the 1970s. The oats market, however, was not discussed in Peck's paper, and we assume that the distribution (between speculation and hedging) for non-reporting traders is the same as that for reporting traders. Allocation of the positions of non-reporting traders was carried out based on this assumption using open-position data. These open-position data were used to measure the supply of and demand for oats futures contracts by hedgers. The demand for and supply of oats futures contracts by long and short speculators (LS_t and SS_t respectively) are also measured by the end-of-month open interest for speculators calculated from the figures reported by the CFTC.

Data on the demand U_t for unhedged storage are unobservable, and U_t is generated by subtracting LH_t or SH_t, whichever is larger, from K_t. In some periods negative U_t values[4] are generated by this procedure. Negative U_t values are not consistent with this model, and so the following procedure is used to adjust these values: in periods when U_t is negative, LH_t or SH_t, whichever is larger,[5] is reduced by the absolute value of U_t, and this absolute value is added to LS_t (if LH_t is decreased) or SS_t (if SH_t is decreased). In this procedure, it is assumed that excess hedging is speculation rather than hedging. The signs and significance of the estimates of the structural parameters of the model are improved if commercial stocks CK rather than total stocks K are employed in the calculation of unhedged storage (see the next section).

Oats consumption data C_t are quarterly observations, in thousands of bushels, of the total domestic use of oats published in the *Commodity Yearbook*, 1978, 1983. These quarterly observations are interpolated to monthly data using the program TRANSF (Wymer 1977).

Exogenous variables

Data on US total stocks of oats K_t are total stocks (in thousands of bushels) at end of month taken from the CBOT *Statistical Annual*, 1982, and data on US commercial stocks of oats CK_t (in thousands of bushels) at end of month are obtained from the same source. The latter do not include stocks on farms.

The marginal risk premium r_t is defined as the (90 day) commercial paper rate less the (90 day) treasury bill rate in per cent per annum, as published in the US *Federal Reserve Bulletin*, 1972–81.

The marginal interest cost is the US prime rate in per cent per annum divided by twelve and multiplied by A_t; the US prime rate is taken from the US *Federal Reserve Bulletin*, 1972–81.

The income variable Y_t is the US total nominal personal income in billion US dollars, taken from the US *Federal Reserve Bulletin*, 1972–81, divided by the consumer price index (base year, 1963) obtained from the *International Financial Statistics*, 1972–81. While Y_t data for the period 1972–5 are monthly observations, data for total personal income for the years 1976–81 are quarterly observations interpolated to monthly data using the program TRANSF (Wymer 1977). Cash prices A_t^c of corn are daily prices in US dollars per bushel, on the median trading day of each month, as published in the CBOT *Statistical Annual*, 1972–82.

Corn futures prices P_t^c are the closing prices on the median trading day of each month for a corn futures contract approximately six months prior to delivery, where that contract is selected according to the rule defined in note 3. These prices are in US dollars per bushel as published in the CBOT *Statistical Annual*, 1972–82.

Tests for unit roots

Tests for unit roots have been of interest in recent research on financial time series, partly because a time series which has an autoregressive representation with a single unit root can be approximated by a random walk, which is of special interest in the study of efficient markets. Moreover, rational expectations models of financial markets require stationarity in order that conditional expectations of prices in such models are time invariant.

Tests for unit roots have been studied by Fuller (1976), Dickey and Fuller (1979, 1981), Evans and Savin (1981, 1984) and Doukas and Rahman (1987). In this chapter tests are reported for a single unit root in oats futures prices, using the test statistics developed by Dickey and Fuller (1979, 1981). This hypothesis is of interest here, given the focus of this chapter on the informational efficiency of the oats market.

In the autoregressive representation of the futures price series

$$P_t = \rho P_{t-1} + e_t \tag{6.23}$$

it is assumed that ρ is a real number and e_t is NID(0, σ^2):

1 if $|\rho| < 1$, P_t converges to a stationary series as $t \to \infty$;
2 if $|\rho| > 1$, the series is non-stationary and the variance of P_t grows exponentially as $t \to \infty$;
3 if $|\rho| = 1$, there is borderline non-stationarity, and if $\rho = 1$, there is a single unit root.

The models used to test the hypothesis of a single unit root are (6.23) together with the following representations:

$$P_t = \mu + \rho P_{t-1} + e_t \tag{6.24}$$

$$P_t = \mu + \beta t + \rho P_{t-1} + e_t \tag{6.25}$$

In these models, P_1 is assumed fixed, (6.24) contains an intercept and (6.25) contains an intercept and a time trend. The tests employed are the Wald test and the likelihood ratio test developed by Dickey and Fuller (1979, 1981). The Wald test requires estimation of the unconstrained model, while the likelihood ratio test requires that the model be re-estimated according to the constraint of the null hypothesis.

The least squares estimator $\hat{\rho}$ is consistent for all values of ρ (Dickey and Fuller 1979: 427). The estimates of the parameters for models (6.23)–(6.25) are presented in Table 6.1 for 119 observations of oats futures prices, together with the relevant Wald test statistics as developed by Dickey and Fuller (1979) which are used to test the hypothesis H($\rho = 1$). These calculated statistics are compared with the tabulated 10 per cent critical values, given by Fuller (1976: 371, 373), which are reproduced in Table 6.1 for sample size $n = 100$. It will be seen that the hypothesis of one unit root H($\rho = 1$) cannot be rejected at the 10 per cent level in any of the versions formulated in (6.23), (6.24) or (6.25). This statement applies whether the test statistic $n(\hat{\rho} - 1)$ or the statistic $\hat{\tau} = (\hat{\rho} - 1)/\text{SD}\hat{\rho}$ is employed, where SD$\hat{\rho}$ is the sample standard deviation of $\hat{\rho}$.

The powers of these various tests in a Monte Carlo study, using

Table 6.1 Parameter estimates and Wald test statistics for unit roots: futures prices

Model	$\hat{\mu}$	$\hat{\beta}$	$\hat{\rho}$		
				$n(\hat{\rho}-1)$	$\hat{\tau}$
(6.23)	–	–	1.0018 (0.0072)	0.2142	0.2500
Critical value (0.1)				−5.6	−1.61
				$n(\hat{\rho}_\mu-1)$	$\hat{\tau}_\mu$
(6.24)	0.1067 (0.0442)	–	0.9358 (0.0283)	−7.6398	−2.2686
Critical value (0.1)				−11.0	−2.58
				$n(\hat{\rho}_\tau-1)$	$\hat{\tau}_\tau$
(6.25)	0.1509 (0.0497)	0.00097 (0.00052)	0.8680 (0.0457)	−15.7080	−2.8884
Critical value (0.1)				−17.5	−3.15

Note: Numbers in parentheses are standard errors.

model (6.23), are given by Dickey and Fuller (1979: 430) for different sample sizes and different values of ρ. For a sample of $n = 100$ with $\rho = 0.95$, the powers of the test statistics $n(\hat{\rho}-1)$ and $\hat{\tau}$ are identical, and both are more powerful than the statistics $n(\hat{\rho}_\mu - 1)$ and $\hat{\tau}_\mu$. When $\rho = 1.02$, the power of $\hat{\tau}$ slightly exceeds that of $n(\hat{\rho}-1)$, and again both these test statistics are more powerful than $n(\hat{\rho}_\mu - 1)$ and $\hat{\tau}_\mu$.

Table 6.2 Likelihood ratio tests for unit roots: futures prices

Hypothesis	*Null model*	*Alternative model*	*Test statistic (calc. value)*	*Critical value*[a]
$H(\alpha,\rho)=(0,1)$	$A_t = A_{t-1} + e_t$	(6.24)	$\phi_1 = 2.9170$	3.86
$H(\alpha,\beta,\rho)=(0,0,1)$	$A_t = A_{t-1} + e_t$	(6.25)	$\phi_2 = 3.1761$	4.16
$H(\alpha,\beta,\rho)=(\alpha,0,1)$	$A_t = \alpha + A_{t-1} + e_t$	(6.25)	$\phi_3 = 4.3955$	5.47

Note: [a]These are tabulated values for 0.9 probability of a smaller value taken from Dickey and Fuller (1981: 1063) (see text).

Likelihood ratio tests are also employed to test for the presence of a single unit root in oats futures prices, and these tests, as noted below, can under some circumstances be more powerful than thc Wald tests reported in Table 6.1. Three likelihood ratio tests are reported here. The first hypothesis considered is $H(\alpha, \rho) = (0, 1)$, in which the alternative model (6.24) is tested against the null model $P_t = P_{t-1} + e_t$ and the test statistic is ϕ_1. The second hypothesis is that $H(\alpha, \beta, \rho) = (0, 0, 1)$, i.e. model (6.25) is tested against the same null as above and the test statistic is ϕ_2. The third hypothesis tested is $H(\alpha, \beta, \rho) = (\alpha, 0, 1)$; here the alternative model (6.25) is tested against the slightly wider null $P_t = \alpha + P_{t-1} + e_t$ and the test statistic is ϕ_3. Table 6.2 gives the calculated values of the relevant statistics for these various hypothesis tests, according to the formulae in Dickey and Fuller (1981: 1059). Empirical distributions of the test statistics ϕ_1, ϕ_2 and ϕ_3 are given for various sample sizes in Tables IV, V and VI of Dickey and Fuller (1981: 1063). Tabulated values for a probability of 0.9 of a smaller value (thus giving 0.1 rejection region) for a sample size $n = 100$, taken from Dickey and Fuller (1981: 1063), are given in Table 6.2. Comparison of the critical values with the calculated values of the test statistics in Table 6.2 supports the view that in none of the three cases is it possible to reject the hypothesis of a single unit root. This result is consistent with the outcome of the Wald tests in Table 6.1.

It is observed by Dickey and Fuller (1981: 1069) that the statistics $n(\hat{\rho}_\mu - 1)$ and $\hat{\tau}_\mu$ display poor power when ρ is close to unity and $\alpha \neq 0$, as in some of the models estimated here. Moreover, these authors note that the test statistic ϕ_1 has more power than ϕ_2 because the alternative model for ϕ_2 is wider (Dickey and Fuller 1981: 1068).

These tests were also executed for oats cash price data for the same sample period, and again in no case could the hypothesis of a single unit root be rejected (the latter tests are not reported here because of space limitations).

ESTIMATION AND RESULTS: SAMPLE PERIOD

The model is linear in the parameters but non-linear in the endogenous variables P and A. Each of the six structural equations is overidentified. Prior to the estimation of the simultaneous system, the initial values of the parameters of the structural equations were estimated by two-stage least squares (2SLS) for each equation. The 2SLS procedure obtains instrumental variable (IV) estimates, and the instrument set used to obtain initial values for equations (6.6), (6.10),

Table 6.3 Oats model: three-stage least squares parameter estimates

Coefficient	*Variable*	*Estimate*	*Asymptotic t value*	*Equation*
ϕ_1	Const.	4,631.2	2.010	(6.6)
ϕ_2	P_t	11,084.0	2.698	
ϕ_3	A_t	−7,829.1	−1.921	
ϕ_4	P_{t-1}	−10,603.0	−3.036	
ϕ_5	A_{t-1}	5,191.3	1.232	
ϕ_6	CK_t	0.298	4.716	
ϕ_7	CK_{t-1}	−0.300	−4.844	
ϕ_8	SH_{t-1}	0.914	11.306	
ϕ_9	Const.	−6,917.2	−1.807	(6.10)
ϕ_{10}	P_t/A_t	28,550.0	4.499	
ϕ_{11}	P_{t-1}/A_{t-1}	−20,670.0	−3.183	
ϕ_{12}	LH_{t-1}	0.935	11.676	
ϕ_{13}	Const.	4,058.5	1.025	(6.12)
ϕ_{14}	A_t	−14,041.0	−2.647	
ϕ_{15}	A_{t-1}	10,971.0	2.232	
ϕ_{16}	r_t	−389.1	−0.252	
ϕ_{17}	r_{t-1}	1,505.2	1.215	
ϕ_{18}	U_{t-1}	0.925	28.921	
ρ_3		0.235	1.680	
ϕ_{19}	Const.	3,048.1	2.248	(6.15)
ϕ_{20}	$P_t - P_t^c$	1,603.4	0.504	
ϕ_{21}	$P_{t-1} - P_{t-1}^c$	232.8	0.076	
ϕ_{22}	LS_{t-1}	0.916	14.681	
ϕ_{23}	Const.	498.4	0.449	(6.18)
ϕ_{24}	$P_t - P_t^c$	3,434.4	1.267	
ϕ_{25}	$P_{t-1} - P_{t-1}^c$	−3,366.1	−1.295	
ϕ_{26}	SS_{t-1}	0.991	17.386	
ϕ_{27}	Const.	84,585.0	−1.488	(6.20)
ϕ_{28}	A_t	-120.37×10^3	−3.464	
ϕ_{29}	A_t^c	55,383.0	3.120	
ϕ_{30}	A_{t-1}	54,376.0	1.612	
ϕ_{31}	A_{t-1}^c	−19,915.0	−1.082	
ϕ_{32}	Y_t	15,891.0	2.184	
ϕ_{33}	C_{t-1}	0.346	2.024	

(6.12), (6.15), (6.18) and (6.20) comprised lagged endogenous variables and current and lagged exogenous variables from the model as a whole. Only in the demand for unhedged storage (equation (6.12)), a spot market relationship, was there evidence of serial correlation among the residuals. In this equation a correction was made for first-order autocorrelation. The signs of the estimates of all parameters in all equations, except for ϕ_{11} in equation (6.10), were as expected. In equation (6.10), the long-hedging relationship, the sign of the estimated coefficient of P_{t-1}/A_{t-1} was contrary to expectation. This may have arisen because the cash price of oats is an imperfect proxy for the forward actuals price of stock feed products, or it may be due to an inadequate understanding of the behaviour of long hedgers.

These 2SLS estimates were employed as initial values for the simultaneous estimation of the structural parameters by three-stage least squares (3SLS) using the program TSP 4.1B (Hall 1986). The 3SLS procedure obtains IV estimates, and the instrument set employed here is as follows: CK_t, CK_{t-1}, r_{t-1}, r_{t-2}, Y_{t-1}, SH_{t-2}, P^c_{t-1}, A^c_{t-1}, LH_{t-2}, SS_{t-2}, LS_{t-2}, U_{t-2}, C_{t-3} and $P_{t-2} - A_{t-2}$. The correction for first-order autocorrelation made in the estimation of the initial values for equation (6.12) was extended to the estimation of the simultaneous system. This was done by means of an autoregressive transformation, obtained by taking equation (6.12), lagging it one period, multiplying by ρ_3 (the autocorrelation coefficient) and subtracting the result from (6.12), which gives

$$\begin{aligned} U_t - \rho_3 U_{t-1} = {} & \phi_{13}(1-\rho_3) + \phi_{14}(A_t - \rho_3 A_{t-1}) \\ & + \phi_{15}(A_{t-1} - \rho_3 A_{t-2}) + \phi_{16}(r_t - \rho_3 r_{t-1}) \\ & + \rho_{17}(r_{t-1} - \rho_3 r_{t-2}) + \phi_{18}(U_{t-1} - \rho_3 U_{t-2}) \\ & + u_{3t} - \rho_3 u_{3t-1} \end{aligned} \tag{6.26}$$

The 3SLS procedure was employed to estimate the structural parameters of the model and the autocorrelation coefficient. The 3SLS estimates are consistent and asymptotically efficient (Hall 1986: 270). These estimates for the sample period October 1972 to September 1978 (seventy-two observations) are presented in Table 6.3, together with asymptotic *t* values.

The main features of the estimates are as follows. First, all adaptive expectations adjustment coefficients are between zero and unity, as economic theory requires. The adaptive hypothesis is evidently an appropriate representation of expectations revision in this market, including anticipations of income. In equation (6.12), for example, the adaptive adjustment coefficient (which is $1 - \hat{\phi}_{20}$) implies that only 7.5 per cent of expectational error is taken into account in revision of expectations of the spot price, and hence implies that expectations of holders of unhedged inventories are somewhat static. While we may be sceptical of such an estimate, the simulation performance of this equation (see below) tends to support the estimate.

Second, the two spot market relationships (6.12) and (6.20) have the signs of all parameter estimates as expected, and the majority of these estimates are significant. These relationships are important, because oats inventories are mostly held unhedged and most oats are consumed domestically. It should be noted that the definition of U as the residual of CK over the volume of hedging (max SH, LH) is more satisfactory, from the viewpoint of signs and significance of parameter estimates, than its definition as the surplus of total stocks K over the volume of hedging, notwithstanding that U is sometimes negative. Hence the variable U should be interpreted here as unhedged commercial inventories, which are evidently more sensitive to market signals than are unhedged total inventories. Moreover, the estimated autocorrelation coefficient in (6.12) is not significant, although omission of the correction for autocorrelation is not warranted. In the consumption equation, the estimate of ϕ_{32} suggests that oats are a normal good, as expected, while the hypothesis of interdependence with the corn market is supported and the two grains are evidently substitutes (see $\hat{\phi}_{29}$).

Third, in the short-hedging equation, which is an important futures market relationship, the hypothesis that the volume of short hedging varies directly with the futures price and inversely with the cash price and expected futures price is supported. The hypothesis that short hedging varies directly with the price spread $P - A$ and inversely with the expected price spread is also supported with alternative estimates (not reported), but this alternative hypothesis results in inferior simulation by the model generally.[6] It is noted that the volume of commercial stocks CK performs well as an indicator of the commitments of short hedgers (see $\hat{\phi}_6$). The estimates of the coefficients of the long-hedging equation provide some support for the hypothesis that long hedgers respond to the ratio of futures to spot prices, although the sign of the estimate of ϕ_{11} is contrary to expectations (equations (6.9) and (6.10) predict that $\phi_{10} > 0$ if $|\alpha_6| < \alpha_7(1 - \lambda)$). It should be noted that there is a comparable degree of support for the hypothesis that long hedgers respond to the

Table 6.4 Intrasample simulation assessment

Variable	*Correlation coefficient*	*Theil's IC*	*%RMSE*
SH	0.9356	0.1445	23.378
LH	0.7034	0.3534	34.417[a]
U	1.0000	0.0000	0.0000
LS	0.7707	0.4132	82.463[a]
SS	0.8771	0.3365	81.707[a]
C	0.5966	0.4666	50.328
P	0.5570	0.2131	22.815
A	0.7406	0.1542	17.308

Note: [a]Values of %RMSE are calculated for LH with the observation for July 1974 deleted, for LS with the observations for December 1973, August 1974, August 1977, and December 1977 deleted, and for SS with the observations for March 1975, August 1975 and August 1977 deleted. The reason for these deletions is that this statistic can be greatly distorted by the presence of a few outliers.

price spread, although substitution of $P_t - A_t$ for P_t/A_t in (6.10) results in the sign of $\hat{\phi}_5$ in (6.6) being contrary to expectations and leads to a slight deterioration in the simulation performance of the model.

Fourth, the general lack of significance in the long and short speculation equations is disappointing, although it is not fatal to model performance in view of the low speculative ratio in the oats market. The hypothesis of interdependence with the corn market receives weak support, rather than the strong support observed in the estimates of the coefficients of the consumption equation.

Notwithstanding these deficiencies in the estimation of the structural parameters, an important test of the appropriateness of a simultaneous model with an expectations function is the ability of the model to simulate values of the endogenous variables both within and outside the sample period. A summary evaluation of intrasample simulation by this model is presented in Table 6.4, which comprises correlation coefficients between simulated and actual values, as well as Theil's inequality coefficient (IC) and the percentage root mean squared error of forecast (%RMSE). The intrasample simulation is also illustrated in Figures 6.1–6.8. It can be seen that the unhedged inventory relationship is the best performing equation, with virtually perfect simulation throughout. This is an important result because, as seen above, most stocks are held unhedged. The short-hedging function also performs quite well, except for some slight underprediction on a rising market, as expected with the adaptive

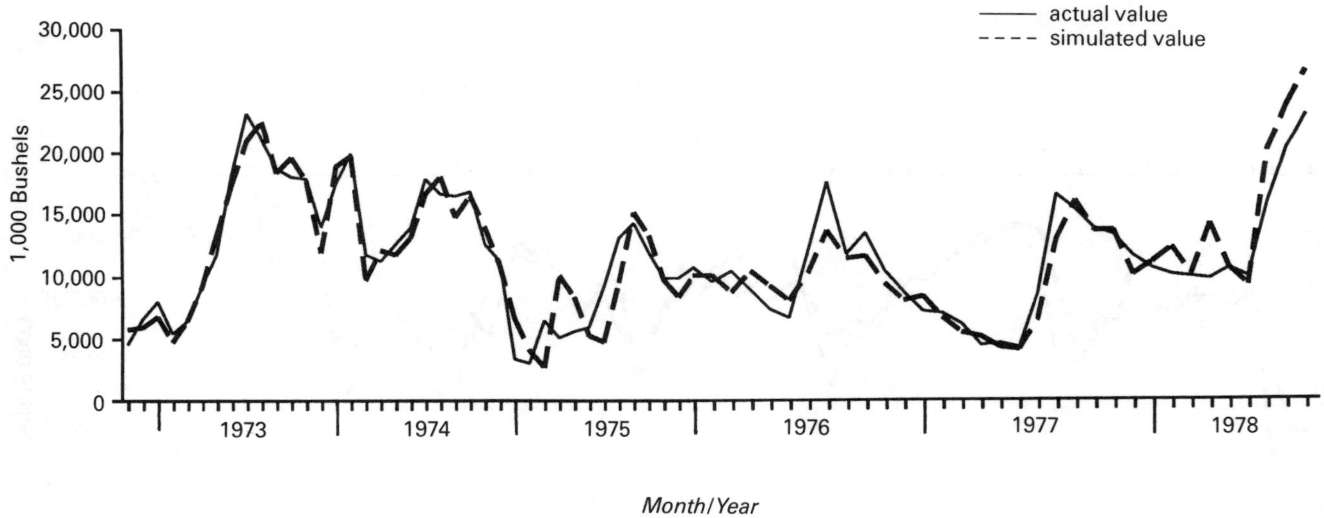

Figure 6.1 Short hedging

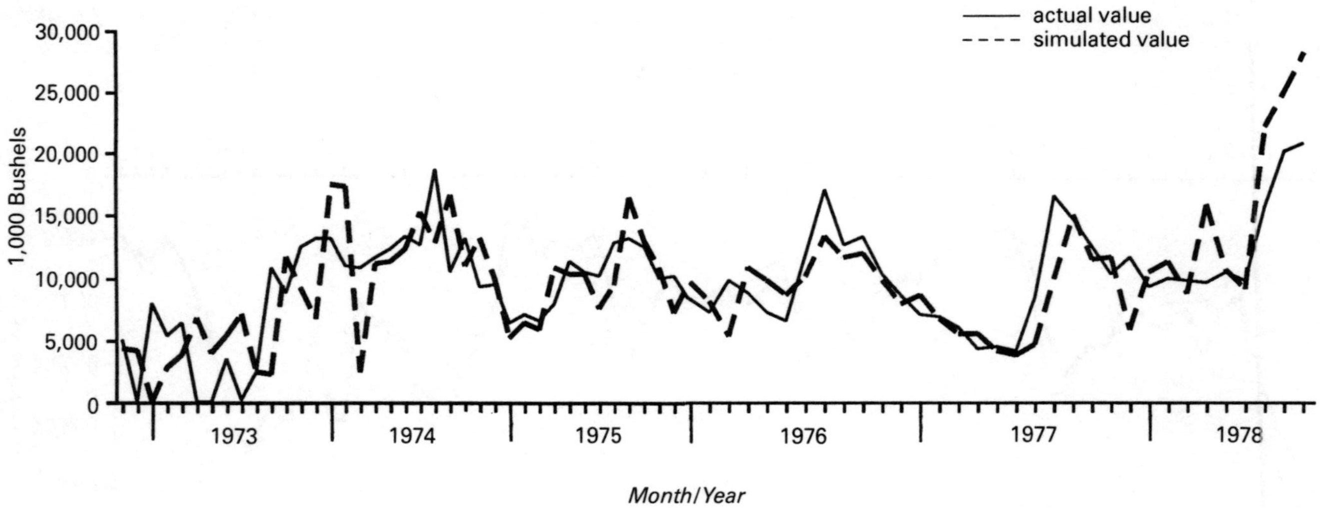

Figure 6.2 Long hedging

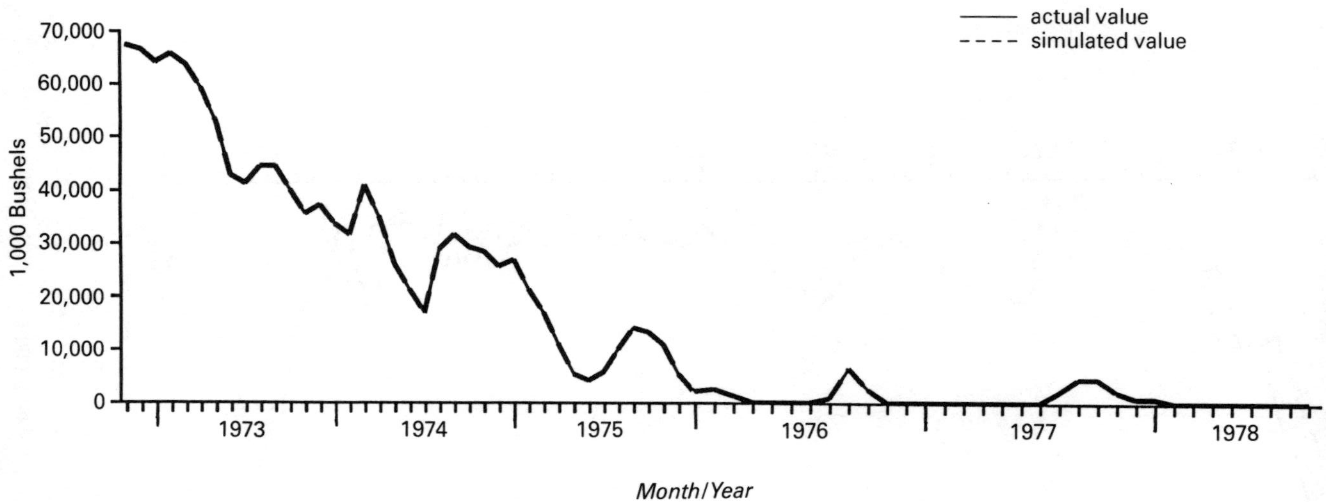

Figure 6.3 Unhedged storage

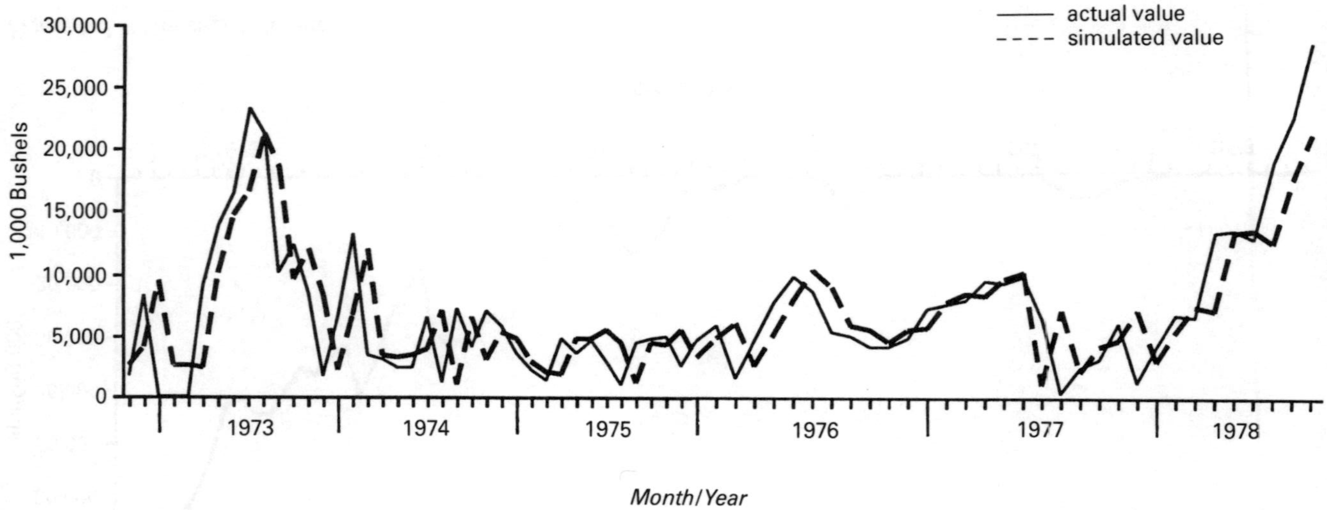

Figure 6.4 Long speculation

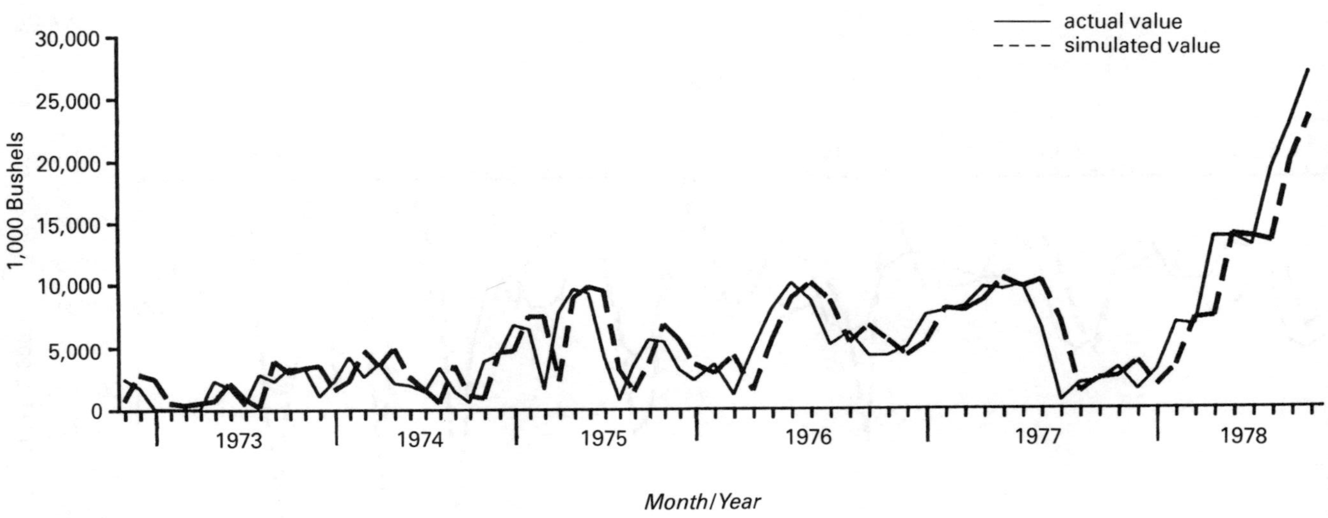

Figure 6.5 Short speculation

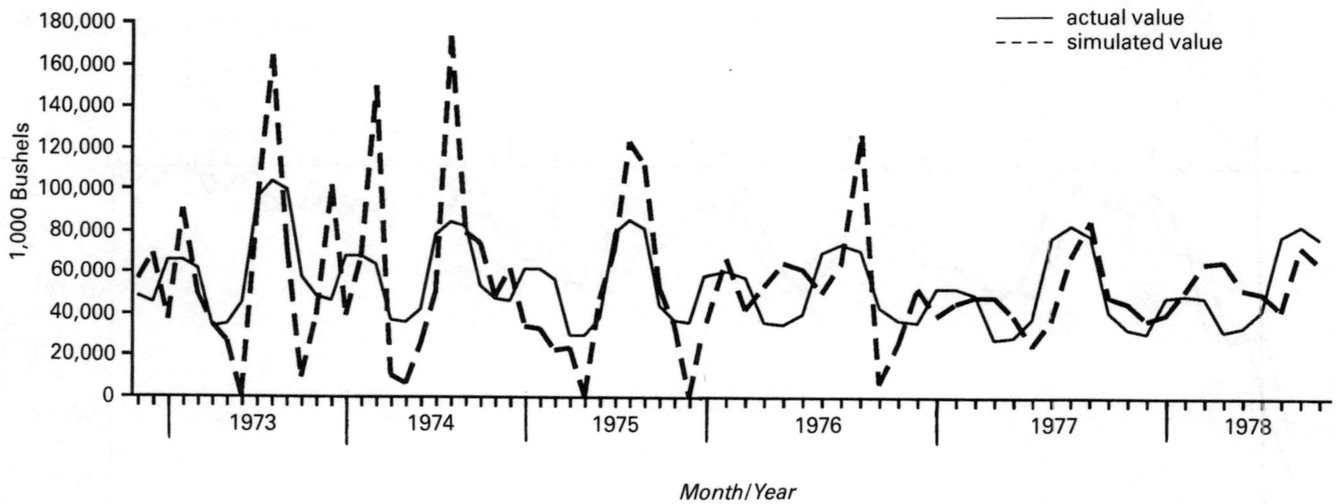

Figure 6.6 Consumption

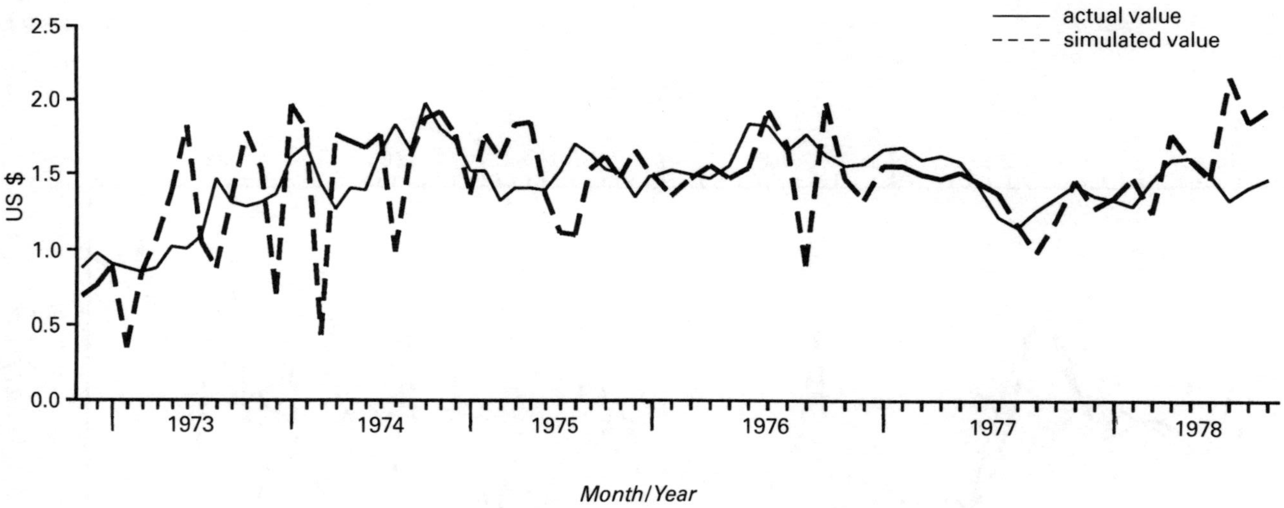

Figure 6.7 Futures prices

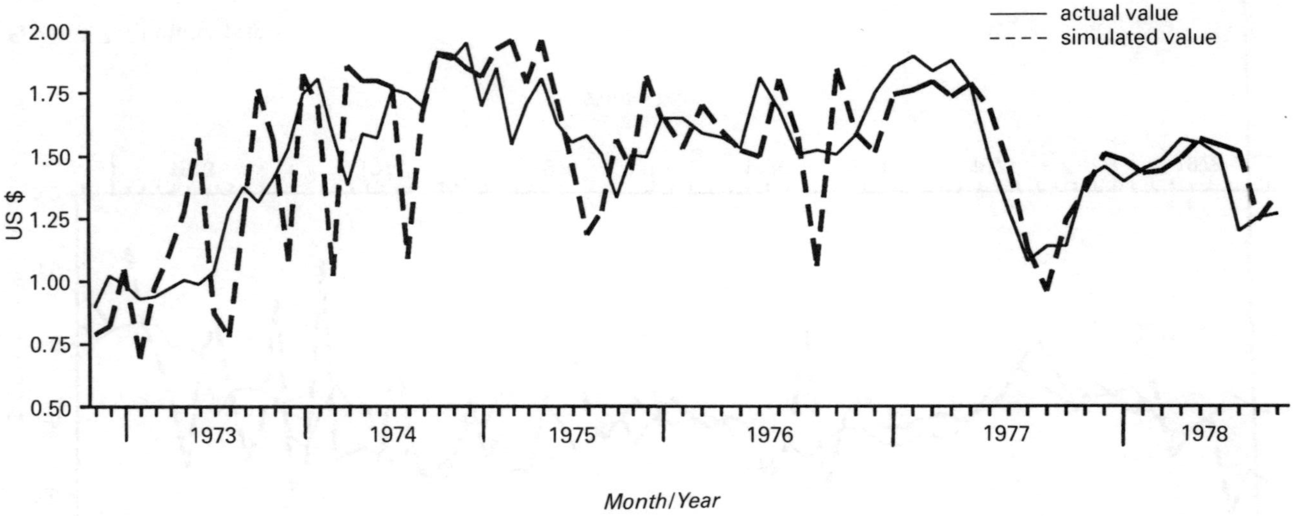

Figure 6.8 Cash prices

hypothesis. This underprediction leads to a delay of around one month in the prediction of peaks, and of course there is a tendency to overpredict on a falling market. The long-hedging function, although exhibiting a relatively high value of Theil's IC, performs tolerably well after December 1974, and not as poorly as the parameter estimates for equation (6.10) would lead us to expect. It may be appropriate to infer that there was some significant change in the behaviour of long hedgers after December 1974 which renders the present model more relevant after that date.

The tracking of consumption reveals a tendency to exaggerate all peaks and troughs, and this is reflected to some extent in the correlation coefficient and Theil's IC for equation (6.20). This deficiency of the model may be due partly to the substantial proportion of the oats crop which is consumed on the farm (see p. 129) and is therefore not the subject of any market transaction.

The simulation of the long and short speculation functions in futures is moderately good, except for the adaptive characteristic of underprediction (overprediction) on a rising (falling) market noted above, which is reflected particularly in Theil's IC and the %RMSE statistics. While the simulation of the futures and cash prices improves after June 1975, prior to that date there is notable exaggeration of the amplitude of fluctuations. Again, the present model seems to be more appropriate in explaining these variables after 1975.

Simulation of the oats cash price is better than that of the soybeans cash price in the study reported by Giles *et al.* (1985), although it is inferior to that of the corn cash price reported in the same paper. Simulation of the oats futures price, however, is inferior to that of both corn and soybeans futures prices in the earlier paper, a feature which may be due to the more successful representation of the (greater) speculative interest in the latter two markets. Of the various structural equations, only the unhedged storage relationship for the oats market clearly outperforms any corresponding function for the corn and soybeans markets, although the performance of the oats short-hedging equation may be comparable (no %RMSEs were reported in the earlier paper).

In any case, the results reported here are sufficiently encouraging to warrant the generation of post-sample forecasts of the cash price, and the use of these forecasts to test the semi-strong form of the EMH.

POST-SAMPLE FORECASTS AND MARKET EFFICIENCY

The model analysed in the previous section was employed to provide forecasts of the cash price of oats six months ahead during a post-sample forecast period (March 1979 to September 1981) comprising thirty-one observations. In order to place the model on the same informational footing as the oats futures price, the model was continuously updated by re-estimating the parameters for each successive forecast during the post-sample period. A test of the EMH requires that these model-derived forecasts of the cash price AS be compared with the six-month-ahead forecasts of the cash price implicit in the futures price P. The performance of these two predictors is compared in Table 6.5, and it will be seen that the model predictor AS clearly outperforms the futures price P, although the difference between the two according to the %RMSE criterion is not statistically significant (see Appendix 2). Incidentally, the hypothesis that each of these two predictors is unbiased cannot be rejected (see Appendix 2).

Each of these predictors, however, contains information which the other does not (Figure 6.9), and so the proportionate contribution of each to an assumed composite predictor was estimated from the relationship

$$\mathrm{CP}_{t-6,t} = \alpha\,\mathrm{AS}_{t-6,t} + \beta P_{t-6,t} + e_t \tag{6.27}$$

where $\mathrm{CP}_{t-6,t}$ is a composite predictor formed at time $t-6$ for the cash price at time t. Equation (6.27) was estimated by ordinary least squares (OLS) for thirty-one observations in the forecast period, $\hat{\alpha}$ and $\hat{\beta}$ were not constrained to add to unity and there is no evidence of serial correlation among the residuals. The results of this estimation are given in Table 6.6, and while multicollinearity would normally be expected to qualify the interpretation of such estimates, the relative magnitudes of the estimated coefficients do confirm the

Table 6.5 Post-sample prediction of cash price

Predictor	*Correlation coefficient*	*Theil's IC*	*%RMSE*
AS	0.8663	0.0880	9.541
P	0.7922	0.1086	10.257
CP	0.8774	0.0829	8.625

Note: AS is the model predictor with continuous updating during the thirty-one observations of the forecast period, P is the futures price and CP is a composite predictor constructed as $0.71\mathrm{AS} + 0.30P$, where the weights are estimated by OLS (see text).

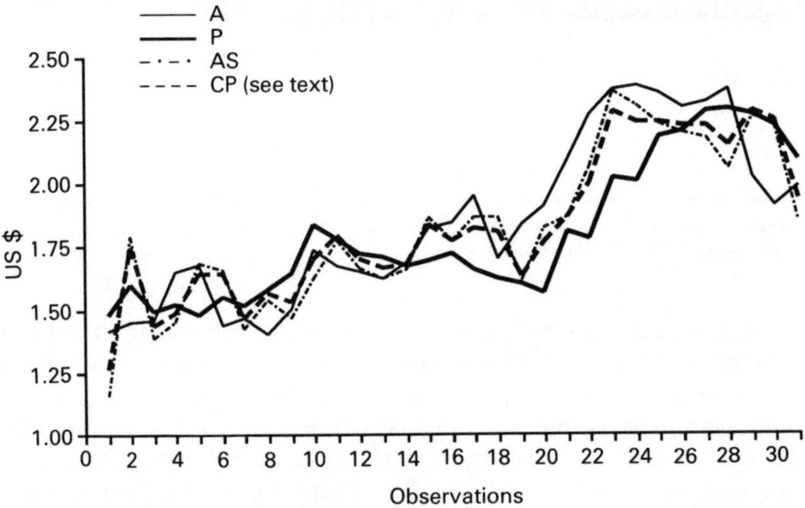

Figure 6.9 Oats: post-sample simulation

view that the model predictor outperforms the futures price as an anticipation of the cash price.

The estimated weights $\hat{\alpha}$ and $\hat{\beta}$ were used to form the composite predictor of the cash price $CP_{t-6,t}$, the performance of which is evaluated in Table 6.5. It will be seen that, as expected, CP outperforms the other two predictors, and moreover that the difference in performance between CP and the model predictor, according to the %RMSE criterion, is statistically significant at the 5 per cent level but not at the 1 per cent level (see Appendix 2).

In this case it would seem more appropriate to reduce the probability of a type 1 error (i.e. reduce the chance of rejecting the EMH when it is true) and so select the 1 per cent level of significance. This is because the EMH is not a purely static concept, but also raises the question of whether there is evidence that agents are learning to use the information contained in the model. Convergence of the two predictors CP and *P*, for example, would constitute such evidence, although in Figure 6.9 it is not clear that these two series do converge. In any case, selection of the 1 per cent level, and hence non-rejection of the EMH, simply has the consequence of calling for further evidence on this market, and in view of the ambiguous results reported in this section that is the decision made here. Non-rejection of the EMH at this level of significance is consistent with the outcome described on pp. 142–4, where the hypothesis of a single unit root could not be rejected.

Table 6.6 Estimation of weights for composite predictor

Equation	$\hat{\alpha}$	$\hat{\beta}$	*DW*
(6.27)	0.713 (4.283)	0.307 (1.815)	1.587

Notes: Estimation is by OLS for thirty-one observations; asymptotic *t* values are in parentheses; DW, Durbin–Watson statistic.

A speculative trading programme also was employed to investigate whether significant profits could be made in the oats futures market, using the information contained in the model. For each month of the forecast period a futures contract, as defined in note 3, was sold if the futures price *P* exceeded the model predictor AS, while the futures contract was purchased if $P \leq$ AS. There were seventeen sell and fourteen buy transactions in this programme, and each position was reversed after six months (or one month prior to the delivery date, whichever was the earlier). The programme resulted in mean gross profits which were significant at the 1 per cent level (two-tail test), but which ceased to be significant when the expense ratio reached 25 per cent of profits. This result suggests a possible inefficiency in the oats futures market, but in the absence of information about actual expenses and confirmation from repeated samples, it cannot be used to reject the EMH.

CONCLUSIONS

Although the area planted to oats in the United States is the fourth largest after wheat, corn and soybeans, oats have been comparatively neglected in grain market studies. This may be because a significant proportion of the crop is consumed on the farm, possibly because of the high bulk-to-weight ratio. Moreover, the oats market has attracted a relatively low speculative ratio and this may have made it a less interesting subject of economic investigation.

In this chapter we have developed a simultaneous model of the oats market, distinguishing functional relationships for holders of unhedged inventories and consumers (mainly stock feed processors), as well as for short and long hedgers and short and long speculators in futures. In the 3SLS estimation of the parameters of the simultaneous system and in intrasample simulation, the best performing equation, with virtually perfect simulation, is the unhedged inventory function.

This is an important result because most inventories are held unhedged. The short-hedging equation performs better when specified in terms of current cash and futures prices and the expected futures price, rather than as a function of the current and expected price spread. Better results are obtained when the long-hedging equation is specified in terms of the current and expected ratio of the futures price to the spot price, rather than the price spread, although this relationship does not perform as well as its short-hedging counterpart. Simulation of long and short speculative positions is acceptable, given the low speculative ratio. The adaptive hypothesis, employed throughout, is an appropriate representation of expectations, including anticipated income in the consumption relationship. There is no evidence of serial correlation except in the unhedged inventory function, in which a correction is made for first-order autocorrelation.

This model is employed to forecast the cash price of oats six months ahead during a post-sample forecast period, and for each monthly forecast the model is updated by extending the sample period one month and re-estimating the parameters. The semi-strong form of the EMH is tested by comparing the model prediction of the cash price with the prediction implicit in the futures price for six months ahead delivery. The model is a superior predictor to the futures price, although the difference between the two is not significant. A composite predictor, with OLS estimated weights, also outperforms the futures price as a predictor of the cash price, and in this case the difference in performance, while significant at the 5 per cent level, is not significant at the 1 per cent level at which the test is conducted. The outcome of this test, therefore, is that the EMH is not rejected. This result is consistent with the outcome of Wald and likelihood ratio tests for a single unit root in futures prices, reported in the data section, a hypothesis which also is not rejected.

A speculative trading programme, in which the future was sold if priced at a premium to the model predictor and bought at a discount, resulted in significant gross profits in the forecast period, although this is insufficient evidence to reject the EMH.

APPENDIX 6.1: AVERAGE MONTH-END RATIO OF LARGE SPECULATORS TO TOTAL OPEN POSITIONS (%)

	Oats		*Corn*		*Soybeans*		*Wheat*	
	Long	*Short*	*Long*	*Short*	*Long*	*Short*	*Long*	*Short*
1970	24.5	17.3	28.7	27.1	31.2	33.5	37.9	31.2
1974	12.3	8.2	18.8	15.0	27.2	29.2	20.6	20.6
1975	13.1	9.1	18.5	15.2	30.0	33.8	16.7	20.6
1976	11.7	10.4	14.2	14.9	41.5	39.6	22.1	21.1
1977	4.3	4.1	13.9	16.3	41.2	35.6	24.4	22.8
1978	13.4	11.5	12.5	9.5	29.7	26.5	24.6	21.1

Source: CFTC, *Commitments of Traders* 1970–9

APPENDIX 6.2: COMPARATIVE PERFORMANCE OF THE FUTURES PRICE, THE MODEL AND COMPOSITE PREDICTOR AS ANTICIPATIONS OF THE CASH PRICE

Comparison of P and AS

Define

$$e_1 = A - \mathrm{AS}$$
$$e_2 = A - P$$

where A is the cash price, P is the futures price and AS is the model predictor of the cash price, all at time t as defined on pp. 133 and 158. For the post-sample forecast period March 1979 to September 1981 (thirty-one observations)

$$\bar{e}_1 = 0.03116 \qquad \mathrm{SD}_{e_1} = 0.16442$$
$$\bar{e}_2 = 0.05307 \qquad \mathrm{SD}_{e_2} = 0.19937$$

Hence neither of the hypotheses $\mathrm{H}(\mu_{e_1} = 0)$ and $\mathrm{H}(\mu_{e_2} = 0)$ can be rejected; i.e. the separate hypotheses that the futures price and the model are each unbiased predictors of the cash price cannot be rejected.

Now define $S = e_1 + e_2$ and $D = e_1 - e_2$. Since it is reasonable to assume that both predictors are unbiased the formula for the coefficient of correlation between S and D is given in Granger and Newbold (1986: 279), and its value is $r = -0.2505$. On the argument in Granger and Newbold (1986: 278–9), if r is significantly different from zero, then it can be inferred that the %RMSEs of P and AS, as forecasts of A, are significantly different. The hypothesis $H(\mu_r = 0)$ can be tested by the statistic

$$t = r/S_r$$

where $S_r = [(1 - r^2)/(n - 2)]^{1/2}$ and n is the number of observations. In this case $t = -1.3936$ and the hypothesis $H(\mu_r = 0)$ cannot be rejected. Hence it should be inferred that the model does not significantly outperform P as a predictor of A.

Comparison of *P* and CP

Define $e_3 = A - \mathrm{CP}$, where CP is a composite predictor as defined on p. 158. For the post-sample period March 1979 to September 1981

$$\bar{e}_3 = 0.01961 \qquad \mathrm{SD}_{e_3} = 0.15646$$

and the hypothesis $H(\mu_{e_3} = 0)$ cannot be rejected.

Now define $S_1 = e_2 + e_3$ and $D_1 = e_2 - e_3$. Since it is reasonable to assume that P and CP are each unbiased predictors of A, the formula for the correlation coefficient between S_1 and D_1 is as employed above, and its value is $r_1 = -0.40338$.

The question of the significance of the difference between the %RMSEs of P and CP can be addressed by testing the hypothesis $H(\mu_{r_1} = 0)$. This hypothesis can be tested by the statistic $t = r_1/S_{r_1}$. In this case $t = -2.3742$, so that the hypothesis $H(\mu_{r_1} = 0)$ is not rejected at the 5 per cent level of significance but is not rejected at the 1 per cent level (two-tail test). If the test is conducted at the 1 per cent level for the reasons given on p. 159 $H(\mu_{r_1} = 0)$ is not rejected, and it is inferred that CP does not significantly outperform P as a predictor of A.

NOTES

Helpful comments by Jerome Stein are acknowledged. An earlier version of this paper was presented at the Australian Economics Congress, Canberra, August 1988.

1 They are said to demand storage because they plan to acquire the physical commodity in the next period, although they do not necessarily plan to take delivery under the futures contract. These traders are using the futures contract as a substitute for a merchandizing contract (see Working 1953).

2 This is not necessarily a cause for concern. Since the equilibrium condition for profit-maximizing short hedgers can be written

$$(P_t - A_t) - (P^*_{t+1} - A^*_{t+1}) = m_t$$

the influence of m_t is taken into account through the variables on the left-hand side of this condition. Similarly in (6.11) if the equilibrium condition for holders of unhedged inventories is

$$A^*_{t+1} - A_t - r_t = m_t$$

then the effect of m_t is taken into account by the presence in (6.12) of the variables on the left-hand side of this equilibrium condition. A similar statement can be made about the marginal risk premium in (6.13).

3 A six-month future is defined as follows:

when the month is January/February, the future is July;
when the month is March/April, the future is September;
when the month is May/June/July, the future is December;
when the month is August/September, the future is March;
when the month is October/November, the future is May;
when the month is December, the future is July.

4 A total of twenty-two such negative values are generated, of which three are in periods when LH > SH, eighteen are in periods when LH < SH and one is in a period when LH = SH.

5 When $LH_t = SH_t$, both LH_t and SH_t are decreased by half the absolute value of U_t, while LS_t and SS_t are each increased by half the absolute value of U_t.

6 It will be recalled that the specification of equation (6.6) does not include the expected cash price; this would have led to a two-period lag of all variables in (6.6) and to an excessive number of parameters.

REFERENCES

Brasse, V. (1986) 'Testing the efficiency of the tin futures market on the LME', in K. Tucker and C. Baden Fuller (eds) *Firms and Markets: Essays in Honour of Basil Yamey*, Chapter 2, London: Croom Helm.

Brennan, M. J. (1958) 'The supply of storage', *American Economic Review* 48: 50–72.

Cargill, T. F. and Rausser, G. C. (1975) 'Temporal price behaviour in commodity futures markets', *Journal of Finance* 30 (4): 1043–53.

Chance, D. M. (1985a) 'A semi strong form test of the efficiency of the treasury bond futures market', *Journal of Futures Markets* 5 (3): 385–405.

—— (1985b) 'The reaction of the Chicago Board of Trade GNMA futures contract to the announcement of inflation rates: a study of market efficiency', *Review of Research in Futures Markets* 4 (1): 132–54.

Commodity Yearbook, New York: Commodity Research Bureau, various years.

Dickey, D. A. and Fuller, W. A. (1979) 'Distribution of the estimators for autoregressive time series with a unit root', *Journal of the American Statistical Association* 74: 327–31.

—— (1981) 'Likelihood ratio statistics for autoregressive time series with a unit root', *Econometrica* 49: 1057–72.

Doukas, J. and Rahman, A. (1987) 'Unit roots tests: evidence from the foreign exchange futures market', *Journal of Financial and Quantitative Analysis* 22: 101–8.

Evans, G. B. A. and Savin, N. E. (1981) 'Testing for unit roots: 1', *Econometrica* 49: 753–79.

—— and —— (1984) 'Testing for unit roots: 2', *Econometrica* 52: 1241–68.

Fama, E. F. (1970) 'Efficient capital markets: a review of theory and empirical work', *Journal of Finance* 25: 383–417.

Fuller, W. A. (1976) *Introduction to Statistical Time Series*, New York: Wiley.

Giles, D. E. A., Goss, B. A. and Chin, O. P. L. (1985) 'Intertemporal allocation in the corn and soybeans markets with rational expectations', *American Journal of Agricultural Economics* 67: 749–60.

Goss, B. A. (ed.) (1986) *Futures Markets: Their Establishment and Performance*, London: Croom Helm.

—— (1987) 'Wool prices and publicly available information', *Australian Economic Papers* 26 (49): 225–36.

Goss, B. A. and Giles, D. E. A (1986a) 'Price determination and storage in commodity markets: soybeans and wool', in K. A. Tucker and C. Baden Fuller (eds) *Firms and Markets: Essays in Honour of Basil Yamey*, Chapter 1, pp. 3–41, London: Croom Helm.

—— and —— (1986b) 'Intertemporal allocation in the Australian wool market', in B. A. Goss (ed.) *Futures Markets: Their Establishment and Performance*, Chapter 4, pp. 93–118, London: Croom Helm.

Granger, C. W. J. and Newbold, P. (1986) *Forecasting Economic Time Series*, 2nd edn, London: Academic Press.

Hall, B. H. (1986) *Time Series Processor Version 4.1B Reference Manual*, Stanford University.

Hansen, L. P. and Hodrick, R. J. (1980) 'Forward exchange rates as optimal predictors of future spot rates: an econometric analysis', *Journal of Political Economy* 88: 829–53.

Inkeles, D. M. (1972) 'Understanding the oats futures market', *Commodity Yearbook*, New York: Commodity Research Bureau.

Larson, A. B. (1960) 'Measurement of a random process in futures prices', *Food Research Institute Studies* 1: 313–24.

Leuthold, R. M. (1972) 'Random walks and price trends: the live cattle futures market', *Journal of Finance*, 27: 879–89.

Leuthold, R. M. and Hartmann, P. A. (1979) 'A semi-strong form evaluation of the efficiency of the hog futures market', *American Journal of Agricultural Economics* 61 (3): 482–9.

Nerlove, M. (1958) 'Adaptive expectations and cobweb phenomena', *Quarterly Journal of Economics* 72: 227–40.

Peck, A. E. (1982) 'Estimations of hedging and speculative positions in futures markets revisited', *Food Research Institute Studies* 18: 181–95.

Peston, M. H. and Yamey, B. S. (1960) 'Intertemporal price relationships with forward markets: a method of analysis', *Economica* 27: 355–67.

Praetz, P. D. (1975) 'Testing the efficient markets theory on the Sydney wool futures exchange', *Australian Economic Papers* 14 (25): 240–9.

Rausser, G. C. and Carter, C. (1983) 'Futures market efficiency in the soybean complex', *Review of Economics and Statistics* 65: 469–78.

Stevenson, R. A. and Bear, R. M. (1970) 'Commodity futures: trends or random walks?' *Journal of Finance* 25: 65–81.

Telser, L. (1958) 'Futures trading and the storage of cotton and wheat', *Journal of Political Economy* 66: 233–55.

Working, H. (1953) 'Futures trading and hedging', *American Economic Review* 43: 313–43.

Wymer, C. R. (1977) 'Computer programs: TRANSF Manual', Mimeo, International Monetary Fund, Washington, DC.

7 Alternative performance models in interest rate futures

Jot Yau, Uttama Savanayana and Thomas Schneeweis

INTRODUCTION

While few studies have questioned the effectiveness of financial futures in providing minimum risk positions, in adding incremental return to established spot portfolios or in improving efficient frontiers, many of the studies of the effectiveness of financial futures have been characterized by *ad hoc* resolution of three potentially important issues in research design: (a) the pricing model used to measure expected price performance, (b) the performance criteria used in determining the inclusion of futures contracts in an asset position and (c) the return form used in the analysis.

For instance, tests on suspected pricing abnormalities in futures markets (for example, futures/spot market arbitrage) require an accurate model of the expected futures contract price. In recent years, new theories and empirical tests have offered additional perspectives on the price behaviour of futures contracts which differ from results obtained from simple cost-of-carry arbitrage models. For example, during the delivery month, treasury bond and treasury note futures contracts have been shown to provide several options to holders of short futures contract positions. These have been identified as the quality option, or the option to choose the 'cheapest' of a number of deliverable commodities, and three timing options involving the choice of when to deliver (Gay and Manaster 1986).

In addition to alternative models of determining expected pricing performance, various approaches have been suggested to test the effectiveness of financial futures in improving the risk–return trade-off. Three principal frameworks have been suggested for determining the effectiveness of interest rate futures in asset management: (a) minimum risk, (b) risk–return enhancement of an established spot portfolio and (c) variable spot/futures (for example, simultaneous multi-asset portfolio choice). Each of these frameworks is based on an alternative view of the portfolio problem. The multi-asset portfolio choice approach with variable spot and futures positions is relevant for the investor who has no commitment to an established spot position. Performance models based on an established spot position are concerned with the evaluation of a spot portfolio and the incremental benefit of futures to the risk–return performance of that portfolio. Likewise, the minimum risk approach is primarily for the individual who is constrained to holding a spot position but does not explicitly consider the expected return on the portfolio and simply derives a minimum risk position.

Lastly, little research has been conducted on the effect of using alternative return measures for financial futures in tests of interest rate futures performance. An analysis of the alternative return measures is important not only because the use of alternative return measures (for example, price change, price relatives) may affect the comparability of the empirical results of previous studies but also because such measures imply different loss functions of the market participants.

In the following sections, we review the current suggested approaches to determining (a) futures effectiveness, (b) futures pricing and (c) return formulations, and discuss the problems and uses of the alternative models. In the next section we review approaches to determining interest rate futures effectiveness. In the third section we discuss the possible impact of alternative return measures in minimum risk hedge analysis and in portfolio/risk optimization. In the fourth section we review the impact of various option pricing effects on the traditional cost-of-carry futures pricing model. In the final section we present our conclusions and discuss future research areas.

ALTERNATIVE PERFORMANCE MODELS

Considerable research in financial futures has been conducted on the effectiveness of futures in obtaining minimum risk positions (Ederington 1979; Dale 1981; Hill and Schneeweis 1982), in improving the risk–return characteristics of an established spot portfolio (Howard and D'Antonio 1984; Chang and Shanker 1986; Elton *et al.* 1987; Gjerde 1987), and in forming an optimal portfolio in which the futures contracts and the spot assets are considered simultaneously (Levy 1987). Each of these studies is sound given their own perspective; however, each deals with a risk–return framework that is specific to a particular portfolio problem. For instance, Ederington (1979) and others analyse the ability of futures contracts to offset potential price risk associated with a given spot position. Ederington's approach is based on risk reduction alone and is devoid of expected return considerations. Howard and D'Antonio (1984), Chang and Shanker (1986) and Gjerde (1987) take into account both return and risk characteristics of the futures contract; however, they do not assume a simultaneous futures/spot asset selection process. Similarly, Elton *et al.* (1987) test for the incremental improvement in the risk–return performance of a spot portfolio compared with adding a portfolio of commodity funds.

In contrast, Levy (1987) views the use of futures as an alternative to spot assets in a multi-asset portfolio framework with variable futures and spot positions. Thus the three frameworks – minimum risk, fixed spot, and variable spot optimal asset allocation – differ both in the procedures required to determine the number of futures contracts and in those used to measure the degree of effectiveness. The differences in the hedging and effectiveness procedures stem primarily from the different objectives of the three frameworks. In the following sections we review briefly the basis for the determination of the optimal futures positions and the approaches used to measure the effectiveness of that position.

The minimum risk hedging framework

Research has shown that futures contracts can be combined with the underlying assets to create minimum risk positions (Ederington 1979; Franckle 1980; Dale 1981; Hill and Schneeweis 1982).[1] For instance, Black (1976) and Ederington (1979) have employed the mean–variance framework in solving the minimum risk hedging problem. The objective of the investor is to minimize the portfolio risk by hedging an existing cash position with an offsetting position in futures. Hill and Schneeweis have used a similar approach in deriving the optimal hedge ratio and the hedging effectiveness measure for interest rate futures. The objective of this approach is to

$$\text{minimize var } R_p = X_c^2 \text{ var } R_c + X_f^2 \text{ var } R_f + 2X_f X_c \text{ cov}(R_c, R_f) \quad (7.1)$$

where var R_c, var R_f, and cov(R_c, R_f) are the variances and co-variance of the returns of cash and futures respectively, R_c and R_f are the expected return for the next period of cash and futures respectively, R_p is the expected return for the next period of the portfolio invested in the cash and the futures contracts, X_c is the given fixed position in the cash ($X_c = 1$) and X_f is the proportion of portfolio held in futures.

It can be shown that the optimal X_f which minimizes the portfolio variance in equation (7.1) is equal to the negative of the regression coefficient obtained from the regression

$$R_c = a + hR_f + e$$

where h is the optimal hedge ratio and is given by

$$h = -\frac{\text{cov}(R_c, R_f)}{\text{var } R_f} \tag{7.2a}$$

$$= -\frac{p(\text{var } R_c \text{ var } R_f)^{1/2}}{\text{var } R_f} \tag{7.2b}$$

where p is the correlation between returns on cash and futures.

The corresponding measure of the hedging effectiveness HE is defined as follows:

$$\text{HE} = \frac{\text{var } R_c - \text{var } R_p}{\text{var } R_c} \tag{7.3}$$

$$= \frac{\text{cov}^2(R_c, R_f)}{\text{var } R_c \text{ var } R_f}$$

$$= R^2$$

where R^2 is the coefficient of determination corresponding to the regression of R_c on R_f. The HE measures the relative reduction in portfolio risk which results from the inclusion of the optimal amount of futures in the portfolio. From the formulation, it is clear that the basic objective of the hedging framework is to obtain the minimum risk position for the combined portfolio. R^2, which is empirically derived, measures the reduction in an existing portfolio variance which results from the use of the minimum risk hedge ratio over the estimation period. If $R^2 = 1$, then the minimum risk is zero. For $R^2 < 1$, the minimum risk point has variance greater than zero.

The portfolio allocation framework

In contrast with risk minimization for an existing portfolio, the portfolio optimization approach focuses on obtaining the optimal number of futures contracts to be combined with either a fixed or a variable spot position to create a portfolio with a risk–return trade-off superior to that of the existing fixed or variable spot position. The optimal futures position is the number of contracts which maximizes the return–risk trade-off for tangency portfolio given a risk-free rate. While measures of effectiveness differ between studies, in this framework effectiveness is measured as a reduction not in the variance of the spot portfolio but in the risk-adjusted return performance of the futures-contract-adjusted spot portfolio relative to the existing spot portfolio(s).

Fixed spot position

In contrast with risk minimization, the potential of futures contracts in enhancing the risk–return characteristic of a portfolio of a spot asset and a risk-free asset has been demonstrated by Howard and D'Antonio (1984) and Chang and Shanker (1986). While they utilize the mean–variance analysis, they do not focus on futures to obtain a minimum risk portfolio for an established spot asset but rather on the marginal benefit of adding futures to an established spot portfolio. Howard and D'Antonio and Chang and Shanker have proposed the following portfolio optimization:

$$\text{maximize } (R_p - i)/S_p \text{ with respect to } C_f$$

where

$$R_p = \frac{C_f P_f R_f + C_c P_c R_c}{C_c P_c}$$

is the expected return from the combined portfolio (per cent), i is the risk-free rate of return

$$S_p = \frac{(C_c^2 P_c^2 S_c^2 + C_f^2 P_f^2 S_f^2 + 2 C_c C_f P_f P_c S_c S_f p)^{1/2}}{C_c P_c}$$

is the standard deviation of the combined portfolio, C_c and C_f are units of cash and futures respectively, P_c and P_f are the current prices per unit of cash and futures respectively, R_c and R_f are the expected one-period returns of cash and futures respectively, S_c and S_f are the standard deviations of the one-period returns of cash and futures respectively and p is the correlation between the returns of spot and futures. The optimal number of futures contracts is

$$C_f^* = C_c b^*$$

where

$$b^* = \frac{B - p}{\tau\pi(1 - Bp)}$$

$$B = \frac{R_f/S_f}{(R_c - i)/S_c}$$

$$\pi = \frac{S_f}{S_c}$$

$$\tau = \frac{P_f}{P_c}$$

b^* is the number of futures contracts per unit of the underlying cash that yields the optimum risk–excess return trade-off. A full derivation of the formula is given in the Appendix.

By combining an appropriate number of futures contracts with an existing cash position, the investor can obtain a portfolio with a risk–return trade-off superior to that of the existing cash position. An implicit assumption of the Howard and D'Antonio formulation is that the investor maintains the existing cash position (i.e. C_c is fixed) while seeking to improve the risk–return characteristic by using futures.

In Figure 7.1, A represents the existing cash position in the risk–return space and i is the expected return on the risk-free asset. By

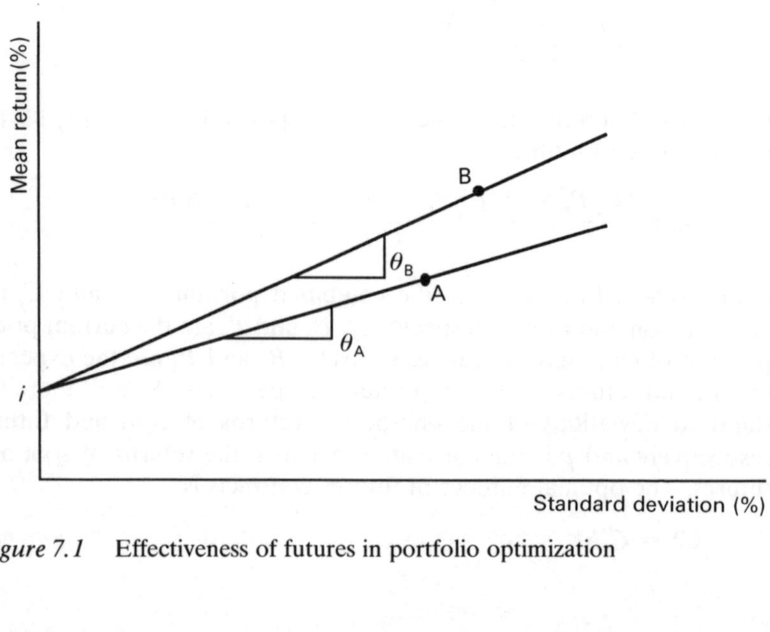

Figure 7.1 Effectiveness of futures in portfolio optimization

combining the optimal number of futures contracts (as determined by the optimization procedure described above) with the existing cash position, the investor can move to position B. He/she can then invest in any portfolio consisting of the combined cash and futures of B and the risk-free assets that lie on the line *i*B to obtain the desired risk–return trade-off. All portfolios on *i*B have superior risk–return trade-off to portfolios of the existing cash and risk-free asset that lie along the line *i*A.

To measure the effectiveness of futures in portfolio optimization, the following excess return–risk measures RE are defined:

$$\text{RE1} = \frac{\theta_{\text{B}}}{\theta_{\text{A}}} \tag{7.4}$$

$$\text{RE2} = \frac{\theta_{\text{B}} - \theta_{\text{A}}}{|\theta_{\text{A}}|} \tag{7.5}$$

$$\text{RE} = \frac{i + \theta_{\text{B}} S_{\text{c}} - R_{\text{c}}}{S_{\text{c}}} \tag{7.6a}$$

$$= \frac{\theta_{\text{B}} S_{\text{c}}}{S_{\text{c}}} - \frac{R_{\text{c}} - i}{S_{\text{c}}} \tag{7.6b}$$

$$= \theta_{\text{B}} - \theta_{\text{A}} \tag{7.6c}$$

where θ_{A} is the slope of line *i*A in Figure 7.1 and θ_{B} is the slope of line *i*B in Figure 7.1. RE1, introduced by Howard and D'Antonio (1984), is the measure of the effectiveness of futures in improving the risk–return trade-off of the combined portfolio over the performance of the existing cash position. RE1, however, is based on a special case of the second-order condition for the optimization problem. As a result, it can yield inconsistent measures of futures effectiveness when $R_{\text{c}} < i$ or $\theta_{\text{A}} < 0$. (If θ_{A} and θ_{B} are both greater than zero, the greater the value of θ_{B}, the higher is the effectiveness. However if $\theta_{\text{A}} < 0$, the greater the value of θ_{B}, the lower is the effectiveness.) Chang and Shanker (1986, 1987) have remedied the problem by developing RE2 which takes into account the complete second-order condition. RE2 yields consistent ranking of futures effectiveness while maintaining the same interpretation as RE1. In replying to Chang and Shanker (1987), Howard and D'Antonio (1987) propose RE3. It is obvious from equations (7.6a)–(7.6c) that RE3 is simply the numerator of RE2. However, RE3 eliminates the potential problem of RE2 in having an undefined value for the futures effectiveness when $\theta_{\text{A}} = 0$ or $R_{\text{c}} - R_{\text{f}} = 0$. (Such a situation can occur when RE1 and RE2 are used to examine an *ex post* performance of futures in improving the risk–return trade-off of the combined cash and futures portfolio.)

It is important to note that the suggestions by Howard and D'Antonio and Chang and Shanker relating to the addition of futures contracts to an established spot portfolio are similar in form. The addition is based on the ability of the futures contract to produce a superior risk–return trade-off (for example, efficient frontier) than that of an established spot position.[2] In brief, as pointed out by Elton *et al.* (1987), futures should be added as long as

$$\frac{R_f - i}{sd_f} > \frac{R_p - i}{sd_p} P_{pf} \tag{7.7}$$

where R_f is the expected return of the futures contract, i is the riskless rate, sd_f is the standard deviation of the futures contract f, R_p is the expected return of the spot portfolio P, sd_p is the standard deviation of the spot portfolio and p_{pf} is the correlation between the futures contract f and the portfolio P.

Variable spot position

Both the minimum risk and the Howard and D'Antonio, Chang and Shanker approaches test the advantages of futures to an established (fixed) spot position. Levy (1987) and others have pointed to the benefits of futures in risk–return performance when the futures and spot positions are both variable and can be substituted. In this case the aim is to minimize

$$\text{var } R_p = X_c^2 \text{ var } R_c + X_f^2 \text{ var } R_f + 2X_c X_f \text{ cov}(R_c, R_f) \tag{7.8}$$

subject to the following constraints:

$$R_p = X_c R_c + X_f R_f = k \tag{7.9}$$

$$X_c + X_f = 1 \tag{7.10}$$

$$X_c, X_f > 0 \tag{7.11}$$

where k is the target return of the portfolio and is a constant, X_c and X_f are fractions of the total wealth invested in cash and futures respectively and the other notation is as defined earlier. This framework differs from both the minimum risk framework and the Howard and D'Antonio, Chang and Shanker approaches in that X_c is to be determined simultaneously with X_f. This model can also be used with the assumption that the agents can take short positions in cash and futures (i.e. $X_c < 0$, $X_f < 0$). The percentage invested in X_f is that amount which maximizes return subject to a constrained risk level or (as in (7.8)) minimizes risk subject to a constrained return level. Note that (7.8) does not choose a single optimal portfolio based on a tangency point from an assumed risk-free rate as in equations (7.4)–(7.6c). Since this simultaneous model generates a series of optimal solutions, tests of effectiveness for it have often compared its risk–return trade-off with that of the efficient portfolio generated from the spot assets included in the futures/spot optimization. Other studies have concentrated on the *ex post* performance of the efficient portfolios relative to expectations for example, (Hill and Schneeweis 1985).

Performance attribution: problems and uses

While both the minimum risk and portfolio allocation models involve the use of futures contracts, there are differences and similarities between them. The models differ in their underlying objectives. The minimum risk framework focuses on the derivation of the optimum hedge ratio, in the sense of minimum risk of the portfolio. It differs from portfolio optimization in that return levels are not considered. Minimum risk hedge ratios for treasury bond and treasury note futures can be obtained using various approaches (for example, regression, duration, yield beta (Besant and Schneeweis 1986)). However, each of the suggested methods contains problems. For instance, since the regression hedge ratio is based on historical data, this means that the minimum risk model is essentially an *ex post* analysis. Consequently, a major assumption in using this model is that the relationship between the cash and futures price changes is time invariant. The simple duration-based hedge ratio assumes small changes only in interest rates (for example, no convexity problems). More importantly, the minimum risk model does not necessarily consider the full portfolio of assets that an investor holds. Hence this method reduces the risk of the assumed spot position only, and does not consider non-tradeable assets or other tradeable assets held by the investor (Hill and Schneeweis 1982).

The portfolio allocation model focuses on the optimal number of futures contracts to be combined with the cash and risk-free assets to create a portfolio with risk–return trade-off superior to that of the existing cash position. Similar to the portfolio analysis by Markowitz

(1952) and Sharpe (1972), the portfolio allocation framework requires expected returns and risk as inputs to the optimization programme. If historical data are used to derive parameter inputs, the effectiveness of this framework, like the regression hedge ratio, relies on the stability of the relationship between cash and futures prices over time. Moreover, the minimum risk and portfolio frameworks of Howard and D'Antonio and Chang and Shanker assumed a fixed cash position. To the degree that this fixed cash position does not reflect the true portfolio of the investor, the portfolio optimization position may be suboptimal.

HE and REs have different interpretations. HE measures the relative reduction in the risk as a result of including futures in the established portfolio. As HE is equivalent to R^2, the coefficient of determination of the regression of R_c on R_f, $p = 1$ is a sufficient condition for $R^2 = 1$, i.e. a perfect hedge position. Conversely, when $p = 0$, HE = 0, indicating that futures are ineffective in reducing the risk of price changes in cash. REs, however, depend not only on the correlation between the cash and futures returns but also on the risk–return trade-off of cash and futures. Thus, even when the futures cash price changes are not highly correlated (relatively low HE), the benefit of futures in improving the risk–return characteristic of the portfolio as measured by REs may still be significant. Therefore REs measure the degree of improvement in risk–return trade-off due to the inclusion of futures.

The assumption of a fixed spot position, however, may significantly restrict the portfolio optimization approach suggested by Howard and D'Antonio and Chang and Shanker. The models of Howard and D'Antonio, Chang and Shanker, Elton *et al.* (1987) and Gjerde (1987) focus on optimizing the risk–return relationships for a fixed spot position and a variable futures position. In contrast, Levy (1987) and others have focused on the effectiveness of futures in improving the risk–return trade-off when investment in both the futures and the spot assets can be varied. The effectiveness measures suggested by Howard and D'Antonio and Chang and Shanker may have little significance in this case. Since the ability of the futures contract to improve the risk–return trade-off depends on the forecast of the parameter, tests of efficiency for the multi-asset portfolio have generally focused on the stability of the forecast risk–return trade-off and the risk–return trade-off obtained during the investment period (Hill and Schneeweis 1982; Yau *et al.* 1990a).

Table 7.1 Return definitions for financial futures

Price change	$R_t = P_{t+1} - P_t$
Percentage change (futures)	$R_t = (P_{t+1} - P_t)/P_t$
Percentage change (margin)	$R_t = (P_{t+1} - P_t + M_t r_t)/M_t$

Notes: R_t, rate of return; P_t, P_{t+1}, price at times t and $t + 1$ respectively; M_t, initial margin at time t; r_t, one-month treasury bills rate at time t.

ALTERNATIVE RETURN MEASURES

In the analysis of security performance in spot markets, return has often been measured as the relative rate of return, i.e. total income divided by the initial investment. In futures markets the definitions of original investment and return have not been unambiguous. As shown in Table 7.1, the definition of return for financial futures has usually been one of the following: absolute price change; relative price change; price relatives based on margin.

Black (1976) argues that there is no investment involved in futures trading since treasury bills can be posted as initial margin. Thus, the return on the futures contract can be simply measured by the price change $P_{t+1} - P_t$. This measure would be relevant for investors who view return in terms of the total dollar change in wealth. Alternatively, the return can be measured as the percentage change in futures prices. The latter measure represents a potential metric for a change in investor wealth under the assumption of 100 per cent margin. For futures contracts which only require a margin deposit, a percentage change in value relative to the margin deposit may offer an accurate representation of investment return.[3] Thus the total return should be computed as $(P_{t+1} - P_t)/M_t$ if the margin is in the form of cash, or as $(P_{t+1} - P_t + M_t r_t)/M_t$ if the margin is in the form of treasury bills, where r_t is the rate of return on the treasury bills in period t, and M_t is the initial margin on futures in period t.[4]

In past studies the choice of return measure would seem to depend primarily on the researcher's preference. Under some circumstances the impact of alternative return measures may be small, although this decision should not be seen as trivial and requires empirical analysis. In their analysis of the effectiveness of futures in improving the risk–return trade-off of an established spot position, Howard and D'Antonio (1984) proposed the use of total return for the spot asset and price change for the futures contract. In contrast Gjerde (1987) used a performance measure based on expected pay-off. In his analysis of the simultaneous multi-asset (spot/futures) portfolio choice problem, Levy (1987) suggested the use of value relatives for the spot asset and the futures contract (for example, futures return based on margin investment), although he used price relatives (futures return based on 100 per cent margin) in his empirical tests.

It is unfortunate, therefore, that little empirical research exists on the impact of the alternative return measures on futures effectiveness. Some evidence, does exist, however. Dale (1981) used price levels in his analysis of the minimum risk hedge effectiveness of currency futures. Hill and Schneeweis (1982) showed the impact on minimum risk hedge ratios of price change compared with price levels. Empirical results may also be sensitive to the use of price changes versus price relatives. For example, Hill and Schneeweis (1982) obtained different measures of hedging effectiveness for currency futures and treasury bond futures when hedge ratios were based on absolute changes compared with percentage changes in price. Witt *et al.* (1987) investigated the impact of alternative return measures on minimum risk hedge ratios for agricultural commodities, although their results did not confirm the superiority of any single measure.

Recently, Yau *et al.* (1990b) have considered the impact of

Table 7.2 Regression-based minimum risk hedge ratios, January 1984 to October 1986

Bond	*Coupon*	*Maturity date*	*Issue date*	*Hedge ratio*		*Hedging effectiveness*
1	10.50	15 Nov 1992	15 Nov 1982	(1)	0.602	0.84
				(2)	0.528	0.90
				(3)	0.012[bc]	0.80
				(3a)	0.600	
2	14.875	15 Aug 1991	17 Aug 1981	(1)	0.558[a]	0.82
				(2)	0.411[a]	0.88
				(3)	0.009[bc]	0.78
				(3a)	0.460	

Source: Yau *et al.* 1990b

Notes: (1) Results from return, $P_{t+1} - P_t$.
(2) Results from return, $(P_{t+1} - P_t)/P_t$.
(3) Results from return, $(P_{t+1} - P_t + M_t r_t)/M_t$.

[a]Significant at 0.05 level for hedge ratios from (1) versus (2).
[b]Significant at 0.05 level for hedge ratios from (1) versus (3).
[c]Significant at 0.05 level for hedge ratios from (2) versus (3).

alternative return measures on various approaches to testing financial futures performance. As shown in Table 7.2, alternative return measures can give different results in hedge ratio analysis. For instance, for bond 2, the hedge ratios based on price changes and price relatives (100 per cent margin) are significantly different, with the hedge ratio derived from return measures based on initial margin being considerably smaller. In order to produce equal dollar changes, the hedge ratio based on margin must be adjusted by the average price of the futures contract. After this adjustment the hedge ratios (3a) approach those under the other return formulations.

Alternative return measures: problems and uses

The results in Table 7.2 do not imply that one return measure is superior to another. The adoption of a particular measure depends primarily on the objective of the agent. For instance, if the agent is concerned about changes in the level of wealth or has a constrained spot position, then a hedge ratio based on the absolute change in prices may be more appropriate than a hedge ratio derived from the percentage change in prices. On the other hand, if the agent is interested in optimizing the total risk–return trade-off of its investment portfolio and is not subject to wealth or trading constraints, the percentage change in prices is more suitable.[5] While Table 7.2 shows that alternative return measures can affect the empirical results, further research is indicated. The effects of alternative return measures (including expectations), loss measures and risk assumptions (for example, skewness) need to be investigated.[6]

FUTURES CONTRACT PRICING

It has been shown that the use of alternative forms of return measurement can have a dramatic impact on model performance in risk management; hence failure to use the most appropriate pricing model can have a significant impact on the measurement of futures contract performance. The use of simple price changes or price relatives may not adequately indicate the importance of futures contracts in risk management. The simple cost-of-carry model for futures implies a future time series of futures prices, so that a change in expectations than to a change in the current market price (Bell and Krasker 1986; Schwarz *et al.* 1986).

Forward/futures pricing

In recent years new theories and empirical tests have offered perspectives on the price behaviour of financial futures which differ from the simple cost-of-carry arbitrage models. For example, during the delivery month, futures contracts have been shown to provide several options to holders of short positions. In particular, emphasis has been placed on the quality option, or the option to choose the 'cheapest' of a number of deliverable commodities, as well as three timing options regarding delivery (Gay and Manaster 1986). Boyle (1987) and others have extended these ideas to the case of several deliverable assets.

If futures contracts for bonds or notes had no embedded delivery options and no variation margin cash flows, they could be valued as forward contracts. When a simple forward pricing model is used, the forward value is the price of the cheapest to deliver (CTD) plus the financing cost less the income earned by carrying the bond or note, all divided by the conversion factor, which can be expressed as

$$\text{FP} = \frac{\text{CP} + (\text{CP} + \text{ACC}_0)(\text{RP}N/360) - (\text{dACC} + C + C\text{RP}M/360)}{F} \tag{7.12}$$

where CP is the price of the CTD, ACC_0 is the accrued interest on the CTD on settlement date, RP is the term repo date on the CTD to contract delivery, N is the number of days from settlement date to delivery, dACC is the change in accrued interest between settlement date and delivery, C is the amount of coupon dropped (if any) between settlement date and delivery, M is the number of days between coupon dropped and delivery, and F is the conversion factor of the CTD. With this formula, the difference between the theoretical forward price and the actual futures price for treasury bond and treasury note futures contracts can be measured using the actual CTD bond. However, significant differences between the actual futures prices and the theoretical forward prices can be attributed, in part, to various options embedded in the futures contract.

The quality option

The quality option arises because any US Government treasury bond with at least fifteen years remaining to call as of the delivery date can be delivered under the five year treasury bond contract. Correspondingly, any US treasury note with between six and a half and seven years to maturity as of the delivery date can be delivered under the treasury note contract. As in other financial and non-financial futures contracts, the short will generally deliver the cheapest qualifying instrument permitted by the contract specifications. To the holder of a short position, the ability to choose the deliverable bond or note is a valuable right. Therefore we would expect treasury futures to trade below the theoretical value obtained from a forward pricing model by an amount equal to the perceived worth of this option.

Timing option: cost of carry

The short may deliver the CTD treasury bond or treasury note at any time during the delivery month. The ability to choose the delivery day gives rise to the right to earn net carry where the yield curve is positively sloped and to avoid a negative carry where the yield curve is negatively sloped. While the value of this choice, if exercised, removes the opportunity of exercising other timing options (for example, wild card and end of the month), it may affect market pricing.

Timing option: wild card

The wild card option arises from the provision in the treasury bond and treasury note contracts allowing the short to announce its intention to deliver until 8.00 p.m. (US Central Time) on any delivery day, although futures trading closes at 2.00 p.m. Since the government cash markets continue to trade until at least 4.00 p.m. the short may benefit from price movements in the cash market during this interval. The value of this option will depend on factors which affect price changes in the cash market (for example, the underlying price volatility of the cash market and the time to delivery).

Timing option: end of month

While delivery can be made on any business day during the delivery month, the contract ceases trading at 12.00 noon on the eighth day prior to the last business day of that month. Deliveries based on a price fixed on business day 1 can be used to establish the delivery invoice priced up to seven business days later. Depending on the portfolio of bonds that the short has to deliver, value gains can be made at delivery.

Valuing quality and timing options

It is clear that the value, to the short, of these various options on the interest rate futures contract will result in the predicted price of that contract's being less than that given in the cost-of-carry model. Nevertheless, attempts to model the value of these options have only just begun. Boyle (1987) estimates that the impact of the quality and timing options has been in the range 2–6 per cent; these estimates are conditional on assumptions regarding the nature of the option model best describing the pricing process. Other tests (Kane and Marcus 1986) have been based primarily on simulation tests, which have assumed interdependence between futures contracts, the underlying deliverables and option pricing theory.

Pricing models: problems and uses

A European call option model is often used as the basis for the pricing effects of the quality option on futures contracts with multiple deliverables. The European call option, however, fits best for an option on forward contracts. For futures contracts, the profit from the exercise of the quality option (as well as the timing options) is not certain, and an arbitrage argument cannot be used to establish the reduced futures price except under certain special assumptions. For example, an important assumption in this context is that interest rates are non-stochastic (see Courtadon (1982) and Rendleman and Bartter (1980) on the need for restrictions on preferences in valuing options when interest rates are stochastic). While there is empirical evidence that differences between futures prices and forward prices are small (Boyle 1987), there is contrary evidence on the importance of stochastic interest rates and variation margin (Hill *et al.* 1983).

The predictions of the basic futures model incorporating option values, however, are helpful. Despite difficulties in the pricing of the quality option, when there are two or more underlying assets that can be delivered to satisfy the terms of the contract, we can assume that the short will always deliver the least valuable assets, and that this benefit will result in a futures price which differs from that of the traditional cost-of-carry model. The standard cost-of-carry model is not appropriate to derive the futures price because, at inception, it is not known which asset will actually be CTD. The actual benefit of the quality option is derived by Stulz (1982) and depends on the individual variances, cross-products and relative prices of the multiple deliverables.[7]

The benefits of the quality option have been questioned, however. Recently, a more complex option available to arbitrageurs has been discussed, where the cash side of the arbitrage is switched multiple times prior to maturity of the futures. Barnhill and Jordan (1986) argue that a 'switching option' is more valuable than the simple quality option to long-cash–short-futures arbitrageurs. Likewise, Livingston (1987) argues that the switching option allows arbitrageurs the opportunity to eliminate the potential cost that they may have to bear from the quality option by continually switching to the bond with the lowest adjusted forward price. Under such conditions Livingston contends that the quality option will have a zero value and will thus not reduce futures prices prior to maturity. Barnhill (1987) suggests that the minimizing strategy of the short-cash–long-futures arbitrageur forms an upper boundary, and that the profit-maximizing strategy of the long-cash–short-futures arbitrageur offers a lower boundary between which observed futures prices will fluctuate. (The mathematics of the switching option is not discussed in this chapter; see Barnhill (1987) and Livingston (1987)).

Research is required to estimate empirically the relative advantages of these models (see also Arak and Goodman 1987).

CONCLUSIONS

The research discussed in this chapter offers an extension of the performance measurement and pricing process of financial futures. It offers a sound basis for the determination of futures prices based on the traditional cost-of-carry model, the use of variable-proportion asset allocations to futures and alternative models of return determination. Recent advances on the impact of other options (for example, location, inventory, switching, wild card, timing) need to be woven into the pricing model. The inclusion of futures in optimal risk–return portfolios requires analysis not only of financial assets but also of an individual's tradeable and non-tradeable real assets. The most appropriate return formulation is determined in part by the loss function of the individual agent who elects to use futures as part of an asset risk management strategy. Future research in this area needs to take account of the issues discussed above, which offer a guide to future research directions.

APPENDIX 7.1

First-order condition

$$\max \theta = \frac{\bar{R}_p - i}{\sigma_p}$$

$$\bar{R}_p = \frac{C_s P_s \bar{r}_s + C_f P_f \bar{r}_f}{C_s P_s}$$

$$\sigma_p = \frac{1}{C_s P_s (C_s^2 P_s^2 \sigma_s^2 + C_f^2 P_f^2 \sigma_f^2 + 2 C_s C_f P_s P_f \sigma_s \sigma_f p)^{1/2}}$$

where $\bar{R}_p$ is the expected return on the combined portfolio, P_s, P_f are the current prices per unit of the spot and futures respectively, C_s, C_f are the units of spot and futures respectively, $\bar{r}_s$, $\bar{r}_f$ are the one-period expected returns of the spot and futures respectively, i is the risk-free rate, p is the correlation between the returns of the spot and futures and σ_p, σ_s, σ_f are the standard deviations of the portfolio, spot and futures respectively.

$$\theta = \frac{(1/C_s P_s)(C_s P_s \bar{r}_s + C_f P_f \bar{r}_f) - i C_s P_s}{(1/C_s P_s)(C_s^2 P_s^2 \sigma_s^2 + C_f^2 P_f^2 \sigma_f^2 + 2 C_s P_s C_f P_f \sigma_s \sigma_f p)^{1/2}}$$

$$= \frac{A}{E^{1/2}} \frac{1/C_s P_s}{1/C_s P_s}$$

$$\frac{d\theta}{dC_f} = P_f \bar{r}_f E^{-1/2} + (C_s P_s \bar{r}_s + C_f P_f \bar{r}_f - i C_s P_s)$$

$$\left[-\frac{1}{2} E^{-3/2}(2 C_f P_f^2 \sigma_f^2 + 2 C_s P_s P_f \sigma_s \sigma_f p)\right] = 0$$

$$E^{-1/2}\{P_f \bar{r}_f - E^{-1}[(C_s P_s \bar{r}_s + C_f P_f \bar{r}_f - i C_s P_s)(C_f P_f^2 \sigma_f^2 + C_s P_s P_f \sigma_s \sigma_f p)]\} = 0$$

$$E = \frac{1}{P_f \bar{r}_f}(C_s P_s \bar{r}_s + C_f P_f \bar{r}_f - i C_s P_s)(C_f P_f^2 \sigma_f^2 + C_s P_s P_f \sigma_s \sigma_f p)$$

We define L and R as follows:

$$L = C_s^2 P_s^2 \sigma_s^2 + C_f^2 P_f^2 \sigma_f^2 + 2 C_s P_s C_f P_f \sigma_s \sigma_f p$$

$$R = \frac{1}{P_f \bar{r}_f}(C_s P_s \bar{r}_s + C_f P_f \bar{r}_f - i C_s P_s)(C_f P_f^2 \sigma_f^2 + C_s P_s P_f \sigma_s \sigma_f p)$$

$$= \frac{1}{P_f \bar{r}_f} (C_f C_s P_s \bar{r}_s P_f^2 \sigma_f^2 + C_f^2 P_f^3 \sigma_f^2 \bar{r}_f - C_f P_f^2 \sigma_f^2 i C_s P_s$$

$$+ C_s^2 P_s^2 \bar{r}_s P_f \sigma_s \sigma_f p + C_f C_s P_s P_f^2 \bar{r}_f \sigma_s \sigma_f p - i C_s^2 P_s^2 P_f \sigma_s \sigma_f p)$$

$$R = (C_f^2) P_f^2 \sigma_f^2 + (C_f)\left(\frac{C_s P_s \bar{r}_s P_f \sigma_f^2}{\bar{r}_f} - \frac{P_f \sigma_f^2 i C_s P_s}{\bar{r}_f} + C_s P_s P_f \sigma_s \sigma_f p\right)$$

$$+ C_s^2 P_s^2 \sigma_s \sigma_f p \, \frac{\bar{r}_s - i}{\bar{r}_f}$$

$$[L] = [R] \Longrightarrow (C_f^*)(C_s P_s P_f \sigma_f)\left(\sigma_s p - \frac{\bar{r}_s \sigma_f}{\bar{r}_f} + \frac{i \sigma_f}{\bar{r}_f}\right)$$

$$= C_s^2 P_s^2 \sigma_s \left(\sigma_f p \, \frac{\bar{r}_s - i}{\bar{r}_f} - \sigma_s\right)$$

$$(C_f^*)(P_f \sigma_f) \, \frac{\sigma_s p \bar{r}_f - \bar{r}_s \sigma_s + i \sigma_f}{\bar{r}_f} = \frac{(C_s P_s \sigma_s)[\sigma_f p(\bar{r}_s - i) - \bar{r}_f \sigma_s]}{\bar{r}_f}$$

$$C_f^* = \frac{P_s \sigma_s(\sigma_f p \bar{r}_s - \sigma_f p i - \bar{r}_f \sigma_s)}{P_f \sigma_f(\sigma_s \bar{r}_f p - \bar{r}_s \sigma_f + i \sigma_f)} \, C_s$$

$$C_f^* = \frac{[\bar{r}_f \sigma_s - \sigma_f p(\bar{r}_s - i)](P_s \sigma_s)}{\sigma_f[P_f \sigma_f(\bar{r}_s - i) - P_f \bar{r}_f \sigma_s p]} \, C_s$$

$$= \frac{[\bar{r}_f \sigma_s - \sigma_f p(\bar{r}_s - i)]/\sigma_f(\bar{r}_s - i)}{[P_f \sigma_f(\bar{r}_s - i) - P_f \bar{r}_f \sigma_s p]/P_s \sigma_s(\bar{r}_s - i)} \, C_s$$

$$= \frac{\{(\bar{r}_f/\sigma_f)/[(\bar{r}_s - i)/\sigma_s]\} - p}{(P_f \sigma_f / P_s \sigma_s)\{1 - (\bar{r}_f/\sigma_f)p/[(\bar{r}_s - i)/\sigma_s]\}} \, C_s$$

$$C_f^* = \frac{B - p}{\tau \pi (1 - Bp)} \, C_s = b^* C_s$$

$$B = \frac{\bar{r}_f/\sigma_f}{(\bar{r}_s - i)/\sigma_s} \qquad \tau = \frac{P_f}{P_s} \qquad \pi = \frac{\sigma_f}{\sigma_s}$$

$$\mathrm{HE}^* = \frac{\theta C_f^*}{(\bar{r}_s - i)/\sigma_s} = \left[\frac{(1 - 2Bp + B^2)}{1 - p^2}\right]^{1/2}$$

Second-order condition

See Chang and Shanker (1986) and Howard and D'Antonio (1984). For

$$\theta^* = \frac{R_p^* - i}{\sigma_p^*}$$

$$\sigma_p^{*2} = (C_s^2 P_s^2 \sigma_s^2 + C_f^{*2} P_f^2 \sigma_f^2 + 2 C_s C_f^* P_s P_f \sigma_s \sigma_f p) \frac{1}{C_s^2 P_s^2}$$

$$C_f^* = \frac{(B-p)}{1-Bp} \frac{C_s}{P_f \sigma_f / P_s \sigma_s}$$

from the first-order condition.

$$\sigma_p^{*2} = \left\{ C_s^2 P_s^2 \sigma_s^2 + C_s^2 P_s^2 \sigma^2 \left[\frac{(B-p)^2}{(1-Bp)^2} + \frac{2p(B-p)}{(1-Bp)} \right] \right\}$$

$$\times \frac{1}{C_s^2 P_s^2} \geqslant 0$$

$$= \sigma_s^2 + \sigma_s^2 \left[\frac{(B-p)^2}{(1-Bp)^2} + \frac{2p(B-p)}{1-Bp} \right] \geqslant 0$$

So,

$$\frac{(B-p)^2}{(1-Bp)^2} \geqslant -1 - \frac{2p(B-p)}{1-Bp}$$

$$(B-p)^2 > -(1-Bp)^2 - 2p(B-p)(1-Bp)$$

$$B^2 - 2Bp + p^2 > -1 + 2Bp - B^2p^2 - 2Bp + 2B^2p^2$$
$$+ 2p^2 - 2Bp^3$$

$$B^2 - 2Bp - B^2p^2 - p^2 + 2Bp^3 + 1 \geqslant 0$$

$$-2Bp(1-p^2) + B^2(1-p^2) + (1-p^2) \geqslant 0$$

$$(1-p^2)(-2Bp + B^2 + 1) \geqslant 0$$

Owing to transactions costs, the returns on futures and spot assets will not be perfectly correlated, i.e. $p < 1$. If $p < 1$, then $1 - p^2 > 0$ and

$$-2Bp + B^2 + 1 \geqslant 0$$

$$2Bp \leqslant B^2 + 1$$

If $B \leq 1$, then $B^2 + 1 \leq 2$. For a discussion of the magnitude of B, the relative risk–return property of futures and spot assets, see Howard and D'Antonio (1984). Thus

$$2Bp \leqslant 2$$

and

$$Bp \leqslant 1 \Longleftrightarrow \frac{p\bar{r}_{\mathrm{f}}}{\sigma_{\mathrm{f}}} < \frac{\bar{r}_{\mathrm{s}} - i}{\sigma_{\mathrm{s}}}$$

which is the second-order condition.

NOTES

1 For a discussion of alternative methodologies used to obtain minimum risk positions, see Schwarz *et al.* (1986) and Toevs and Jacob (1986).

2 For Ederington (1979), Gjerde (1987), Howard–D'Antonio and Chang–Shanker, the hedging effectiveness measures have different interpretations. Ederington measures the relative reduction in risk as a result of including futures in an established portfolio. This is equivalent to the coefficient of determination of the regression of R_{c} on R_{f}. If $p = 1$, i.e. $R^2 = 1$, there is a perfect forecast hedge position, and if this is held in proper proportions there will be a zero risk. Conversely, when $p = 0$ the effectiveness is zero, indicating that futures are ineffective in reducing the risk of price changes in the spot asset. For Howard–D'Antonio, Chang–Shanker, Elton *et al.* and Gjerde, however, the hedging effectiveness (the REs) depends not only on the correlation between the spot and futures returns but also on the risk–return relatives of spot and futures. Thus, even when the futures and spot price changes are not highly correlated, the benefit of futures in improving the risk–return characteristics of the portfolio may still be significant.

3 While an initial margin is required for a futures position, the margin can be put up in the form of treasury bills which may not represent a direct investment for firms which hold treasury bills as a source of cash liquidity.

4 For a discussion of the benefit of geometric versus arithmetic returns, see Francis and Archer (1979).

5 Others argue that the price at which a futures contract is initiated could be discounted to present value and the discounted price viewed as what the investor would have paid if immediate cash settlement were required (Dale 1981). None of the measures in this study attempts to incorporate the opportunity cost of the treasury bill investment as margin.

6 Bell and Krasker (1986) point out that not all these models include expectations. For a discussion of anticipatory hedging see Schwarz *et al.* (1986) and Witt *et al.* (1987).

7 Boyle (1987) shows that the quality option is important in explaining futures contract pricing even when the underlying assets are highly correlated. He also shows that when there is more than one deliverable asset there is an interaction between the timing option and the quality option. As the correlation between the assets increases, the timing option moves closer to the futures price for the single-asset case.

REFERENCES

Arak, M. and Goodman, L.S. (1987) 'Treasury bond futures: valuing the delivery options', *Journal of Futures Markets* February: 269–86.
Barnhill, T. (1987) 'Valuation of the quality and the switching options and their impact on treasury bond futures prices', *Center for Study of Futures Markets, Columbia University* no. 152, May.
Barnhill, T. and Jordan, J. (1986) 'Perspectives on selection of the optimal cash bond for arbitraging against the treasury bond futures contract', *Center for Study of Futures Markets, Columbia University* no. 146, December.
Bell, D.E. and Krasker, W.S. (1986) 'Estimating hedge ratios', *Financial Management* Summer: 34–39.
Besant, L. and Schneeweis, T. (1986) 'Hedge ratio determination for financial futures: measurement and methodology', in D. Logue (ed.) *Handbook of Modern Finance* pp. 12.1–12.28, Boston, MA: Warren, Gorham & Lamont.
Black, F. (1976) 'The pricing of commodity contracts', *Journal of Financial Economics* January: 167–79.
Boyle, P. (1987) 'The quality option and the timing option in futures contracts', presented at the 3rd Annual International Futures Conference and Research Seminar, Toronto, October 1987.
Chang, J. and Shanker, L. (1986) 'Hedging effectiveness of currency options and currency futures', *Journal of Futures Markets* Summer: 289–305.
—— (1987) 'A risk–return measure of hedging effectiveness: a comment', *Journal of Financial and Quantitative Analysis* 22 (3): 373–6.
Courtadon, G. (1982) 'The pricing of options on default-free bonds', *Journal of Financial Quantitative Analysis* March: 75–100.
Dale, C. (1981) 'The hedging effectiveness of currency futures market', *Journal of Futures Markets* Spring: 77–88.
Ederington, L.H. (1979) 'The hedging performance of the new futures markets', *Journal of Finance* March: 157–70.
Elton, E., Gruber, G. and Rentzler, J. (1987) 'Professionally managed, publicly traded commodity funds', *Journal of Business* April: 175–99.
Francis, J.C. and Archer, S.H. (1987) *Portfolio Analysis*, 2nd edn, Englewood Cliffs, NJ: Prentice-Hall.
Franckle, C. (1980) 'The hedging performance of the new futures markets: a comment', *Journal of Finance* December: 1272–9.
Gay, G. and Manaster, S. (1986) 'Implicit delivery options and optimal delivery strategies for financial futures contracts', *Journal of Financial Economics* May: 41–72.
Gjerde, O. (1987) 'Measuring hedging effectiveness in a traditional one period portfolio framework', *Journal of Futures Markets* December: 663–4.
Hill, J. and Schneeweis, T. (1982) 'The hedging effectiveness of foreign currency futures', *Journal of Financial Research* Spring: 95–104.
—— (1985) 'On the estimation of hedge ratios for corporate bond positions', in F. Fabozzi (ed.) *Advances in Financial Planning and Forecasting*, Greenwich, CT: JAI Press.
Hill, J., Schneeweis, T. and Mayerson, B. (1983) 'An analysis of the impact of

variation margin in hedging fixed-income securities', *Review of Research in Futures Markets* 2 (1): 136–59.

Howard, C.T. and D'Antonio, L.J. (1984) 'A risk–return measure of hedging effectiveness', *Journal of Financial and Quantitative Analysis* March: 101–12.

—— (1987) 'A risk–return measure of hedging effectiveness: a reply', *Journal of Financial and Quantitative Analysis* September: 377–81.

Kane, A. and Marcus, A.J. (1986) 'The quality option in the treasury bond futures market: an empirical assessment', *Journal of Futures Markets* April: 231–48.

Levy, H. (1987) 'Futures, spots, stocks and bonds: multi-asset portfolio analysis', *Journal of Futures Markets* August: 383–95.

Livingston, M. (1987) 'The delivery option on forward contracts', *Journal of Financial and Quantitative Analysis* March: 79–87.

Markowitz, H. (1952) 'Portfolio selection', *Journal of Finance* March: 77–81.

Rendleman, R. and Bartter, B. (1980) 'The pricing of options on debt securities', *Journal of Financial and Quantitative Analysis* March: 11–24.

Schwarz, E., Hill, J. and Schneeweis, T. (1986) *Financial Futures: Fundamentals, Strategies and Applications*, Homewood, IL: Dow–Jones, Irwin.

Sharpe, W. (1972) 'Simple strategies for portfolio diversification: a comment', *Journal of Finance* March: 127–9.

Stulz, R. (1982) 'Options on the minimum or maximum of the two risky assets: analysis and applications', *Journal of Financial Economics* (2): 161–85.

Toevs A.L. and Jacob, D.P. (1986) 'Futures and alternative hedge ratio methodologies', *Journal of Portfolio Management* Spring: 60–70.

Witt, H.J., Schroeder, T.C. and Hayenga, M.L. (1987) 'Comparison of analytical approaches for estimating hedge ratios for agricultural commodities', *Journal of Futures Markets* April: 135–46.

Yau, J., Hill, J. and Schneeweis, T. (1990a) 'An empirical analysis of the effectiveness of the Nikkei 225 futures contracts in risk/return management', *Global Financial Journal* Fall: 255–76.

Yau, J., Savanayana, U. and Schneeweis, T. (1990b) 'The effect of alternative return measures in financial research', in F. Fabozzi (ed.) *Advances in Futures and Options Research*, vol. 4, Greenwich, CT: JAI Press.

8 A rational expectations model of the Australian wool spot and futures markets

Barry A. Goss and S. Gulay Avsar

INTRODUCTION

Australia is the world's leading producer and exporter of fine wool, and typically more than 70 per cent is exported as greasy wool, especially to Japan, the USSR and the European Community. Most of this wool is sold in competitive auction markets in Australia, and since May 1960 agents have been able to use the merino wool contract on the Sydney Futures Exchange (SFE) to improve management of their wool market risks and/or support their expectations of wool prices. Turnover of the wool futures contract peaked at an average of 15,500 lots per month in 1973, although since 1981 interest in this contract has waned with the growth of trading in financial futures on the SFE. The merino wool contract on the SFE provides for delivery of greasy wool 22 micron type 78 (64 type 78 prior to 1976), equivalent to 1,500 kilograms clean weight, in the months of March, May, July, October and December at specified delivery points in Australia.

The Australian Wool Corporation (AWC), a government instrumentality, administers a price support scheme and since 1971 has been a major holder of supply stocks, with proportions varying from 39 to 90 per cent. AWC inventories are not hedged on the SFE.

The Australian wool market has been studied by Snape (1968), who investigated price relationships, Praetz (1975), who tested the weak form efficient markets hypothesis (EMH) and Giles and Goss (1980), who studied forward pricing; Fisher (1983) developed a rational expectations model of the wool spot market, while Goss and Giles (1986) developed a model of wool spot and futures markets with adaptive expectations and Goss (1987) tested the semi-strong form EMH using the forecast error approach. In this chapter we extend the work of Fisher (1983) by incorporating the consumption of wool and the futures market into the analysis, and extend the work of Goss and Giles (1986) by representing expectations according to the rational expectations hypothesis (REH) rather than the adaptive hypothesis.

Theoretical rational expectations models of futures markets have been analysed by Dewbre (1981), Bray (1985) and Stein (1986), and Giles *et al.* (1985) have developed an empirical rational expectations model of the US corn and soybeans markets.

In subsequent sections of this chapter we discuss the specification of the model to be estimated, and the data and estimation. Intra-sample results and post-sample forecasts are presented and analysed, and the model is employed to test the semi-strong form EMH. Some conclusions are presented in the final section.

MODEL SPECIFICATION

Hedging interest in the Australian wool futures market has come from inventory holders, from agents who have sold wool forward (especially Australian exporters), from wool processors (mainly overseas) and only to a minor extent from Australian wool growers. Trading interest has also come from agents who employ risk capital to support their expectations in pursuit of uncertain gain.

The model developed in this chapter has its theoretical foundations in Peston and Yamey (1960), whose model has four categories of agents, namely short hedgers, long speculators in futures, holders of unhedged inventories and consumers, and does not include any explicit representation of expectations. The empirical model of the wool market in Goss and Giles (1986) contains, *inter alia*, behavioural relationships for long and short hedgers and for long and short speculators in futures. The disaggregation of turnover data in that paper is based on interview data which are not available beyond 1978 (and hence do not cover the last six years of the sample period of this paper). The model developed here therefore contains behavioural relationships for four groups of agents:

1 sellers of futures contracts for both hedging and speculative purposes;
2 buyers of futures for both hedging and speculative purposes;
3 holders of unhedged inventories;
4 consumers of raw wool, whose demand is a derived demand.

This classification of agents' actvities gives rise to four separate behavioural relationships. The model contains six endogenous variables, and is completed with the inclusion of two identities. The specification of the behavioural equations is discussed in this section.

Sales of futures are undertaken by short hedgers and short speculators. Whether this combined hedging–speculative equation should be predominantly a hedging relationship or predominantly speculative, or whether the two types of activity should be given approximately equal weight, has been treated as an essentially empirical question.

Specification of such a relationship should reflect the equilibrium conditions for the various types of agent. Following the important contributions of Holbrook Working (for example, see Working 1953a, b), sales of futures by short hedgers, who are assumed to pursue the joint objectives of risk reduction and profit, are taken to be an increasing function of the forward premium (short hedgers gain when the forward premium declines). Sales of futures by short speculators, who expect the futures price to fall, are assumed to vary directly with the current futures prices and inversely with their expected futures price and marginal risk premium (if risk aversion is assumed). Preliminary estimation shows that a version of this equation which includes the current futures price, the expected futures price and non-AWC stocks of wool (to represent the commitments of short hedgers) marginally outperforms, in terms of percentage root mean square error (RMSE) in intrasample and post-sample simulation, a version which includes these variables as well as the cash price (rather than the price spread). Hence the specification of this relationship includes both hedging and speculative elements, and is as follows:

$$\mathrm{HSS}_t = \theta_1 + \theta_2 P_t + \theta_3 P^*_{t+1} + \theta_4 \mathrm{NK}_t + e_{1t} \tag{8.1}$$

where, P_t is the current futures price of wool,[1] P^*_{t+1} is the expected futures prices of short speculators for period $t + 1$ formed in period t, NK_t denotes the non-AWC stocks of raw wool and e_{1t} is an error term. The expected signs of the coefficients are θ_1 constant, θ_2, $\theta_4 >$ 0 and $\theta_3 < 0$.

It is assumed that P^*_{t+1} is a rational expectation of the futures price in period $t + 1$, conditional on the set of information available at time t (see Muth 1961). The relevant information set is all publicly available information, and the REH assumes that agents use such information efficiently. The REH also assumes that agents correctly anticipate future prices, in the sense that the subjective probability distributions of agents equal the objective probability distribution of the system.[2] In an operational sense this means that the mean of agents' subjective probability distributions of prices for $t + 1$ coincides with the one-step-ahead prediction of the model. The REH implies that agents have this model in mind in forming their expectations, so that any test of the REH is necessarily a joint test of the expectations hypothesis and the economic model. That is, the REH implies that the model which agents believe determines returns is the same as the model driving returns in reality. If this were not so, then abnormal returns would occur.

Since the REH assumes that agents use all relevant information efficiently, expectational errors will have an expected value of zero and will not be serially correlated with the elements of the information set. This does not mean, of course, that the error terms in the equations in this study will necessarily be serially independent, because unknown specification errors could occur.

The literature on economics suggests that one way in which agents in reality learn to form rational expectations is by using consistently the same forecasting rule, and by having a long history of decision-making in the industry in question (see, for example, Hirsch and Lovell 1969; Blume, *et al.* 1982). This idea is, at least, not inconsistent with the Australian wool industry. Some experimental support for the notion of achievement of rational expectations equilibrium in the short term in futures markets has been found by Friedman *et al.* (1983), and experimental support for the concept of rationality is further discussed by Harrison in Chapter 4 of this volume.

The demand for futures contracts is provided by long hedgers and long speculators. Long hedgers are agents who have sold raw wool and/or wool products forward, such as processors or Australian wool exporters, and who use the futures contract as a substitute for a merchandising contract (see Working 1953b). Their demand for futures can be expected to vary inversely with the current forward premium and directly with their expected forward premium. Long speculators expect the futures price to rise, and hence their purchases of futures contracts can be expected to vary directly with their expected futures price and inversely with the current futures price and their marginal risk premium. Initial estimation showed that the hedging components dominated this equation, and the inclusion of variables to represent purely speculative activities had a detrimental effect on the signs of the estimated coefficients. Hence the specification of the demand function for futures contracts is

$$\mathrm{HSL}_t = \theta_5 + \theta_6(P_t - A_t) + \theta_7(P_{t+1} - A_{t+1})^* + \theta_8 X_{t+2} + e_{2t} \tag{8.2}$$

where $\theta_6 < 0$, θ_7, $\theta_8 > 0$ and X_{t+2}, which is exports of raw wool two periods ahead, represents the commitments of long hedgers. It is assumed that current planned exports are realized two periods later, this lead being suggested by initial estimation. Long hedgers' rational expectation of the price spread next period is represented by $(P_{t+1} - A_{t+1})^*$.

Unhedged inventories of wool are held by the AWC, which buys wool at times of deficient demand and sells it at times of buoyant demand, and by private sector agents, who expect the spot price to rise. Hence no theoretical distinction is made in the unhedged inventory equation between the holding of unhedged stocks by these two groups of agents. This relationship exhibits the characteristics of a speculative demand function (see Kaldor 1939; Brennan 1958), and the volume of unhedged inventories varies inversely with the current spot price, the marginal net cost of storage and the marginal risk premium, and directly with the expected spot price. In initial estimation, superior results were obtained with versions of this equation which did not contain the storage cost or risk premium variables (although this is not a cause for concern[3]). Therefore specification of the unhedged inventory relationship is

$$U_t = \theta_9 + \theta_{10}A_t + \theta_{11}A^*_{t+1} + e_{3t} \qquad (8.3)$$

where U_t is the volume of unhedged inventories at time t, A^*_{t+1} is the rational expectation of the spot price at time $t + 1$ (formed at time t) by agents holding unhedged stocks, and $\theta_{10} < 0$, $\theta_{11} > 0$.

Raw wool is an input in the production of woollen garments and other wool products. The demand for raw wool, which is a derived demand, is a function of the current spot price, the parameters of the demand for final products and the parameters of the supply of other inputs. In this study, the parameters of end-product demand are represented by expected real household disposable income, and the relative price of synthetic fibres, which are a substitute for wool, is employed to represent the parameters of supply of other inputs. In initial estimation, less satisfactory results were obtained with the REH, and hence expected real income is represented by the adaptive hypothesis (Nerlove 1958). In preliminary estimation also, the signs of estimated coefficients in this equation were more consistent with expectations if the price of wool relative to that of synthetics is lagged one period. The last two factors suggest that decisions of consumers of raw wool may not adjust to changes in market conditions as rapidly as those of other agents represented in this model. The consumption of raw wool, which is taken as log linear following research by the

Bureau of Agricultural Economics (1967), is given by the following relationship:

$$\ln C_t = a_1 + b_1 \ln Y^*_{t+1} + b_2 \ln\left(\frac{A}{S}\right)_{t-1} + u_{4t} \tag{8.4a}$$

where C_t is the consumption of raw wool, Y^*_{t+1} is the expected real household disposable income according to the adaptive expectations hypothesis, S_t is the spot price of synthetic fibres, $b_1 > 0$ and $b_2 < 0$, and

$$Y^*_{t+1} = (1-\lambda)\frac{Y_t}{1-\lambda L} \qquad 0 < \lambda < 1$$

where L is the lag operator. Substitution for Y^*_{t+1} in (8.4a) gives the following specification for the consumption equation:

$$\ln C_t = \theta_{12} + \theta_{13} \ln Y_t + \theta_{14} \ln\left(\frac{A}{S}\right)_{t-1} + \theta_{15} \ln\left(\frac{A}{S}\right)_{t-2} + \theta_{16} \ln C_{t-1} + e_{4t} \tag{8.4b}$$

where $\theta_{13}, \theta_{15} > 0$, $\theta_{14} < 0$ and $0 < \theta_{16} < 1$.

This model, with six endogenous variables (HSS, HSL, U, C, P, A), is completed with the identities

$$\text{HSS}_t \equiv \text{HSL}_t \tag{8.5}$$

$$K_t \equiv U_t + \text{HSL}_t \tag{8.6}$$

where K_t represents total stocks of raw wool. Identity (8.5) is a futures market clearing identity, and (8.6) states that total stocks of raw wool comprise unhedged stocks and hedged stocks.[4] Each of the structural equations in the model is overidentified.

DATA AND ESTIMATION

Data

Data on HSS and HSL are the monthly turnover of wool contracts on the SFE for the period February 1974 to March 1984 from the SFE *Statistical Yearbook*, 1980–4 (weekly summaries prior to 1980). Cash price data are daily prices (see Gilbert 1986) for 22 micron type 78 (21 micron in 1976, good 64s prior to 1976) on the median trading day of each month from AWC *Wool Market News*. Similarly, futures price data are daily prices for the median trading day each month for the contract grade for a future approximately six months prior to delivery from the SFE *Statistical Yearbook* (see note 1). Wool spot and futures prices are quoted in Australian cents per kilogram clean basis.

Data on NK, *C*, *K* and *X* are from the Australian Bureau of Statistics (ABS), in million kilograms clean basis converted to contracts. Data on *U* are unobservable, and identity (8.6) was used to calculate *U*. This resulted in three negative values of *U* (January–March 1980), which were deleted because this model is not defined for negative storage.

Real disposable income is Australian household disposable income divided by the consumer price index from the ABS, while synthetic price data are for 70 denier Japanese acrylic tow from the *Japan Textile News* (various issues), converted to Australian dollars at the Reserve Bank of Australia spot rate. Data on *C* and NK are on an annual basis interpolated to monthly, while data on *Y* are quarterly interpolated to monthly.

Estimation

Since, as far as we are aware, there is no existing computer program designed for the estimation of a simultaneous rational expectations model with forward expectations, the method of McCallum (1979) was employed to estimate the coefficients of the structural equations of this model. This method uses the instrumental variable (IV) technique to obtain consistent estimates of the parameters. The property of simultaneity is imparted to the estimation by defining the rational expectations information set to include all exogenous and predetermined variables in the system (see below).

In equation (8.1), for example, the expected futures price is conditional on the set ϕ_t of publicly available information at time *t*, so that

$$P^*_{t+1} = \mathrm{E}(P_{t+1}/\phi_t)$$
$$P_{t+1} = \mathrm{E}(P_{t+1}/\phi_t) + \eta_t$$

where rational expectations requires that $\mathrm{E}(\eta_t) = 0$ and η_t is uncorrelated with the elements of ϕ_t. In this case the information set ϕ_t is defined to comprise all exogenous and predetermined variables in the model (including lagged endogenous variables). A suitable proxy for P^*_{t+1} is found by regressing P_{t+1} on a representative subset of variables in ϕ_t using ordinary least squares (OLS). This yields a least squares prediction $\hat{P}_{t+1}$, which is a valid instrument for P^*_{t+1}.

Where the residuals of the structural equation are not serially correlated, estimation of that equation is straightforward, as in the case of equation (8.3) (demand for unhedged storage) in this model. The IV technique is employed, with current values of exogenous variables in the relevant equation acting as their own instruments, and lagged values of endogenous variables in that equation acting as instruments for those variables. The instrument for the rational expectation of the price variable is the least squares prediction, obtained as described above, for that variable for the next period. In (8.3), for example, $\hat{A}_{t+1}$, derived as above, is employed as a proxy for A^*_{t+1}. These instruments will yield consistent estimates, and the INST routine in TSP (Hall 1986) can be used.[5]

Where the residuals of the structural equation are serially correlated, a simple autoregressive (AR) correction with IV estimates will yield inconsistent estimates, as noted by Flood and Garber (1980). Instead, the method of McCallum (1979) has been employed. This involves first making an AR transformation of the relevant equation. In (8.1), for example, where there was evidence of first-order autocorrelation, the equation was lagged one period and multiplied by the AR coefficient ρ_1, and the result was subtracted from (8.1). Each of the variables in the transformed equation was then regressed on a representative subset of the variables in the relevant ϕ, using OLS, to obtain predicted or fitted values of each, which were then substituted into the transformed equation. For equation (8.1) this procedure gives

$$\begin{aligned} \mathrm{HSS}_t = {} & \theta_1(1-\rho_1) + \rho_1 \mathrm{H\hat{S}S}_{t-1} + (\theta_2 - \theta_3\rho_1)\hat{P}_t \\ & - \theta_2\rho_1\hat{P}_{t-1} + \theta_3\hat{P}_{t+1} + \theta_4 \mathrm{N\hat{K}}_t \\ & - \theta_4\rho_1 \mathrm{N\hat{K}}_{t-1} + (e_{1t} - \rho_1 e_{1t-1}) \end{aligned} \tag{8.7}$$

Consistent estimates of the coefficients in (8.7) were obtained by using the non-linear least squares option LSQ in TSP (Hall 1986). This method of estimation was employed for equations (8.1) and (8.2).

In equation (8.4b), where expected real disposable income is represented according to the adaptive hypothesis, a correction for first-order autocorrelation was made. The transformed equation was then estimated by the IV technique to yield consistent estimates of the coefficients.[6]

RESULTS

The coefficients of the structural model contained in relationships (8.1)–(8.6) were estimated according to the procedure described in the previous section for the sample period February 1974 to December 1980 (eighty observations). The estimated values of these coefficients, together with asymptotic *t* values, are given in Table 8.1. It will be seen that all twelve structural parameter estimates have the anticipated sign, although only 42 per cent are clearly significant while another 16 per cent are almost significant at the 5 per cent level (one-tail test). Of the three rational expectations coefficients, that in

Table 8.1 Parameter estimates: equations (8.1)–(8.4)

Coefficient	*Variable*	*Estimate*	*Asymptotic t Value*	*Equation*
θ_1	Const.	−7,762.500	−0.847	(8.1)
θ_2	P_t	66.400	2.147	
θ_3	P^*_{t+1}	−47.213	−1.583	
θ_4	NK_t	0.905	1.780	
$\hat{\rho}_1$		0.702	3.698	
DW = 1.8089				
θ_5	Const.	1,491.700	0.386	(8.2)
θ_6	$P_t - A_t$	−38.893	1.065	
θ_7	$(P_{t+1} - A_{t+1})^*$	19.825	0.384	
θ_8	X_{t+2}	0.180	1.608	
$\hat{\rho}_2$		0.782	8.546	
DW = 1.8718				
θ_9	Const.	180.250×10^3	8.576	(8.3)
θ_{10}	A_t	−2,835.500	−3.292	
θ_{11}	A^*_{t+1}	2,476.600	2.905	
DW = 1.9409				
θ_{12}	Const.	1.212	1.199	(8.4b)
θ_{13}	$ln\, Y_t$	0.048	0.406	
θ_{14}	$ln(A/S)_{t-1}$	−0.599	−0.799	
θ_{15}	$ln(A/S)_{t-2}$	0.447	0.702	
θ_{16}	$ln\, C_{t-1}$	0.913	13.692	
$\hat{\rho}_4$		0.345	3.242	
DW = 2.1105				

Note: DW, Durbin–Watson statistic.

Table 8.2 Intrasample simulation assessment

Variable	*Correlation coefficient*	*Theil's inequality coefficient*	*%RMSE*
P	0.9706	0.0487	5.377
A	0.9843	0.0368	3.969
U	0.9957	0.0474	39.196[a]
$ln\ C$	0.9574	0.0070	0.713[b]
HSS,HSL	0.6659	0.3772	72.788

Notes: [a]This %RMSE value is affected by six outliers; when these outliers are clipped the %RMSE for U is 8.758%.
[b]This is the %RMSE for the difference between simulated and actual values of $ln\ C$. The corresponding figure for the difference between simulated and actual values of C is 5.253%.

the unhedged inventory equation is clearly significant and that in the sales of futures function approaches significance, while the other is clearly not significant. Hence there is at least adequate support for the REH, although the first result is important because most inventories are held unhedged.

The Durbin–Watson (DW) statistics suggest that there is no serial correlation in equation (8.3), and no remaining serial correlation in (8.1), (8.2) and (8.4b) after the AR1 correction (although the DW test is only approximate under IV estimation).

In equation (8.4b) the estimated income elasticity of demand $\hat{\theta}_{13}$ indicates that wool is a superior good, as anticipated, and the adaptive expectations coefficient $\hat{\theta}_{16}$ is between zero and unity as required.

An assessment of the intrasample simulation performance of this model is presented in Table 8.2 and Figures 8.1–8.3, and is of a high standard for the cash and futures prices, consumption and unhedged inventories, but is only moderately good for sales (and purchases) of futures contracts. Compared with the intrasample simulation performance of an essentially similar model but with adaptive expectations for the same sample period, reported by Goss (1990), it is apparent that the simulation of the cash and futures prices by the Muth rational expectations (MRE) model presented here is clearly superior, while that of the other variables is essentially the same for both models. This difference is perhaps attributable to the characteristic of the MRE model which permits agents to use all available information, while the adaptive model restricts agents to using only a fraction (endogenous) of prior expectational error.

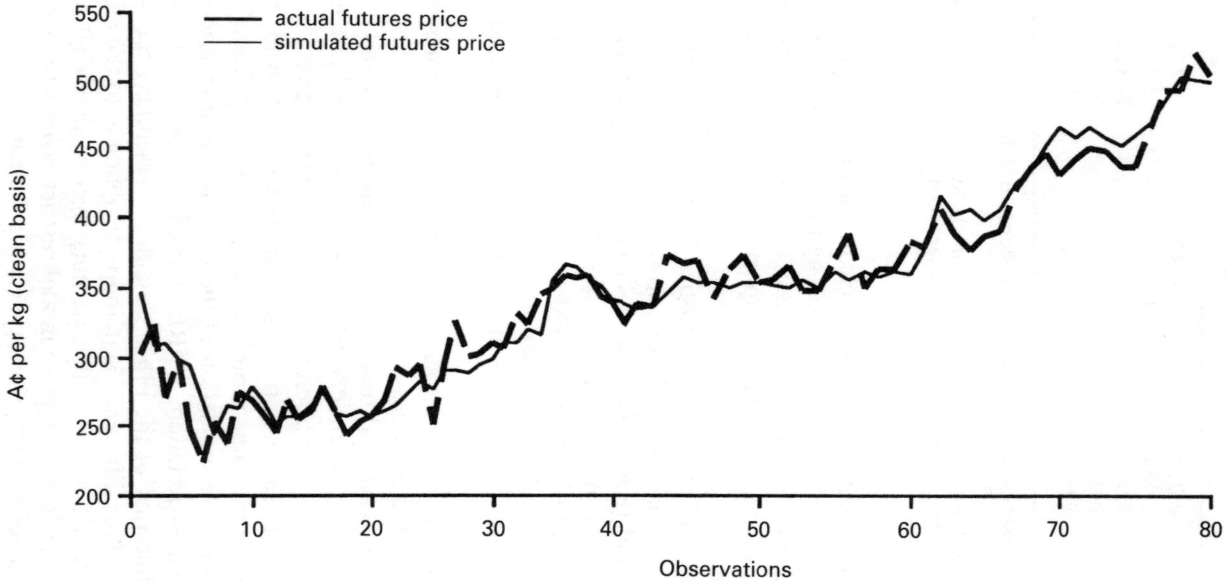

Figure 8.1 Futures prices

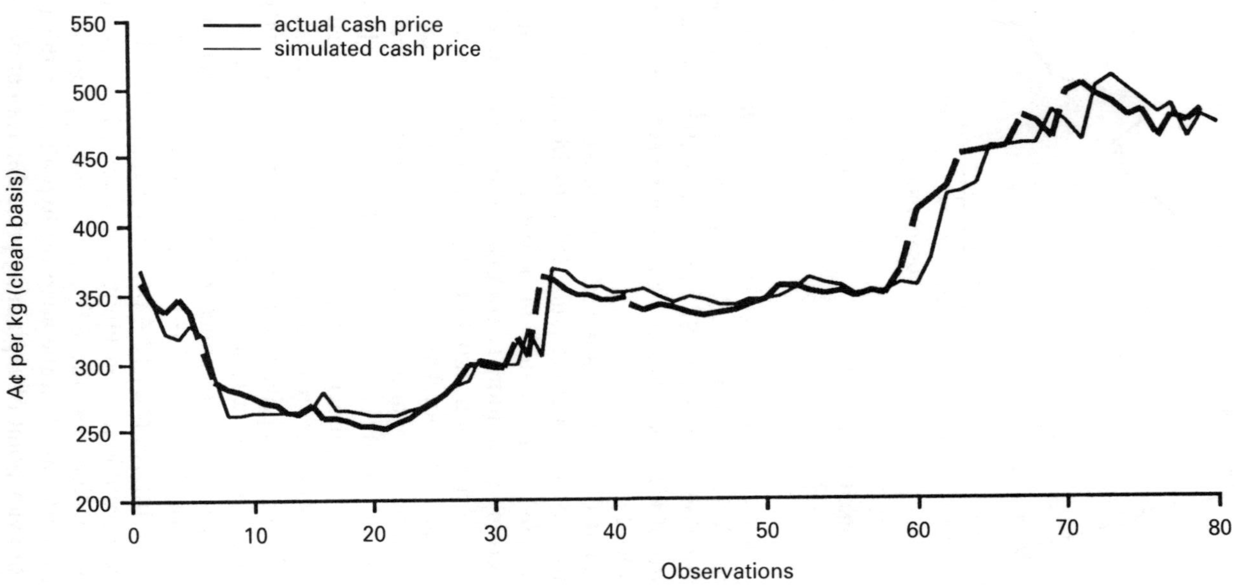

Figure 8.2 Cash prices

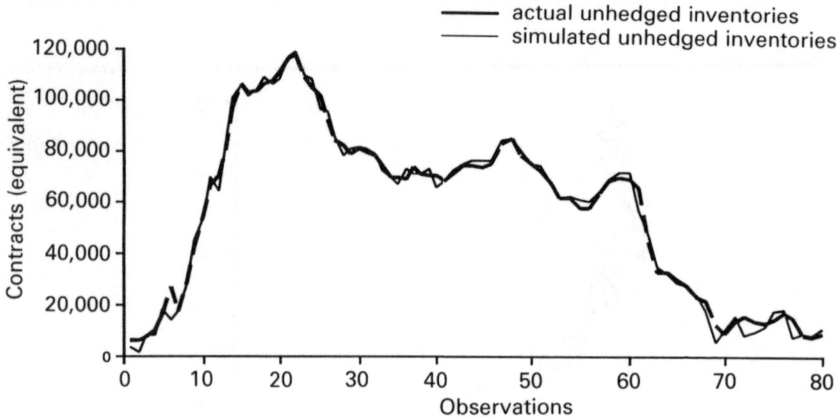

Figure 8.3 Unhedged inventories

These results suggest that the REH is a more appropriate representation of the Australian wool market than the adaptive model. The mediocre simulation of HSS (=HSL) by both models may be due to the thin nature of the wool futures market in recent years (see Goss 1990: Appendix 1).

An assessment of the simulation of the endogenous variables for the post-sample forecast period (July 1981 to March 1984, thirty-three observations) is presented in Table 8.3. According to the %RMSE criterion, simulation is comparatively good for cash and futures prices, consumption and unhedged inventories and is relatively poor for sales (and purchases) of futures contracts. Post-sample simulation is either comparable with, or superior to, intrasample simulation for all variables except HSS (=HSL) for which it is noticeably inferior, a result which may be due to the continual decline in turnover of the wool futures contract (which is now virtually zero).

Compared with the adaptive model reported by Goss (1990), again according to the %RMSE criterion for the same post-sample forecast period, the simulation performance of the MRE model presented here is superior for the cash price (4.7 per cent compared with 6.5 per cent) and the futures price (3.4 per cent compared with 19.8 per cent), and is comparable for consumption and unhedged inventories.[7] This confirms the view that the REH is a more appropriate representation of expectations than the adaptive hypothesis in this market, at least from the viewpoint of explaining price determination.

Table 8.3 Post-sample simulation assessment

Variable	*Correlation coefficient*	*Theil's inequality coefficient*	*%RMSE*
P	0.8802	0.0336	3.411
A	0.8572	0.0475	4.667
U	0.9978	0.0391	6.845
ln C	0.5323	0.0040	0.403[a]
HSS,HSL	0.3462	0.8723	148.252

Note: [a]This is the%RMSE for the difference between simulated and actual values of *ln C*. The corresponding figure for the difference between simulated and actual values for *C* is 2.958%.

The post-sample simulation referred to above was executed with continual updating of the model, i.e after each monthly forecast, the sample period was extended by one month and the model coefficients were re-estimated. The purpose of this updating was to facilitate the test of the EMH discussed in the following section. For the same reason the forecast period does not abut the sample period, but the post-sample forecasts are always six months ahead.

TESTS OF THE EFFICIENT MARKETS HYPOTHESIS

To some authors (for example, Sheffrin 1985: 112), the REH and the EMH are identical, with the latter being merely an application of the former to asset markets. To others (for example, Minford and Peel 1986: 123), the EMH is a joint hypothesis about expectations and market behaviour. The second view seems more persuasive, since the EMH requires not only the formation of expectations which use all relevant information, but the elimination of abnormal gains from expected returns. Hence it is assumed here that the EMH requires rational expectations (i.e. that agents know the model determining actual returns), risk neutrality and the use of all information to the point where marginal return equals marginal cost.

As explained in the first section, the semi-strong EMH is tested in this chapter by employing the structural model presented here to forecast the cash price six months ahead during the post-sample forecast period. These forecasts are compared with those implicit in the futures price six months ahead, and the EMH must be rejected if the model significantly outperforms the futures price as an anticipation of the cash price. The updating of the model, which was

Table 8.4 Post-sample forecasts of the cash price

Variable	*Correlation coefficient*	*Theil's inequality coefficient*	*%RMSE*
P	0.8006	0.0407	4.009
AS	0.8572	0.0475	4.667
CP[a]	0.9104	0.0217	2.182

Note: [a]CP = 0.64AS + 0.37*P* (see text).

undertaken in producing the post-sample forecasts, ensures that the futures price and the model are put on the same informational footing so that the comparison is valid.

Assessments of post-sample forecasts of the cash price are presented in Table 8.4. It will be seen that according to the %RMSE criterion the futures price *P* outperforms the model predictor AS in anticipating the cash price six months ahead, although the difference between the two is not statistically significant (see Appendix).

Nevertheless, each of these two predictors contains information which the other does not, as is clear from Figure 8.4. Hence a composite predictor, which is a weighted average of these two, would

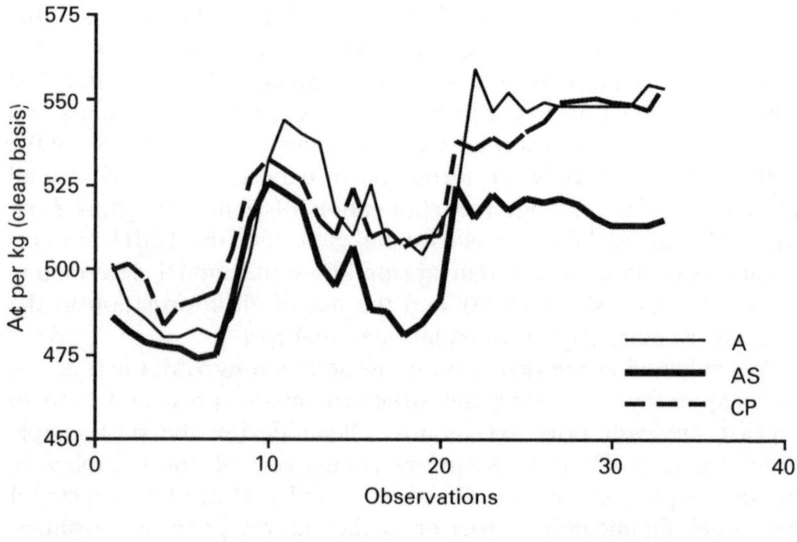

Figure 8.4 Post-sample simulation

be expected to outperform both P and AS. To investigate this possibility a composite predictor CP was formed as a weighted average of P and AS. The weights were estimated by OLS as follows (the weights were not constrained to add to unity, and the asymptotic t statistics are in parentheses):

$$\underset{}{\mathrm{CP}_{t-6,t}} = \underset{(5.756)}{0.64\mathrm{AS}_{t-6,t}} + \underset{(3.589)}{0.37P_{t-6,t}} \tag{8.8}$$

$$\mathrm{DW} = 2.1168$$

It can be seen from Table 8.4 that CP clearly outperforms P as an anticipation of the cash price during the post-sample forecast period, and that the difference in performance between the two is statistically significant (See Appendix). This result is similar to that given by Goss (1990) in which a composite predictor, derived from the adaptive model and the futures price, significantly outperformed the futures price.

This outcome is evidence against the semi-strong EMH, although caution should be exercised in rejecting that hypothesis until evidence is obtained on the question of whether agents are learning, over time, to utilize the information contained in the model presented here.

The conclusion in this section, therefore, is that some evidence against the EMH has been obtained in that the rational expectations model presented here contains information which can be utilized to improve the prediction of the cash price which is contained in the futures price.

CONCLUSIONS

The REH is an appropriate representation of expectations formation in the Australian wool spot and futures markets, and is preferred to the adaptive hypothesis in the sense that the structural model presented here yields superior intrasample and post-sample price forecasts when the REH is employed.

There is strong support for the REH in the unhedged inventory demand function, moderate support in the formation of futures price expectations in the supply of futures function (speculative and hedging) and weak support in the formation of expectations of the price spread in the futures demand function (essentially hedging).

On the other hand, the REH appears inappropriate to represent expected income in the consumption demand for raw wool, and in this function the adaptive hypothesis is preferred. In all cases, of course, any test of the REH is a joint test of the expectations hypothesis and of the appropriateness of the economic model under review.

The simultaneous model presented here evidently contains information which can be used to improve significantly the post-sample forecast of the cash price contained in the futures price, and in that sense evidence against the semi-strong form EMH has been obtained.

APPENDIX 8.1

Relative performance of AS and *P* as predictors of *A* (post-sample forecast period)

Let

$$A - \mathrm{AS} = e_1$$

$$A - P = e_2$$

where

$$\bar{e}_1 = 20.172 \qquad \mathrm{SD}_{e_1} = 14.699$$

$$\bar{e}_2 = -10.052 \qquad \mathrm{SD}_{e_2} = 19.041$$

Neither of the hypotheses $\mathrm{H}(\mu_{e_1} = 0)$ and $\mathrm{H}(\mu_{e_2} = 0)$ can be rejected. Define $S = e_1 + e_2$ and $D = e_1 - e_2$. It is reasonable to assume that both AS and P are unbiased predictors of A; hence the formula for the correlation coefficient between S and D is as given by Granger and Newbold (1986: 279). It can be inferred that the difference between the %RMSEs of P and AS, as forecasts of A, are significantly different from zero. The value of r is 0.1657. The hypothesis $\mathrm{H}(\mu_r = 0)$ can be tested by the statistic

$$t = r/s_r$$

where $s_r = [(1 - r^2)/(n-2)]^{1/2}$ and n is the number of observations. In this case r is not significantly different from zero, and it must be inferred that AS does not significantly outperform P as a predictor of A.

Relative performance of CP and *P* as predictors of *A*

Let

$$A - \mathrm{CP} = e_3$$

where

$$\bar{e}_3 = -0.05664 \qquad SD_{e_3} = 11.517$$

Hence the hypothesis $H(\mu_{e_3} = 0)$ cannot be rejected. Define $S_1 = e_2 + e_3$ and $D_1 = e_2 - e_3$. It can be inferred that CP is significantly superior to P, as a predictor of A, if the coefficient of correlation r_1 between S_1 and D_1 is significantly different from zero. The value of r_1 is -0.6254, using the formula given by Granger and Newbold (1986: 279). The significance of r_1 can be tested by the statistic $t = r_1/s_{r1} = -4.462$, which is significant. Hence it can be inferred that the composite predictor CP significantly outperforms the futures price P as a post-sample predictor of the cash price, according to the %RMSE criterion.

NOTES

An earlier version of this chapter was presented at the Economics Seminar, University of Bologna, Italy, in November 1989 and at the Workshop on Financial Econometrics, University of Canterbury, Christchurch, New Zealand in June 1990. Thanks are due to David Giles, Giorgio Basevi, Gian Paulo Casadio and Massimo Ricottilli, for helpful comments. Remaining errors are the sole responsibility of the authors. The research reported in this chapter was supported by a grant from the Australian Wool Corporation.

1 In order to generate a continuous series of futures prices the following rule was applied:

> when the month is January/February, the future is July;
> when the month is March/April, the future is October;
> when the month is May/June/July, the future is December;
> when the month is August/September, the future is March;
> when the month is October/November, the future is May;
> when the month is December, the future is July.

2 It is not necessary to assume identical expectations as between agents, and the participation of all agents is not necessary for the elimination of excess returns (see Sheffrin 1985).

3 The equilibrium condition for agents holding unhedged stocks can be written $A^*_{t+1} - A_t = m_t + r_t$. Hence the effect of the variables on the right is already taken into account by the variables on the left.

4 In (8.6) it is assumed that all futures market turnover relates to hedging, which is possibly an overstatement. In the absence of disaggregated data on hedging, however, no superior alternative is available.

5 In the IV estimation of (8.3) the instruments employed are A_{t-1}, $\hat{A}_{t+1}$ and U_{t-1}.

6 In the IV estimation of (8.4b) the instruments employed are $ln\, Y_{t-1}$, $ln(A/S)_{t-3}$, $ln(A/S)_{t-4}$ and $ln\, C_{t-2}$.

7 Post-sample forecasts of HSS (=HSL) by the MRE model are noticeably inferior to those of the adaptive model.

REFERENCES

Blume, L.E., Bray, M.M. and Easley, D. (1982) 'Introduction to the stability of rational expectations equilibrium', *Journal of Economic Theory* 26: 313–17.

Bray, M.M. (1985) 'Rational expectations, information and asset markets: an introduction', *Oxford Economic Papers* 37: 161–95.

Brennan, M.J. (1958) 'The supply of storage', *American Economic Review* 48: 50–72.

Bureau of Agricultural Economics (1967) '*The price elasticity of demand for wool in the United Kingdom*, Wool Economic Research Report 11, Canberra.

Dewbre, J.H. (1981) 'Interrelationships between spot and futures markets: some implications of rational expectations', *American Journal of Agricultural Economics* 63: 926–33.

Fisher, B.S. (1983) 'Rational expectations in the Australian wool industry', *Australian Journal of Agricultural Economics* 27 (3): 212–20.

Flood, R.P. and Garber, P.M. (1980) 'A pitfall in estimation of models with rational expectations', *Journal of Monetary Economics* 6: 433–5.

Friedman, D., Harrison, G.W. and Salmon, J.W. (1983) 'The informational role of futures markets: some experimental evidence', in M.E. Streit (ed.) *Futures Markets: Modelling, Managing and Monitoring Futures Trading*, Oxford: Basil Blackwell.

Gilbert, C.L. (1986) 'Testing the efficient markets hypothesis on averaged data', *Applied Economics* 18: 1149–66.

Giles, D.E.A. and Goss, B.A. (1980) 'The predictive quality of futures prices, with an application to the Sydney wool futures market', *Australian Economic Papers* 19: 291–300.

Giles, D.E.A., Goss, B.A. and Chin, O.P.L. (1985) 'Intertemporal allocation in the corn and soybean markets with rational expectations', *American Journal of Agricultural Economics* 67 (4): 749–60.

Goss, B.A. (1987) 'Wool prices and publicly available information', *Australian Economic Papers* 26 (49): 225–36.

—— (1990) 'The forecasting approach to efficiency in the wool market', *Applied Economic Papers* 22: 973–93.

Goss, B.A. and Giles, D.E.A. (1986) 'Intertemporal allocation in the Australian wool market', in B.A. Goss (ed.) *Futures Markets: Their Establishment and Performance*, London: Croom-Helm, Chapter 4, pp. 93–118.

Granger, C.W.J. and Newbold, P. (1986) *Forecasting Economic Time Series*, 2nd edn, London: Academic Press.

Hall, B.H. (1986) *Time Series Processor Version 4.1B Reference Manual*, Stanford University.

Hirsch, A.A. and Lovell, M.C. (1969) *Sales Anticipations and Inventory Behaviour*, New York: Wiley.

Kaldor, N. (1939) 'Speculation and economic stability', *Review of Economic*

Studies 7: 1–27. Reprinted in N. Kaldor, *Essays in Economic Stability and Growth*, pp. 17–58, London: Duckworth, 1961.

McCallum, B.T. (1979) 'Topics concerning the formulation, estimation and use of macroeconomic models with rational expectations', *Proceedings of the Business and Economic Statistics Section*, pp. 65–72, Washington, DC: American Statistical Association.

Minford, P. and Peel, D. (1986) *Rational Expectations and the New Macroeconomics*, Oxford: Basil Blackwell.

Muth, J. (1961) 'Rational expectations and the theory of price movements', *Econometrica* 29: 315–35.

Nerlove, M. (1958) 'Adaptive expectations and cobweb phenomena', *Quarterly Journal of Economics* 72: 227–40.

Peston, M.H. and Yamey, B.S. (1960) 'Intertemporal price relationships with forward markets: a method of analysis', *Economica* 27: 355–67.

Praetz, P.D. (1975) 'Testing the efficient markets theory on the Sydney Wool Futures Exchange', *Australian Economic Papers* 14 (25): 240–9.

Sheffrin, S.M. (1985) *Rational Expectations*, Cambridge: Cambridge University Press.

Snape, R.H. (1968) 'Price relationships on the Sydney Wool Futures Market', *Economica* 35: 169–78.

Stein, J.L. (1986) *The Economics of Futures Markets*, Oxford: Basil Blackwell.

Working, H. (1953a) 'Futures trading and hedging', *American Economic Review* 43: 313–43.

—— (1953b) 'Hedging reconsidered', *Journal of Farm Economics* 35: 544–61.

9 The announcement effects of economic variables

Ting-Yean Tan

In this chapter, the announcement effects of economic variables on interest rate futures prices on the Sydney Futures Exchange (ninety-day bank accepted bills) will be investigated. We shall be concerned with the abnormal return on the day of the announcement of the money supply, the inflation rate and the balance of payments. The null hypothesis to be tested here is that the expected rate of return to the interest rate futures contract should be equal to zero if there is no abnormal market performance. Two similar methods will be used based on the daily rates of return of the interest rate futures contract. The first is the cumulative average abnormal returns (CAAR) approach which was introduced by Ball and Brown (1968) and Fama *et al.* (1969)[1] without statistical tests. The second approach is that of Patell, Dodd and Warner which is based on the cumulative abnormal returns method, where the abnormal returns are standardized by their estimated standard deviations. The latter method was developed by Patell (1976: 256), improved by Dodd (1980: 111–21) and published by Dodd and Warner (1983: 436–7).

Since market price is assumed to be sensitive to any new information in the market, it is relevant to examine whether prices react to new information contained in government announcements. Prices are expected to respond to any important news or surprises contained in those announcements, and if the market is efficient these responses will be immediate. Researchers have argued that it is the unanticipated events (news or surprises) contained in the particular announcement which would give rise to changes in financial prices, because all expected events have already been incorporated in the price prior to the announcement. Dornbusch (1980) and Frenkel (1981) were among the first to suggest that exchange rate movements respond basically to unexpected new information.

Conklin (1983) was probably the first economist to apply the methodology of event studies in the area of futures markets. He used cross-spectral analysis to examine whether announcements of grain export sales have any effect on grain futures prices. His empirical results showed that futures prices react immediately to the unexpected component of the announcements. He therefore concluded that the grain futures market in the United States is semi-strong form efficient.

Woodward (1986) examined the effects of monetary surprises on futures prices in the US treasury bill and treasury bond markets. However, he was not interested in testing the efficient markets hypothesis. Nevertheless, conclusions on market efficiency can be inferred from his empirical results. He regressed unexpected changes in the money supply on changes in futures prices, and found most coefficients to be significant. These results suggest that the futures markets in his study are efficient, and they also support the expected inflation hypothesis.

The method used by Chance (1985a, b) in his studies on US financial futures (treasury bond futures and Government National Mortgage Association futures) is an example of the CAAR approach in which he defined the return of the cumulative average price change. His results suggest that inflation rate announcements provide useful information to the market and that futures prices respond immediately to this information, so that the markets are considered to be semi-strong form efficient.

The procedure employed is (a) to compute the daily rates of return[2] from the period surrounding the announcement events, (b) to net out general market movements by deducting the market rate of return from the particular rate of return and (c) to analyse the relation between the residual rates of return and the events using test statistics.

In this chapter, both parametric tests and non-parametric tests, such as the binomial test, the sign test and the Wilcoxon signed rank test, will be conducted to test the null hypothesis of no abnormal returns.

METHODOLOGY

The following models are most commonly used by researchers to generate abnormal returns:

$$\mathrm{AR} = R - \bar{R} \tag{9.1}$$

$$\mathrm{AR} = R - \bar{R}_{\mathrm{m}} \tag{9.2}$$

$$\mathrm{AR} = R - (a + bR_{\mathrm{m}}) \qquad (9.3)$$

$$\mathrm{AR} = R - [(1 - b)R_{\mathrm{f}} + bR_{\mathrm{m}}] \qquad (9.4)$$

Model (9.1) is the mean adjusted returns model introduced by Masulis (1980). Model (9.2) is a special case of the market model (9.3) used by Fama *et al.* (1969). It is a zero–one market model where $a = 0$ and $b = 1$. Model (9.4) is the simple capital asset pricing model (CAPM). Since many problems involved in the application of CAPM to the area of futures markets are yet to be resolved, model (9.4) will not be pursued here. Therefore, only models (9.1) and (9.3) will be used in this chapter to generate abnormal returns. They will be called the mean adjusted returns model and the market adjusted returns model respectively.

To examine the response of prices to a particular announcement, we must neutralize the movements in prices that result from other factors in the market. The most important factor is the general market condition, and the market model can be utilized to neutralize the effect of this factor.

Market adjusted returns model

The market model[3] is used to generate the expected rate of return for the interest rate futures contract:

$$R_{jt} = a + b_j R_{\mathrm{m}t} + e_{jt} \qquad (9.5)$$

where j is the announcement of economic variable j, $R_{\mathrm{j}t}$ is the daily rate of return of the interest rate futures contract, $R_{\mathrm{m}t}$ is the daily rate of return for the market portfolio (the Australian All Ordinaries Share Index is used as a proxy for the market portfolio), e_t is a random error term and a, b are coefficients to be estimated.

In order to estimate the coefficient in (9.5) it is necessary to have two series of price data for the period studied. These are the price data during the announcement periods and the price data during the non-announcement periods. The announcement period, or the event period, is defined as the period from two days before to two days after an announcement is made. Only domestic announcements are considered.[4] They include the major announcements, such as that of M3, the inflation rate and the balance of payments, as well as policy announcements such as the annual budget and mini-budget. The time period covered in this study is from 1980 to 1987. The non-announcement period is a period in which no announcement is made. It is derived by excluding all the announcement periods from the whole sample period. In this way, it should be possible to compare the changes in futures prices around the announcement periods with those when no announcement is made. The returns from the non-announcement period, or the non-event period, are taken as normal returns. The returns from the announcement period are then tested to see whether they are significantly different from the normal returns.

To obtain an estimate of normal returns, a time series of the interest rate futures contract returns was regressed on a time series of returns based on the Australian All Ordinaries Share Index, both from the non-announcement periods. The return on the Australian All Ordinaries Share Index is used as a proxy for market returns. Expected rates of return are generated using this estimated equation. The deviation of the actual return from the expected return represents the abnormal return AR of the interest rate futures contract for announcement *j* at time *t*:

$$\mathrm{AR}_{jt} = R_{jt} - (\hat{a}_j - \hat{b}_j R_{\mathrm{m}t}) \tag{9.6}$$

Equation (9.6) is assumed to have the following properties:

$$E(\mathrm{AR}_{jt}) = 0 \tag{9.7}$$

$$\sigma(\mathrm{AR}_{jt}, \mathrm{AR}_{it}) = 0 \qquad \forall i \neq j \tag{9.8}$$

Based on the data collected from the non-announcement periods, the daily rate of return of the interest rate futures contract is regressed on the daily rate of market return. The following result is estimated for equation (9.5) using ordinary least squares (OLS) estimation:

$$R_{jt} = 0.022{,}36 \times 10^{-5} + 0.048{,}368 R_{\mathrm{m}t}$$
$$(t = 0.003{,}03) \qquad (t = 5.697)$$

$$R^2 = 0.030 \qquad \mathrm{SER} = 0.002{,}4 \qquad \mathrm{DW} = 1.83$$

$$F_{1,1038} = 32.46$$

From this, the estimated abnormal returns equation is obtained:

$$\mathrm{AR}_{jt} = R_{jt} - (0.022{,}36 \times 10^{-5} + 0.048{,}368 R_{\mathrm{m}t})$$

The *t* statistics show that the coefficient *a* is not statistically different from zero while the coefficient *b* is significant.

Mean adjusted returns model

The mean adjusted returns model was first introduced by Masulis (1980). Although it is simple to use, it can robustly identify abnormal returns in an event study. It also avoids the complicity of using a market index in the study of futures markets. It assumes that the stochastic process generating returns is stationary and is of the form $r_t = u + e_t$, where $E(e_t) = 0$, $\text{cov}(e_t, e_{t-1}) = 0$. The abnormal return is the deviation of the actual return from the estimated mean return $\bar{R}_j$:

$$\text{AR}_{jt} = R_{jt} - \bar{R}_j \tag{9.9}$$

Using the returns from the non-announcement period, the mean return is estimated to be equal to 0.003 per cent with a *t* statistic equal to 0.335,3, which is not significantly different from zero. The corresponding mean market return from the Australian All Ordinaries Share Index is equal to 0.051 per cent with a *t* statistic of 1.908,1, which is statistically significant.

CUMULATIVE AVERAGE ABNORMAL RETURN

The abnormal return AR represents the prediction error which is computed using either the market adjusted returns model or the mean adjusted returns model. These abnormal returns around the time of announcement are the results of many influences, not just the announcements of a particular economic variable in which we are interested. Therefore it is inappropriate to examine the abnormal return of an *individual* announcement. We must neutralize announcement-specific price changes caused by events other than the announcements under study. An appropriate method is to average the abnormal returns using cross-sectional data. Since announcements are made at different times over a long period, cross-sectional average abnormal returns will be effective in neutralizing effects of factors other than the announcements in which we are interested. The average abnormal return AAR on the event day *t* is calculated from

$$\text{AAR} = \sum_{i=1}^{N} \frac{\text{AR}_t}{N} \qquad t = -8 \ldots +8 \tag{9.10}$$

where N is the number of announcements made in the period of this study and AR_t is the daily abnormal return on the interest rate futures contract on day *t*. For example, AR_{-3} is the average daily abnormal return three days before the announcement, where the announcement is made on day $t = 0$. If we sum all AR_{-3} of the N announcements in the study and divide by N, we obtain the average daily abnormal return AAR three days before the announcements. In this study, AARs of the days $t = -8, -7, \ldots, +7, +8$ will be calculated.

In order to measure the cumulative day-by-day effect that the announcement may have, the AARs are summed chronologically over a period of time from eight days before the announcement to eight days after the announcement. By doing this, we obtain the cumulative average abnormal returns CAAR over T days defined as

$$\text{CAAR} = \sum_{t=T_1}^{T_2} \text{AAR} \tag{9.11}$$

where $T = T_2 - T_1 + 1$ and CAAR is computed from event day T_1 to event day T_2. Thus, T_1 to T_2 is the event interval.

TEST STATISTICS

Parametric tests

To test whether the abnormal return on day t is significantly different from zero, we follow Vermaelen (1981) by using the following t test:

$$T = \frac{\text{AR}_t}{s(\text{AR}_t)} \tag{9.12}$$

where $s(\text{AR}_t)$ is the standard deviation of the daily abnormal returns over event days -8 to $+8$. It is assumed that returns are independent and identically distributed.

In order to use the test statistics recommended by Dodd and Warner (1983), it is necessary to convert abnormal returns to standardized abnormal returns SAR. Standardization also reduced bias resulting from the month or year effects which may be present in the seven years time period of this study. This is done by dividing AR by the estimated standard deviation of its prediction errors (see Patell 1976: 256):

$$\text{SAR}_t = \frac{\text{AR}_t}{s_t} \tag{9.13}$$

where

$$s_t = \left[\sum_{t=-8}^{+8} \frac{(\text{AR} - \overline{\text{AR}})^2}{15} \right]^{1/2}$$

in which $\overline{\text{AR}}$ is the average daily abnormal return over the event days -8 to $+8$.

The cumulative standardized abnormal return CSAR for the announcement j over the event interval T_1 to T_2 is

$$\mathrm{CSAR}_j = \sum_{t=T_{1j}}^{T_{2j}} \frac{\mathrm{SAR}_{jt}}{(T_{2j} - T_{1j} + 1)^{1/2}} \tag{9.14}$$

For CSAR, the statistic Z can be computed using the following formula:

$$Z_t = \sum_{i=1}^{N} \frac{\mathrm{SAR}}{N^{1/2}} \tag{9.15}$$

where N is the total number of announcements made in this study. If the AR follow a normal distribution, SAR will follow a univariate Student's t distribution with zero mean. Under the central limit theorem, each SAR is assumed to be distributed unit normal with mean zero and variance $1/N$ in the absence of abnormal performance. If this is the case, the test statistic Z is also distributed unit normal. The null hypothesis to be tested is that the abnormal return on the announcement day is equal to zero.

Therefore the statistical significance of the abnormal return is tested by two parametric statistics, the T and the Z statistics. In this study, statistical significance is also tested by non-parametric tests.

Non-parametric tests

Three different non-parametric tests, namely the binomial test, the sign test and the Wilcoxon signed rank test, will be employed to test the announcement effects.

Binomial test

Binomial statistics (B statistics) are computed using the following formula:

$$B_{jt} = \frac{\%P_{jt} - E(\%P)}{\{E(\%P)[1 - E(\%P)]/n_{jt}\}^{1/2}} \tag{9.16}$$

where P is the probability, $\%P_{jt}$ is the actual percentage of positive abnormal returns for the announcement j on day t observed, $E(\%P)$ is the expected percentage of positive abnormal returns and is assumed to be 0.5, and n is the sample size.

Sign test

The sign test is based on the signs of the abnormal returns only. It is a non-parametric statistical test of significance depending on the signs of differences between matched or unmatched pairs and not on the magnitudes of the differences. If the futures prices do not respond to the announcements, the proportion of positive signs and the proportion of negative signs should be approximately equal at 50 per cent. For example, for size greater than 25, we can conduct the sign test using the following statistic:

$$S = \frac{y0.5n}{0.5n^{1/2}} \tag{9.17}$$

where n is the sample size and y is the number of abnormal returns which are negative. When n is large, S is approximately normally distributed.

Wilcoxon test

The Wilcoxon signed rank test is more powerful than the sign test in that the relative magnitudes of the differences within pairs are used rather than just the signs of these differences. The abnormal returns on day $t = 0$ for each announcement are computed and ranked without regard to sign. The sign of the abnormal returns is affixed to each rank, and those ranks with the same sign are summed. If futures prices do not respond to announcements, the sums of the ranks with positive and negative signs should be roughly equal. For example, for size greater than 25, we can use the following test statistic:

$$W = \{R - [n(n+1)/4]\}/\{[n(n+1)(2n+1)]/24\}^{1/2} \tag{9.18}$$

where n is the sample size and R is the rank sum of positive or negative abnormal returns, whichever is smaller. When n is large, W, is approximately normally distributed,

DATA

Daily price data on the ninety-day bank accepted bill contract are taken from the *Sydney Futures Exchange Statistical Yearbooks*, 1980–5 and *Daily Sheets*, for 1986–7 (see the Appendix for contract specification). Spot price data are daily observations on the Australian All Ordinaries Share Index taken from the *Australian Stock Exchange Journal*, 1980 to June 1983, and from *Personal Investment*, July 1983 to July 1987.

Details of the announcements are as follows:

Consumer price index

The Australian consumer price index figures are released by the Australian Bureau of Statistics (ABS) each quarter, normally in the months of March, June, September and December on any day between day 22 and day 31 of the month. An announcement made in quarter t refers to the inflation rate in quarter $t - 1$. The figures are the weighted average of eight capital cities. Two different rates of change are contained in the release: the twelve months rate of change and the quarterly rate of change. In this study, data on quarterly rate of change are used as announcement data. The period of study of the inflation rate announcement effects is from the March quarter of 1980 to the June quarter of 1987, giving a total of thirty observations in the sample.

Money supply

The Australian M3 announcements are made monthly, in a press release called 'Money Aggregates M3,' by the Reserve Bank of Australia.[5] An announcement in month t refers to the money supply in month $t - 1$. The announcements are not scheduled on any particular day of the month.[6] Normally, however, the announcement is made near the end of the month, from day 24 to day 31. Before December 1985, the release was made at noon, but has been made at 9.30 a.m. since that date. This study covers the period from January 1983 to July 1987, giving a sample of fifty-five observations.

Balance of payments

Balance of current account data are used for balance of payments in this study. They are announced monthly by ABS, normally from day 10 to day 14 of each calendar month. Most announcements are made on Wednesday or Thursday. Before October 1983, the figures were announced at noon, but since then the announcement has been made at 11.30 a.m. An announcement made in month t refers to the balance of payments in month $t - 1$. The sample period of the announcement effects of balance of payments in this study is from May 1980 to July 1987, giving a total of eighty-four observations.

EMPIRICAL RESULTS

Since the purpose of this study is to examine whether abnormal returns from the interest rate futures contract are significantly

Table 9.1 M3 announcements: average abnormal returns, cumulative average abnormal returns and associated test statistics

Event day	*N*	*P*	*AAR (%)*	*Z*	*T*	*B*	*CAAR (%)*
Market adjusted returns model							
−8	55	23	0.021	0.643	0.657	−0.668	0.021
−7	55	20	−0.043	−1.888**	−1.346	−1.479	−0.022
−6	55	25	−0.021	−1.013	−0.657	−0.127	−0.043
−5	55	30	0.041	1.432	1.283	1.225	−0.002
−4	55	25	−0.036	−1.016	−1.126	−0.127	−0.038
−3	55	31	−0.014	−0.456	−0.438	1.495	−0.052
−2	55	26	0.018	0.232	0.563	0.143	−0.034
−1	55	29	0.024	0.773	0.751	0.954	−0.010
0	55	30	0.050	0.522	0.156	1.225	−0.005
1	55	22	−0.028	−1.446	−0.876	−0.939	−0.033
2	55	23	−0.062	−2.135*	−1.940**	−0.668	−0.095
3	55	26	−0.032	−0.697	−1.001	0.143	−0.127
4	55	27	0.020	0.808	0.626	0.414	−0.107
5	55	21	−0.059	−1.327	−1.846**	−1.209	−0.166
6	55	26	−0.060	−1.802**	−1.877**	0.143	−0.226
7	55	24	−0.027	−1.784**	−0.845	−0.398	−0.253
8	55	25	−0.001	−0.006	−0.019	−0.127	−0.254
Mean adjusted returns model							
−8	55	22	0.023	0.584	0.761	−0.907	0.023
−7	55	19	−0.042	−2.050*	−1.390	−1.719+	−0.019
−6	55	23	−0.020	−0.991	−0.662	−0.636	−0.039
−5	55	30	0.045	1.585	1.490	1.257	0.006
−4	55	25	−0.035	−0.826	−1.159	−0.095	−0.029
−3	55	30	−0.030	−0.046	−0.993	1.257	−0.059
−2	55	26	0.018	0.195	0.596	0.175	−0.041
−1	55	31	0.031	1.021	1.026	1.528	−0.010
0	55	29	0.001	0.423	0.013	0.987	−0.009
1	55	24	−0.023	−1.115	−0.761	−0.367	−0.032
2	55	21	−0.066	−2.363*	−2.185*	−1.178	−0.098
3	55	24	−0.031	−1.063	−1.026	−0.367	−0.129
4	55	29	0.014	0.402	0.463	0.987	−0.115
5	55	23	−0.050	−0.868	−1.655	−0.636	−0.165
6	55	26	−0.018	−0.010	−0.596	0.175	−0.183
7	55	23	−0.019	−1.637	−0.629	−0.636	−0.202
8	55	26	0.015	0.412	0.497	0.175	−0.187

Notes: *N*, number of observations; *P*, number of positive abnormal returns.
*Significance at the 5% level.
**Significance at the 10% level.

different from zero after the announcement of various economic variables, emphasis will be placed on the daily abnormal return on the day of announcement, i.e. day 0, and not other days.

M3 announcements

Table 9.1 reports the average abnormal return and cumulative average abnormal returns using both market adjusted returns and mean adjusted returns for the eight days before and eight days after the M3 announcements. Values of the five test statistics discussed above are given in the table.

The empirical results obtained show that interest rate futures prices do not respond significantly to the announcements of M3. The test statistics for the announcement days ($Z = 0.522$, $T = 0.156$ for the market adjusted returns model, and $Z = 0.423$, $T = 0.013$ for the mean adjusted returns model) show that the abnormal returns are not significantly different from zero. Both Z and T show that abnormal returns are significant at the 5 per cent level on day 2, i.e. two days after the announcements of M3. This may be due to the arrival of other information rather than a reflection of the market's slow response to the M3 information. Note that since 1983 the inflation rate announcements have often been made on the same day as or one day after the M3 announcements. The inflation announcement is also a more important piece of information than M3 from the trader's point of view.

Table 9.2 M3 announcements: non-parametric tests

Event day	*N*	*P*	*AAR (%)*	*B*	*S*	*W*	*CAAR (%)*
Market adjusted returns model							
−1	55	29	0.024	0.95	0.40	0.72	−0.010
0	55	30	0.050	1.22	0.67	0.06	−0.005
1	55	22	−0.028	0.93	1.48	1.43	−0.033
Mean adjusted returns model							
−1	55	31	0.031	1.52	0.94	0.87	−0.0100
0	55	29	0.001	0.98	0.40	0.19	−0.0096
1	55	24	−0.023	0.36	0.94	0.94	−0.0326

Notes: *N*, number of observations in the sample; *P*, number of positive abnormal returns; *B, S, W*, statistics of the binomial test, the sign test and the Wilcoxon test respectively.

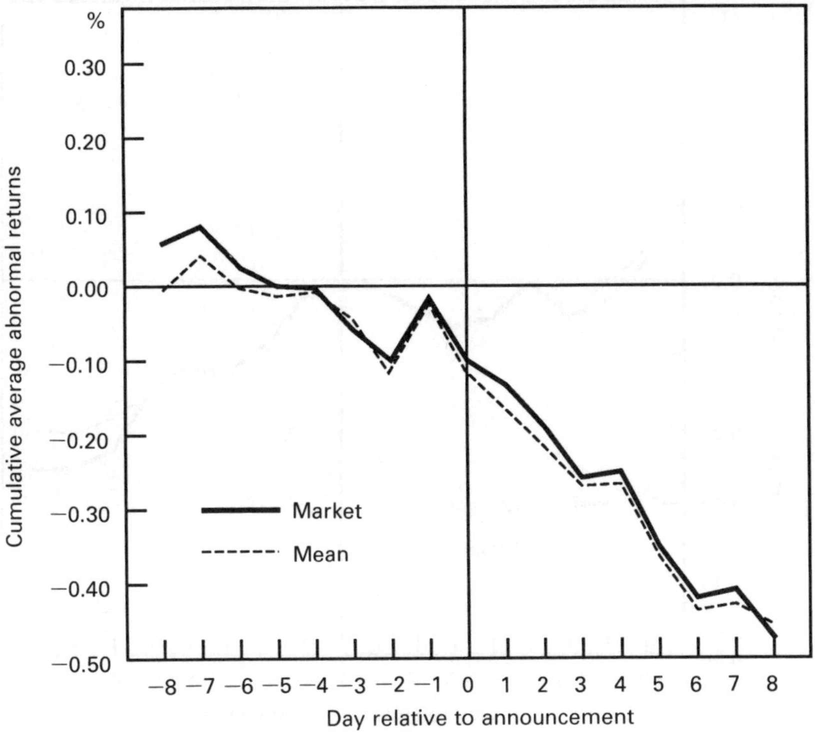

Figure 9.1 M3 announcements: cumulative average abnormal returns

Figure 9.1 presents a plot of CAAR from eight days before to eight days after the M3 announcements. Day 0 represents the day on which M3 is announced. If the market is efficient, the plot of CAAR should exhibit dramatic changes before and on the day of announcements. After the announcements, the CAAR should exhibit relative stability if there is no arrival of other new information. The plot of CAAR in the case of M3 announcements does show this pattern in day −2, i.e. two days before the announcements. There are no dramatic changes after or on the day of announcements.

None of the three non-parametric tests (binomial, sign and Wilcoxon) has recorded any significant response of futures prices to the M3 announcements on days −1, 0 and +1. The test statistics for day 0 are $B = 1.22$, $S = 0.67$ and $W = 0.06$ for the market adjusted returns model, and $B = 0.98$, $S = 0.40$ and $W = 0.19$ for the mean adjusted returns model. These results are reported in Table 9.2.

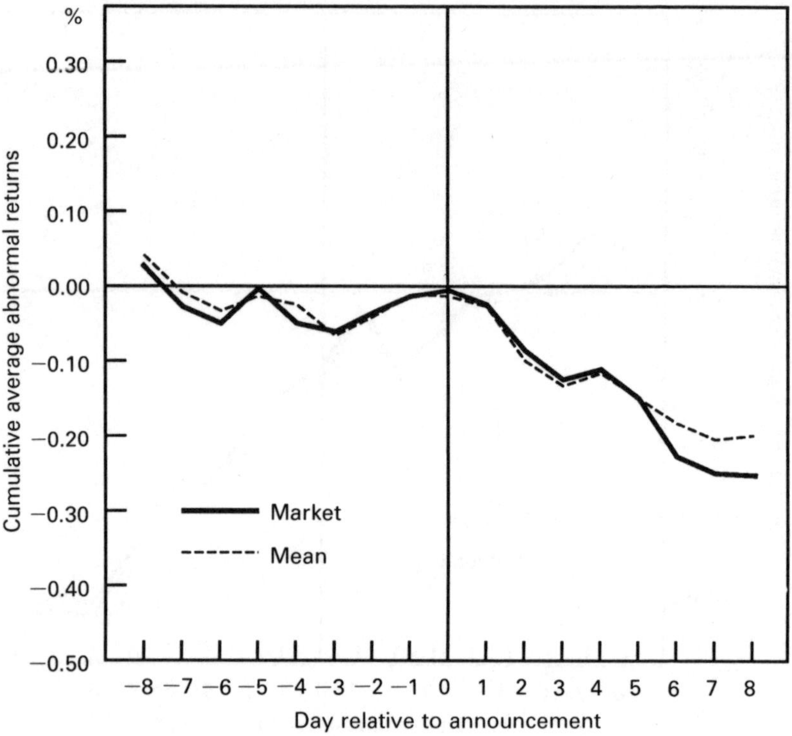

Figure 9.2 Consumer price index announcements: cumulative average abnormal returns

Inflation rate announcements

Table 9.3 presents a summary of the average abnormal returns and cumulative average abnormal returns (both market adjusted and mean adjusted) for eight days before and eight days after the inflation rate announcements. The test statistics again show that the abnormal returns are not significantly different from zero at the 5 per cent level. In this case, $Z = 1.057$, $T = 1.558$ for the market adjusted returns model and $Z = 0.535$, $T = 1.685$ for the mean adjusted returns model on day 0. However, this table shows that futures price response to inflation rate announcements is much stronger than that to the M3 announcements.

Figure 9.2 shows that there are substantial changes of CAAR on the day of inflation rate announcements, although test statistics show that these are not significant at the 5 per cent level (see T in Table 9.3).

Table 9.3 Consumer price index announcements: average abnormal returns, cumulative average abnormal returns and associated test statistics

Event day	*N*	*P*	*AAR (%)*	*Z*	*T*	*B*	*CAAR (%)*
Market adjusted returns model							
−8	30	19	0.043	0.803	0.770	2.007	0.043
−7	30	14	0.030	0.642	0.537	0.173	0.073
−6	30	9	−0.050	−1.642	−0.896	−1.662**	0.023
−5	30	15	−0.028	−0.674	−0.502	0.540	−0.005
−4	30	17	−0.003	−0.270	−0.054	1.273	−0.008
−3	30	9	−0.068	−1.966*	−1.218	−1.662**	−0.076
−2	30	11	−0.032	−0.955	−0.573	−0.928	−0.108
−1	30	21	0.092	1.623	1.648	2.741*	−0.016
0	30	12	−0.087	−1.057	−1.558	−0.561	−0.103
1	30	16	−0.029	−0.102	−0.519	0.907	−0.132
2	30	12	−0.056	−1.996*	−1.003	−0.561	−0.188
3	30	13	−0.060	−1.131	−1.075	−0.194	−0.248
4	30	12	0.007	0.355	0.125	−0.561	−0.241
5	30	9	−0.103	2.233*	−1.845**	−1.662**	−0.344
6	30	10	−0.075	1.422	−1.343	−1.295	−0.419
7	30	19	0.004	0.089	0.072	2.007*	−0.415
8	30	12	−0.055	1.577	−0.985	−0.561	−0.470
Mean adjusted returns model							
−8	30	15	−0.006	−0.067	−0.126	0.518	−0.006
−7	30	15	0.053	1.222	1.117	0.518	0.047
−6	30	10	−0.049	−1.768**	−1.032	−1.316	−0.002
−5	30	15	−0.019	−0.347	−0.400	0.518	−0.021
−4	30	17	0.004	0.026	0.084	1.251	−0.017
−3	30	11	−0.054	−1.231	−1.138	−0.949	−0.071
−2	30	11	−0.051	−1.643	−1.074	−0.949	−0.122
−1	30	17	0.088	1.415	1.854**	1.251	−0.034
0	30	14	−0.080	−0.535	−1.685	0.151	−0.114
1	30	14	−0.036	−0.333	−0.758	0.151	−0.150
2	30	12	−0.055	−1.984*	−1.159	−0.583	−0.205
3	30	15	−0.061	−1.275	−1.285	0.518	−0.266
4	30	13	−0.001	−0.308	0.021	−0.216	−0.265
5	30	9	−0.101	−2.030*	−2.128	−1.683**	−0.366
6	30	10	−0.076	−1.239	−1.643	−1.316	−0.444
7	30	18	0.001	0.416	0.105	1.618	−0.439
8	30	15	−0.038	−0.931	−0.590	0.518	−0.467

Notes: *N*, number of observations; *P*, number of positive abnormal returns.
*Significance at the 5% level.
**Significance at the 10% level.

Table 9.4 Consumer price index announcements: non-parametric tests

Event day	*N*	*P*	*AAR (%)*	*B*	*S*	*W*	*CAAR (%)*
Market adjusted returns model							
−1	30	21	0.092	2.74*	2.19*	1.85	−0.016
0	30	12	−0.087	0.56	1.10	1.66	−0.103
1	30	16	−0.029	0.90	0.37	0.38	−0.132
Mean adjusted returns model							
−1	30	17	0.088	1.25	0.73	1.61	−0.034
0	30	14	−0.080	0.15	0.37	1.14	−0.114
1	30	14	−0.036	0.15	0.37	0.74	−0.150

Notes: *N*, number of observations in the sample; *P*, number of positive abnormal returns; *B*, *S*, *W*, statistics of the binomial test, the sign test and the Wilcoxon test respectively.
*Significance at the 5% level

Results of the non-parametric tests are reported in Table 9.4. The empirical results from all non-parametric tests conducted here have also documented insignificant response to the inflation rate announcements on day 0. Test statistics for day 0 are $B = 0.56$, $S = 1.10$ and $W = 1.14$ for the mean adjusted returns model. Significant response is documented in day −1 based on the market adjusted returns model at the 5 per cent level.

Balance of payments announcements

Table 9.5 presents a summary of the average abnormal returns and cumulative average abnormal returns (market adjusted and mean adjusted) for the eight days before and eight days after the balance of payments announcements.

For balance of payments announcements, market price response is the strongest among the three announcements in this study. On the announcement day it is significant at the 5 per cent level according to the Z test (Z is 3.167 and 2.737 for the two models respectively) but is not significant according to the t test (T is 1.477 and 1.493 for the two models respectively). It is also significant on day −1 and day +1 according to the Z statistics.

Figure 9.3 shows that a dramatic change occurs in CAAR on the day of balance of payments announcements. This is supported by the

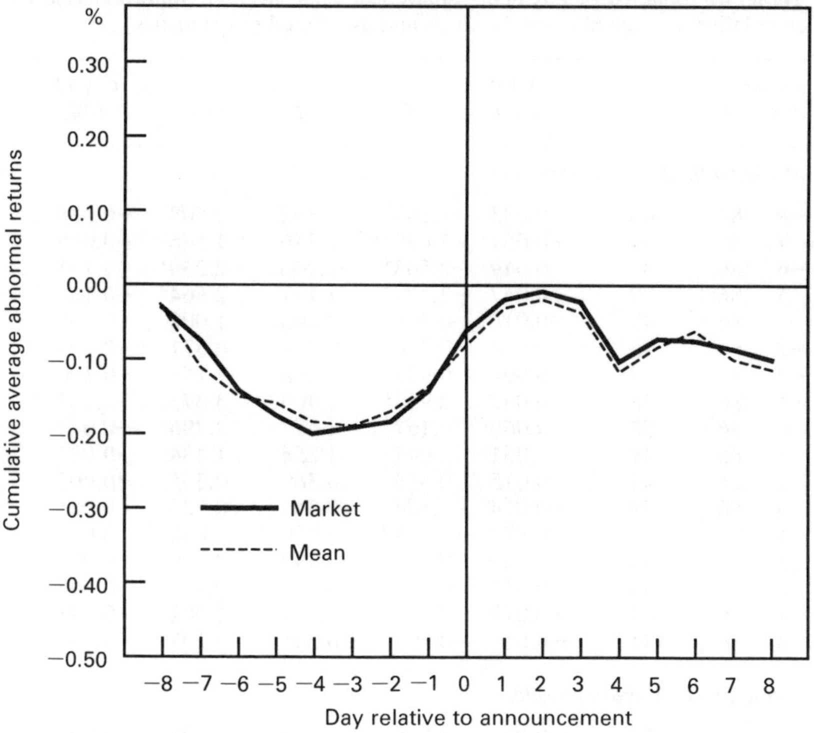

Figure 9.3 Balance of payments announcements: cumulative average abnormal returns

test statistics in Table 9.5 which show that CAAR is significant at the 5 per cent level as noted above.

On the announcement day, significant response is also documented by all non-parametric test statistics for balance of payments announcements (except the sign test based on the mean adjusted returns model). The results are summarized in Table 9.6. Test statistics for day 0 are $B = 2.29$, $S = 2.16$ and $W = 2.45$ for the market adjusted returns model and $B = 1.99$, $S = 1.51$ and $W = 2.21$ for the mean adjusted returns model. The Wilcoxon test is more powerful than the sign test because the ranking is also taken into account in the computation of test statistics. Significant response is also recorded on day −1 by all test statistics. The response on day +1 is generally insignificant.

Table 9.5 Balance of payments announcements: average abnormal returns, cumulative average abnormal returns and associated test statistics

Event day	*N*	*P*	*AAR (%)*	*Z*	*T*	*B*	*CAAR (%)*
Market adjusted returns model							
−8	86	40	−0.035	−1.168	−0.862	−0.508	−0.035
−7	86	35	−0.051	−1.829**	−1.256	−1.586	−0.086
−6	86	32	−0.049	−2.503*	−1.206	−2.233*	−0.135
−5	86	30	−0.047	−2.777*	−1.157	−2.664*	−0.182
−4	86	47	−0.016	−0.266	−0.393	1.002	−0.198
−3	86	45	0.004	0.216	0.098	0.571	−0.194
−2	86	37	0.004	0.949	0.098	−1.155	−0.190
−1	86	58	0.057	2.989*	1.403	3.375*	−0.133
0	86	53	0.060	3.167*	1.477	2.296*	−0.073
1	86	49	0.051	2.047*	1.256	1.434	−0.022
2	86	44	0.015	0.514	0.369	0.355	−0.007
3	86	39	−0.014	−1.484	−0.345	−0.723	−0.021
4	86	34	−0.078	−2.917*	−1.920**	−1.802**	−0.099
5	86	43	0.020	0.704	0.492	0.140	−0.079
6	86	46	0.011	0.023	0.271	0.787	−0.068
7	86	47	−0.017	−0.208	−0.419	1.002	−0.085
8	86	41	−0.014	−0.504	−0.345	−0.292	−0.099
Mean adjusted returns model							
−8	86	38	−0.037	−1.078	−0.952	−0.597	−0.037
−7	86	36	−0.056	−2.270*	−1.442	−1.029	−0.093
−6	86	33	−0.045	−2.534*	−1.159	−1.677**	−0.138
−5	86	29	−0.034	−2.008*	−0.875	−2.541*	−0.172
−4	86	46	−0.015	−0.158	−0.386	1.131	−0.187
−3	86	38	−0.007	−0.188	−0.180	−0.597	−0.194
−2	86	37	0.006	0.894	0.154	−0.813	−0.188
−1	86	56	0.053	2.644*	1.365	3.290*	−0.135
0	86	50	0.058	2.737*	1.493	1.994*	−0.077
1	86	48	0.048	1.873**	1.236	1.563	−0.029
2	86	42	0.007	0.116	0.180	0.267	−0.022
3	86	37	−0.008	−1.310	−0.206	−0.813	−0.030
4	86	27	−0.078	−3.204*	−2.008*	−2.973*	−0.108
5	86	41	0.018	0.761*	0.463	0.051	−0.090
6	86	51	0.024	0.815	0.618	2.210*	−0.066
7	86	44	−0.024	−0.741	−0.618	0.699	−0.090
8	86	40	−0.018	−0.859	0.463	−0.165	−0.108

Notes: *N*, number of observations; *P*, number of positive abnormal returns.
*Significance at the 5% level.
**Significance at the 10% level.

Table 9.6 Balance of payments announcements: non-parametric tests

Event day	*N*	*P*	*AAR (%)*	*B*	*S*	*W*	*CAAR (%)*
Market adjusted returns model							
−1	86	58	0.057	3.37*	3.23*	3.32*	−0.133
0	86	53	0.060	2.29*	2.16*	2.45*	−0.073
1	86	49	0.051	1.43	1.29	1.86	−0.022
Mean adjusted returns model							
−1	86	56	0.053	3.29*	2.80*	2.91*	−0.135
0	86	50	0.058	1.99*	1.51	2.21*	−0.077
1	86	48	0.048	1.56	1.08	2.10*	−0.029

Notes: *N*, number of observations in the sample; *P*, number of positive abnormal returns; *B, S, W*, statistics of the binomial test, the sign test and the Wilcoxon test respectively.
*Significance at the 5% level

SUMMARY

In this chapter we have examined the reaction of abnormal returns in the interest rate futures market to the announcements of the economic variables M3, inflation rate and balance of payments.

The response of interest rate futures prices is found to be statistically significant at the 5 per cent level with regard to the balance of payments announcements on day 0, nearly significant with regard to the inflation rate announcements and not significant in relation to the M3 announcements. Similar results are reported for both market adjusted returns and mean adjusted returns models. There is no strong evidence to suggest that the interest rate futures market is inefficient. The lack of response of futures prices to the announcements of the inflation rate and M3 in particular may be due to the following reasons.

First, the efficient markets hypothesis requires that prices reflect all information without delay. Therefore, price responses to a relevant announcement are expected to be completed within a very short period on the day that the announcement is made. The use of closing prices to calculate abnormal returns is not an optimal measure to examine the announcement effects. As the announcements of M3, inflation rate and balance of payments are made either at 9.00 a.m. or 11.30 a.m., and futures trading closes at 4.00 p.m., this allows the arrival of other new information which may affect the price on the same day. In this case it is not possible to isolate the effects of the information as contained in the announcements from those of other information also arriving on day 0 if closing prices are used. Until better data are available, it will not be possible to improve the test results in this respect.

Second, not all information but only that which is important will affect futures prices. In Australia, the announcement of M3 seems to have virtually no impact on interest rate futures prices. In the United States, where the figures of M1 are watched closely by the market, an unexpected change in M1 will have a significant effect on interest rates. In Australia, traders have not paid much attention to the announcement of M3. Announcements of the inflation rate and balance of payments have been given better coverage in Australian newspapers, perhaps because they are regarded as containing more important economic information. The lack of attention paid to M3 announcements may have contributed to the lack of response of futures prices on the event days concerned.

Third, an implicit assumption of the Patell–Dodd–Warner approach is that trading in futures markets is based on fundamental analysis. Any significant change in the fundamental variables is expected to change futures prices. However, this is not necessarily the case, because a significant proportion of trading is based on the results of technical analysis, especially program trading, which uses computers for trading decisions. Therefore if an announcement of an economic variable has led to a significant change in the fundamentals, traders may not react or may react with a delay if they rely greatly on technical analysis. This may explain, in part, the lack of response of futures prices to the announcements of some economic variables discussed in this study.

Fourth, the lack of response on day 0 to the announcement may also be attributable to the market's ability to predict correctly the changes contained in the announcements. On the other hand, there may be information leaks. In that case, futures prices would already have been adjusted before the announcements to reflect the expected (or leaked) information, and the responses to the announcements would then be insignificant. This would be a sign of market efficiency rather than inefficiency.

Therefore the Australian interest rate futures market can be considered semi-strong form efficient after taking into account the potential biases that may be present in the market. Further study, with better data, needs to be conducted in order to produce improved results.

APPENDIX 9.1 CONTRACT SPECIFICATION, NINETY-DAY BANK ACCEPTED BILLS, SYDNEY FUTURES EXCHANGE

Contract unit: $A500,000 face value ninety-day bank accepted bills of exchange

Standard delivery: five ninety-day bank accepted bills each of face value $A100,000, or one ninety-day bank accepted bill of face value $500,000 maturing eighty-five to ninety-five days from settlement day

Quotations: One hundred minus annual percentage yield to second decimal place (the minimum fluctuation of 0.01 per cent equals approximately $11 per contract, varying with the level of interest rate)

Deposit: as determined by the clearing house, and subject to change from time to time

Commission round turn: negotiable between brokers and their clients

Clearing House: International Commodities Clearing House

Clearing House fee: $4.00 round turn, subject to change from time to time

Exchange levy: $1.50 round turn, subject to change from time to time

Delivery months: spot month plus next six consecutive calendar months, and then March, June, September and December up to two years ahead.

Termination of trading: the Wednesday prior to the second Friday of the delivery month; trading on this day ceases at 12.00 noon

Settlement date: the second Friday of the delivery month

Approved accepters
Australia and New Zealand Banking Group Ltd
Australian Bank
Bank of New Zealand

Banque Nationale de Paris
Commonwealth Trading Bank of Australia
National Australia Bank Ltd
State Bank of New South Wales
State Bank of Victoria
Westpac Banking Corporation

Approved settlement facility: Commonwealth Trading Bank of Australia

NOTES

1 For a discussion of the traditional cumulative average abnormal returns approach, see Larcker *et al.* (1980).
2 According to Black (1976), care must be taken in calculating the rate of return on futures contracts since only margin is placed for futures contract which is thus not considered as an investment in an asset. He suggested using *price changes* rather than *rates of return* in the analysis of futures returns.
3 For a discussion of the market model, see Fama (1976).
4 It is assumed that market prices respond to domestic announcements only, and not to foreign announcements. Whether market prices respond to foreign, especially US announcements is still to be tested.
5 Broad money figures are also released regularly by the Reserve Bank. However, the financial markets have paid more attention to the announcements of M3 than to those of broad money. The announcements of M3 are used.
6 In the United States, M1 announcements are scheduled weekly on every Friday.

REFERENCES

Ball, R. and Brown, P. (1968) 'An empirical evaluation of accounting income numbers', *Journal of Accounting Research* 6: 159–78.
Black, R. (1976) 'The pricing of commodity contracts', *Journal of Financial Economics* 3: 167–79.
Chance, D.M. (1985a) 'The reaction of the Chicago Board of Trade GNMA futures contract to the announcement of inflation rates: a study of market efficiency', *Review of Research in Futures Markets* 4: 132–54.
—— (1985b) 'A semi-strong form test of the efficiency of the treasury bond futures market', *Journal of Futures Markets* 5: 385–405.
Conklin, N.C. (1983) 'Grain exports, futures markets and pricing efficiency', *Review of Research in Futures Markets* 2: 1–25.
Dodd, P. (1980) 'The market for corporate control and stockholder wealth', Monograph and Thesis Series MERC MT-80-04, Managerial Economics Research Center, Graduate School of Management, University of Rochester, New York.

Dodd, P. and Warner, J. (1983) 'On corporate governance: a study of proxy contests', *Journal of Financial Economics* 11: 401–38.

Dornbusch, R. (1980) 'Exchange rate economics: where do we stand', *Brookings Papers on Economic Activity* 143–85.

Fama, E.F. (1976) *Foundations of Finance*, New York: Basic Books.

Fama, E.F., Fisher, L., Jensen, M.C. and Roll, R. (1969) 'The adjustments of stock prices to new information', *International Economic Review* 10: 1–21.

Frenkel, J.A. (1981) 'Flexible exchange rates, prices and the role of 'news': lessons from the 1970s', *Journal of Political Economy* 89: 665–705.

Larcker, D.F., Gordon, L.A. and Pinches, G.E. (1980) 'Testing for market efficiency: a comparison of the cumulative average residual methodology and intervention analysis', *Journal of Financial and Quantitative Analysis* 15: 267–87.

Masulis, R.W. (1980) 'The effects of capital structure change on securities prices: a study of exchange offers', *Journal of Financial Economics* 8: 139–79.

Patell, J.M. (1976) 'Corporate forecasts of earnings per share and stock price behaviour: empirical tests', *Journal of Accounting Research* 14: 246–76.

Vermaelen, T. (1981) 'Common stock repurchases and market signalling: an empirical study', *Journal of Financial Economics* 9: 139–83.

Woodward, R.S. (1986) 'The effects of monetary surprises on financial futures prices', *Journal of Futures Markets* 6: 375–83.

Index